INTO ALL TRUTH

MILTON WALSH

INTO ALL TRUTH

What Catholics Believe—and Why

IGNATIUS PRESS   SAN FRANCISCO

Nihil Obstat: Reverend Monsignor J. Warren Holleran
Censor Librorum

Imprimatur: † Most Reverend Salvatore Cordileone
Archbishop of San Francisco
November 28, 2012

Cover art
Icon of the Trinity by Andrei Rublev (1360–c. 1430)
Rublev Museum, Moscow, Russia
Scala/Art Resource, New York

Cover design by Riz Boncan Marsella

© 2013 by Ignatius Press, San Francisco
All rights reserved
ISBN 978-1-58617-486-6
Library of Congress Control Number 2012945578
Printed in the United States of America ∞

A Word of Thanks, and Dedication

For two thousand years, the Holy Spirit has guided the community of believers into all truth, writing a living Gospel in the faith of the Catholic Church. I would like to dedicate this work to three communities of learning who taught me that Gospel, but before doing so I should acknowledge some individuals who assisted me in this project. I am grateful to several theologians who reviewed different sections of this book and made very helpful corrections and suggestions: Msgr. Dennis Mikulanis; Fr. Gerald O'Collins, S.J.; Fr. Francis Sullivan, S.J.; and Fr. Ronald Witherup, S.S. Mr. Anthony Dolan offered valuable assistance regarding the style and organization of the material presented here.

Three people deserve special thanks because they read and re-read each chapter of *Into All Truth* and by their questions and observations helped a great deal: Sr. Mary Edel, O.C.D.; Mr. David Kent; and Mr. Alexander Stepanov.

I have been greatly blessed in the Catholic education I have received, and I gratefully dedicate this book to three communities:

— The Sisters of the Holy Names of Jesus and Mary at Saint Cecilia School, San Francisco
— The Sulpician Fathers at Saint Joseph's College and Saint Patrick's Seminary
— The Jesuit community at the Gregorian University

and their lay and religious colleagues. By word and example, they have been a living Gospel for me, and for countless others.

When the Spirit of truth comes, he will guide you into all the truth; for he will not speak on his own authority, but whatever he hears he will speak, and he will declare to you the things that are to come. He will glorify me, for he will take what is mine and declare it to you. All that the Father has is mine; therefore I said that he will take what is mine and declare it to you.

John 16:13–15

Contents

Introduction

When Pope John Paul II visited the United States in 1987, I spent about a week at a local television station providing background information to the newscasters covering the papal visit. Toward the end of the week, one of them asked me, "Why does the Catholic Church have such a hang-up about sex?" For several days we had been continually discussing several "hot button" topics: birth control, abortion, divorce, homosexuality, celibacy, and the ordination of women. I pointed out that these were the issues she had brought up, and I mentioned several subjects we had not talked about: our beliefs, our music, our art, our philosophy, our schools, our social services, our literature, and our saints.

Purpose

This book is about the first item on my list, and the most fundamental: our beliefs. What do we believe as Catholics, and why? I am writing first for my fellow Catholics. Over the past fifty years, we have given much attention to Church structures, liturgical changes, and moral issues. Important as these matters are, what we believe is—or should be—more basic. But how can we deepen our understanding of our Catholic faith? For most of us, our only adult education takes place at the Sunday homily. While it is appropriate for a preacher to speak about doctrine, the homily is not the occasion for an in-depth presentation of the faith. For this, there is no substitute for personal study. You may have grown up before the Second Vatican Council, and wonder what the connection is between what you learned then and what the Church teaches now; you may be younger and have never received much instruction on the Creed. I hope that this book will help you learn more about the basic beliefs we profess. I am writing for the general reader and will try to avoid theological terms, except where these are necessary to express the nuances of Catholic faith.

I also have an ecumenical purpose in mind. Sometimes non-Catholics reject what they mistakenly believe to be Catholic teaching; if this book helps dispel misunderstandings, it may further, in some small

I

way, the cause of Christian unity. There are also Catholic doctrines that other Christians understand correctly, but do not accept. If we are interested in fostering unity among the followers of Christ, these differences cannot be papered over. I will note where Catholic doctrines create difficulties for other Christians, but my aim is exposition, not controversy. I am guided by the advice given in the First Letter of Saint Peter: "Always be prepared to make a defense to any one who calls you to account for the hope that is in you, yet do it with gentleness and reverence" (1 Pet 3:15).

The most important common ground Christians share is the Bible. Throughout this book, I will refer frequently to the Scriptures, citing the Revised Standard Version of the Bible, which is itself a good example of ecumenical cooperation.[1] The other two resources upon which I will draw are the documents of the Second Vatican Council and the *Catechism of the Catholic Church (CCC)*.[2] These are the principal sources of authoritative Church teaching; they provide many biblical citations in their presentation of the Catholic faith; and they are readily accessible to everyone. Appendix B at the end gives suggestions on how to use the *Catechism* and references to appropriate paragraphs for each chapter of this book. There is also a study guide that relies heavily on the *Catechism*. This study guide is available online at www.intoalltruthbook .com and is designed to be used in RCIA, in the classroom, or by adult study groups in a parish.

Structure

The plan of this book is very simple. Part One brings us into the heart of the Christian faith, the mystery of the Trinity, beginning with the Resurrection. Why begin there? That extraordinary event prompted

[1] The Revised Standard Version is a revision of the Authorized (King James) Version of the Bible published by American Protestant scholars in 1952. In 1966, a Catholic edition was produced that made a few changes in the New Testament, some of which were incorporated into the second edition of the Protestant RSV published in 1971. The only significant differences between the 1966 Catholic RSV and the 1971 Protestant RSV are a preference in the former to use the term *brethren* for *brothers* in passages referring to the relatives of Jesus, and the rendering of the angel's salutation of Mary in Luke 1:28 as "full of grace" rather than "highly favored". Biblical citations in this book are taken from the 2006 Second Catholic edition of the RSV, published by Ignatius Press.

[2] Throughout this book, *CCC* refers to the second edition of *The Catechism of the Catholic Church* (1997); the number following refers to the specific paragraph in the *Catechism*.

Jesus' followers to reflect on his mission and identity, which in turn led them to see the one God as an eternal communion of Father, Son, and Holy Spirit. The Good News is that we are invited to enter into that communion of love, so Part Two shows how other Catholic beliefs are rooted in the mystery of the Trinity. In conclusion, I offer a brief reflection on the role played by the Roman Catholic Church in handing on the Gospel over the past two thousand years.

Each chapter explores "the Catholic Gospel" in three stages: first, a simple statement of what we profess about a particular doctrine; second, a summary of how the Catholic understanding of this doctrine has developed over the centuries; finally, some application of the doctrine to our lives. I use the phrase "the Catholic understanding" intentionally—not in the sense that I claim some authority to declare which teachings are truly Catholic, but because I have sought to present all of the doctrines that the Church herself has proposed as essential to our faith. In Catholic theology, these basic beliefs are called *dogmas*. I realize that this is a freighted word for many people. However, it is important for us to distinguish core beliefs from the many secondary doctrines and theological explanations of those beliefs that are also part of our Catholic patrimony. To take one simple illustration: the Catholic concepts of Purgatory and Limbo are so well known that the terms have passed into common speech; are they dogmas? Purgatory is, but Limbo is not; it is a theological opinion that Catholics are free to accept or reject. There are in fact relatively few Catholic dogmas, and it is these that are the subject of this book.[3]

Three Presuppositions

By way of conclusion to this introduction, I would like to set down three assumptions I make in presenting the Catholic Gospel. To justify them would require a book in itself (at least), so I will simply state them and say why they must be presumed before examining the subjects treated in the following chapters.

---

[3] I had originally planned to provide here an explanation of the meaning and importance of *dogma* in Catholic thought. Upon reflection, I have decided that a rather technical discussion at the outset might be rather daunting; this material instead has been included as Appendix A. If we ignore the distinction between essential dogmas and other ideas, we are in danger of exalting a particular theological explanation—however venerable—to the level of a dogma, or dismissing a fundamental belief as "just one more opinion".

4

Objective Truth

My first assumption is that truth pertains to objective reality and it can be known, to some degree, by the human intellect. Obviously, a complete skeptic would dismiss the truth claims of any statement, let alone statements claiming divine authority, but a complete skeptic—if such a person exists in real life—would not be interested in this book. A more likely obstacle is an attitude that holds truth to be entirely subjective. Thus someone might say, "Well, that may be true for *you*, but . . .". At its most benevolent, this statement is simply a convenient social convention in a pluralistic society, but followed to its logical conclusion, it suggests that truth is not something we apprehend; it is something we create. Do any of us really believe this about the most important things we hold to be true? Be that as it may, my first assumption is that there is objective reality, and that ideas are true to the extent that they correspond to reality.

While assuming the existence of objective truth, I would add two cautions when considering Catholic beliefs. First, while truth is objective, our statements about it are culturally conditioned. Any dogmatic statement, even the most definitive, is always partial and provisional. The Catholic Church holds that such solemn definitions are infallible. What she understands by that will be considered later, but the point to be noted here is that this is a negative guarantee: it simply means that a particular doctrinal formulation is not wrong. This does not mean that it is necessarily the best way to express the truth, or that it cannot be improved upon; the same truth can be expressed in other ways, provided they do not contradict the meaning intended by the formula. In studying the Catholic Gospel, we need to be attentive to the cultural limitations of language.

Such limitations pertain to any statement of truth. But there is another limitation peculiar to dogmatic statements: here we are touching the mystery of God, a mystery beyond our finite comprehension as creatures. Any human word about divine realities is bound to be inadequate. One of the great mystics of the Catholic Church, Saint John of the Cross, was fond of quoting a dictum of the Fourth Lateran Council: no similarity between God and creatures can be expressed that does not imply an even greater dissimilarity (see *CCC*, no. 43). We can know *something* about God, but what we do not know, and can never know, is infinitely greater. We must assume a stance of humble reverence before the mystery of God.

Creator of the Universe and Lord of History

My second assumption is that God created the universe and has revealed himself in history. In effect, I assume the traditional Jewish understanding of God. Through the events related in the Old Testament, the chosen people gradually came to believe that there is only one God, infinitely transcendent, who freely chose to involve himself in their history. The fundamental dogma of the Jewish religion is stated in the Book of Deuteronomy: "Hear, O Israel: the LORD our God is one LORD; and you shall love the LORD your God with all your heart, and with all your soul, and with all your might" (Deut 6:4). This God has entered into a covenant with the Jewish people so that, although he possesses sovereign freedom in regard to his creation, he can be spoken of as "their God", and what gives them their identity is that they are "his people". Utterly transcendent in being, this God is nonetheless intimately present in history.

Libraries could be filled with books giving arguments for and against the existence of God, whether or not such a God is personal, and what it means to hold that the experience of the Jewish people represents a unique intervention of God in human affairs. All of that is presumed here, because Christian revelation is rooted in the Jewish faith. The arrival of Jesus on the stage of history represents an undreamt-of manifestation of God in our world, but when he arrived the play had been going on for some time.

Reliability of the New Testament

The reference to history brings me to my third assumption: the New Testament provides a reliable record of how the first disciples saw Jesus. The oldest writings in the New Testament, some of Saint Paul's Letters, were composed within only twenty or thirty years of Jesus' lifetime. These Letters deal with specific issues in the communities addressed, and they tell us very little about the life of Christ. However, several fundamental ideas about the *meaning* of his life are clearly affirmed; indeed, Paul refers to them as beliefs with which his readers are very familiar: Jesus' Resurrection, the salvific meaning of his death, his unique status as "Lord" and "Son of the Father", his expected return as Judge of the living and the dead, and the sanctifying activity of the Holy Spirit. The Gospels, although they incorporate earlier material, were probably written from thirty to sixty years after Jesus' life. This means they are just one generation removed from the events they relate: they record the reminiscences of those who saw Jesus himself, or those who received the testimony of these eyewitnesses firsthand. The Gospels are not biographies as we understand that genre today, but they do contain "the memoirs of the apostles", the recollections of those who could testify to that "which we have heard, which we have seen with our eyes, which we have looked upon and touched with our hands" (1 Jn 1:1)".[4]

Of course, this proximity does not necessarily guarantee that the Gospel stories are true, but it tells against the notion that Christian beliefs about the identity and mission of Jesus were projected onto him long after his death. The fundamental conviction of the first Christians was that Jesus had risen from the dead. This event fueled their interest in his teaching and deeds and their desire to preserve the recollections of the original eyewitnesses. Why they believed he rose from the dead will be the subject of our first chapter, but that assertion runs through the whole of the New Testament, beginning with Letters written within twenty-five years of Jesus' life.

The Catholic faith is called "apostolic" because it flows from the experience of the apostles and other original disciples who, in the light of Christ's Resurrection, came to believe that he was God's unique agent of salvation for all people. The New Testament preserves a reliable record of what the first generations of disciples believed about Jesus; their experience is the origin of the Catholic Gospel.

With these three assumptions in mind—that we can know the truth, that a personal God made the universe and revealed himself in the history of the Jewish people, and that the New Testament records the meaning of what Jesus said and did as understood by the first two generations of his followers—we are ready to begin our exploration of the Catholic Gospel. And our journey begins where most journeys end: at the grave.

---

[4] Writing around the year 155, Saint Justin Martyr said that the "memoirs of the apostles" were read at the Sunday Eucharist (*CCC*, no. 1345). In another work, he states that these memoirs were produced by the apostles and their followers.

PART ONE

TO THE MYSTERY OF THE TRINITY

Chapter One

The Resurrection of Jesus

On Pentecost morning, Saint Peter proclaimed to the crowds in Jerusalem: "This Jesus God raised up, and of that we all are witnesses" (Acts 2:32). At the heart of the Good News is the proclamation that Jesus of Nazareth, who endured the shameful death of crucifixion, lives again. This has been the primary assertion of Christianity for twenty centuries; whatever conflicts divide the followers of Jesus, all believers are one in declaring, "He is risen!"

What We Believe

Jesus of Nazareth died on a Cross, and his body was laid in a tomb. When his followers returned to complete the burial rites, they found the tomb empty. For a period of time, the risen Christ appeared to his disciples. He still had his human body, which bore the marks of his crucifixion, but this body was transformed. After these appearances, Jesus ascended to Heaven. From there, he will come at the end of time to judge the living and the dead; then all who have died will experience a bodily resurrection. Christ's Resurrection has transformed all of creation, and by the outpouring of the Holy Spirit, he has made the community of disciples into his Mystical Body, the Church. The Body of the risen Lord is present sacramentally in the Eucharist.

Some History

We believe Jesus rose from the dead on the testimony of his followers, "who were chosen by God as witnesses, who ate and drank with him after he rose from the dead" (Acts 10:41). It would be naïve to think that the Acts of the Apostles preserves verbatim the first sermons delivered by the apostles, but this is their core message: Jesus went about

9

doing good and performing wondrous deeds; his death on the Cross
was part of God's plan; God has raised Jesus from the dead and exalted
him at his right hand as Messiah and Lord; in the death and Resurrection of Christ, God has accomplished his great work of salvation,
and he invites us to repent and receive the new life of the Holy Spirit
(see Acts 2:14–39; 4:10–12; 5:30–32; 10:34–43; 13:16–41). The sermons in Acts are packed with theology, and several chapters of this
book will examine different strands of that theology. But our starting
point is the momentous event of Christ's Resurrection and its impact
on his followers. What happened?

In attempting to answer that crucial question, we need to exercise caution for two reasons. First, we have relatively little evidence to go on: the
scriptural accounts of the appearances of the risen Christ are brief and
somewhat confused. Second, whatever the nature of those encounters,
they were unique; the biblical narratives represent halting efforts to describe
events unlike anything men have ever experienced, before or since.

The Witness of Saint Paul

The oldest written testimony to the Resurrection is found in Saint Paul's
First Letter to the Corinthians, written in the middle of the first century. Paul states that the risen Christ appeared to him. This encounter is
particularly significant because Paul had not been a disciple of Jesus; on
the contrary, he had been actively persecuting his followers. It is also
noteworthy because it marks the last such appearance of Christ, "as to
one untimely born" (1 Cor 15:8). Saint Paul is recalling something that
happened to him within a few years of Jesus' death. But there is more. In
introducing this personal testimony, Saint Paul links it to a tradition he
had received and had handed on in turn to the Corinthians:

> That Christ died for our sins in accordance with the Scriptures, that he
> was buried, that he was raised on the third day in accordance with the
> Scriptures, and that he appeared to Cephas, then to the Twelve. Then
> he appeared to more than five hundred brethren at one time, most of
> whom are still alive, though some have fallen asleep. Then he appeared
> to James, then to all the apostles. (1 Cor 15:3–7)

The wording suggests that Paul learned this list of appearances from
those who were believers before him; for example, this is the only

time he uses the term "the Twelve". What we have in this Letter is not only Saint Paul's report of his own encounter with the risen Jesus, but also his recital of a list of Resurrection appearances formulated within a few years of Jesus' lifetime. It would be anachronistic to describe this as a page from "the Jerusalem Catechism", but its structure suggests something of the sort: Saint Paul is reminding the Corinthians of the "lesson" of Resurrection appearances he had learned from the Jerusalem community, and which he had passed on to the Corinthians when he first preached the Gospel to them.

Gospel Accounts of the Resurrection

Paul affirms the reality of Jesus' Resurrection in all of his Letters, but what did he experience? All he says in First Corinthians is that Christ "appeared" to him; he does not tell us where or when this happened—he reports no words of Jesus. He alludes to this encounter in his Letter to the Galatians, although there he simply states that God "was pleased to reveal his Son to me, in order that I might preach him among the Gentiles" (Gal 1:16). (It is not surprising that Paul gives no details of these appearances in writing to the Corinthians and Galatians; he is simply reminding them of an event that he must have described when he first preached the Gospel to them.) It is when we turn to Acts and the Gospels that we find more detailed descriptions of this and other Resurrection appearances—but we also encounter several inconsistencies in the accounts. The list Paul gives in First Corinthians mentions appearances not recorded in the Gospels (such as to James, and to the five hundred), and the Gospels relate appearances not enumerated in Paul's list (notably, Christ's appearances to women). Saint Luke confines the appearances to Jerusalem and its environs, while the other Evangelists record appearances in Galilee as well. Details of these appearances vary from one Gospel to the next, as do the words of the risen Jesus.

Do these inconsistencies weaken the veracity of the accounts? It could be argued that the opposite is the case: if the first Christians had invented the stories, they would have made them more consistent. In fact, we find discrepancies even in writings by the same author. Saint Luke's stated purpose was to write an orderly account so that his reader would know the truth (Lk 1:3–4). However, he implies in his Gospel that Christ ascended at Easter, and in Acts, says that he ascended forty days later; his three accounts of the meeting between Christ and Saint Paul on the road to Damascus vary in some details (Acts 9:1–9; 22:4–16; 26:9–18). Nor should inconsistencies between authors surprise us: each Gospel has its own perspective on the story of Jesus, and the Evangelists' theologies influenced how they told that story.

Despite these differences, the accounts of the Resurrection appearances follow a common pattern. Initially, the disciples are sorrowful and disconsolate; although the followers of Jesus would recall later that he had spoken to them about his Resurrection, they were not expecting it when it happened. Jesus takes the initiative in appearing to his followers, and he meets them in the places hallowed by associations: the site of his death and burial, the upper room, Galilee. He speaks words of comfort to them, but also takes them to task for their lack of faith. At first, the disciples do not believe that they are meeting their Master, but then they rejoice. Finally, the risen Jesus sends them to share the Good News of his Resurrection with others; then he is no longer seen. In these appearances, Jesus breaks in upon the sadness and discouragement of his friends, convinces them that he is alive, and commissions them to carry the news to others.

The Gospels make it clear that Christ is not only alive, but he is also changed; it is not just the case of a corpse come back to life. On the one hand, there is continuity: he has the same body that was laid in the tomb, which bears the marks of the nails and spear; on the other hand, his friends often do not recognize him at first. He can be touched and he eats with them, but he is able to pass through locked doors. Were these encounters hallucinations, the product of wishful thinking? The disciples were not expecting to see Jesus alive; even those Jews who looked forward to some kind of resurrection at the end of time did not expect the glorious resurrection of one individual before then. In any event, this explanation cannot account for the appearance to Saint Paul, who certainly had no longing to meet the dead teacher whose disciples he was persecuting. Were they visions? The New Testament describes visions, mystical experiences, dreams, and locutions, but the testimony of the disciples is that these experiences were different from any of those, and that the risen Christ was tangible in some way. There are historical aspects to these encounters: Jesus' empty tomb is evidence to which Saint Peter can point without fear of contradiction, and these appearances are experienced by particular individuals and groups, and at specific places. But it also seems that what has happened has broken out of history; while grounded in time and space, the Resurrection bursts open our three-dimensional world.

All we can say with certainty is that, whatever the precise nature of these meetings, they changed Jesus' followers radically. Formerly, they had hoped that he would bring some kind of political liberation and prosperity to Israel. That hope was crushed in the humiliating death of their leader, a leader they had denied and deserted. Yet, within months of Jesus' execution, the disciples appear as courageous witnesses to his Resurrection and exaltation in the very city where he had been put to death. The apostles and their fellow disciples were now willing to endure imprisonment, torture, and death rather than deny that Christ was risen. Their testimony is the foundation of the Christian faith.

Do we believe them? The alternatives are either that Jesus somehow faked his death in order to fool people, or that his followers perpetrated a hoax. The former idea flies in the face of what we know about Jesus; even many who do not believe him divine honor Jesus as a great teacher, notable for his honesty and humility. The latter idea flies in the face of what we know about his disciples: Would those who had abandoned Jesus to a cruel death undergo torture and death themselves for the sake of a fraud? The most reasonable explanation is that the disciples were telling the truth. But there is a vast chasm between saying that something is reasonable and affirming that we believe it is true. To believe in Jesus risen from the dead requires faith, and faith is a gift of God. There was an element of faith at work when the disciples saw the risen Lord. They did not witness the actual Resurrection itself. Saint Thomas Aquinas has an interesting observation here: he suggests that just as faith comes from hearing and leads to vision, so it was fitting that the disciples were prepared to see the risen Christ by hearing of the Resurrection from the angels. Their human sight was enlightened by faith. This faith was fueled by love. The disciples were mourning because they had truly *loved* Jesus. They had not lost only a Teacher, but a Friend—the kindest, most compassionate friend they had ever known.

Sometimes people ask, "If the Resurrection was the vindication of Jesus' mission, why didn't he appear to his enemies?" In the case of

Paul, he did. Certainly other such appearances would have had a remarkable effect: one can imagine the High Priest or Pilate experiencing a conversion and paying obeisance to the glorified Christ. But Christ did not come for adulation; he came for love. It was love that prompted him to gather his band of followers, it was love that led him to lay down his life, and it was love that moved him to seek out his friends after his Resurrection. The Easter message the disciples carried to the whole world was not "God is great", but "God is love."

Why do we find it difficult to accept their testimony? Sometimes we equate skepticism with sophistication. We have been told, "If something seems too good to be true, it probably is." Or a lack of resolution is equated with an open mind. If we study the Scriptures and conclude that the testimony of the apostles is reasonable, but do not believe it is true, let us ask God for the gift of faith. To ask for faith is also to ask for love, since it is only into a heart open to love that God can enter. All that Jesus taught and did, his miracles of compassion, his parables of forgiveness, his tiring journeys from village to village; all that Jesus suffered in his agony and death; all that he manifested after his Resurrection—all these things were done to show God's love for us, and to invite us to love God in return. Fundamentally, the Resurrection proclaims that love is stronger than death, and that we are invited into communion with the God who is the God of the living, not of the dead. Is this news "too good to be true"? At times it can seem so, and part of being a believer is to struggle with doubts. It is comforting to remember that even those who were privileged to meet the risen Christ wrestled with doubts. Like the man who asked Jesus to heal his son, we need to cry out, "I believe; help my unbelief!" (Mk 9:24).

Implications

The Resurrection of Christ is a stone dropped into the lake of human history; its ripples are the whole experience of Christianity. In the wake of this event, his followers had to examine the meaning of Christ's death and to ask who he was. This in turn led them to ask what Jesus tells us about God. Two thousand years of prayer, art, music, and theological exploration were set in motion by the Resurrection. The rest of this book, in fact the whole panorama of Catholic faith, can be seen as "implications" of Easter. Here we will limit our reflection to the Resurrection itself.

The most immediate question is "What does it matter to *me* if Jesus rose from the dead?" The Resurrection means that the dreadful dominion of death has been broken, and that we are offered the gift of life eternal. In the triumphant words of a paschal hymn of the East:

> Christ is risen from the dead!
> Dying, he conquered death;
> To the dead, he has given life.[1]

The New Testament repeatedly brings home the conviction that the risen Christ tasted death so that we might have life; he is the "first-born" of many brothers and sisters. Saint Paul discusses the appearances of the risen Christ in the First Letter to the Corinthians because some in the community doubted *their* future resurrection. In a fascinating twist of logic, Paul asserts that to deny the resurrection of the dead is to deny the Resurrection of Christ: "But if there is no resurrection of the dead, then Christ has not been raised" (1 Cor 15:13). The assurance that we are destined to share in the resurrection occurs throughout the Letters of Saint Paul.

How do we share in this experience? We rise with Jesus only if we have died with him (Rom 6:4–11; 2 Tim 2:11; Col 2:12). The God who raised Jesus will raise us up, too (1 Thess 4:14; 2 Cor 4:14; Eph 2:6). It is "the Spirit of God" or "the Spirit of Christ" who is the agent of resurrection: "If the Spirit of him who raised Jesus from the dead dwells in you, he who raised Christ Jesus from the dead will give life to your mortal bodies also through his Spirit who dwells in you" (Rom 8:11).

Christ's Bodily Resurrection—and Ours

This reference to our mortal bodies prompts a question: What kind of body will we have? This, too, is a matter Saint Paul deals with in First Corinthians. Recall that he was one of the few people privileged to encounter the risen Christ; yet all he says is that the resurrected life involves a celestial body that differs from, and yet is related to, our physical body. He draws an analogy from a seed and a plant:

[1] The Byzantine Liturgy, Troparion of Easter, quoted in *CCC*, no. 638.

What you sow does not come to life unless it dies. And what you sow is not the body which is to be, but a bare kernel. . . . But God gives it a body as he has chosen, and to each kind of seed its own body. . . . So is it with the resurrection of the dead. What is sown is perishable, what is raised is imperishable. It is sown in dishonor, it is raised in glory. It is sown in weakness, it is raised in power. (1 Cor 15:36–43)

It would be impossible to picture an oak tree if all you had ever seen was an acorn. Similarly, Saint Paul suggests, it is futile for us to attempt to imagine the qualities of a spiritual body. Human curiosity being what it is, it is not surprising that Paul's admonition has been ignored; over the centuries, people have speculated about the attributes of a resurrected body. Catholic dogma affirms *that* there will be a bodily resurrection, but the Church has never defined *what* a "spiritual body" is, or what qualities it possesses. The doctrine of a bodily resurrection goes back to the apostolic preaching, which in turn is based on the appearances of the risen Christ.

Belief in the resurrection of the body underscores the importance of the body-soul integrity in Christian thought: I do not "have" a soul and a body—I *am* a soul and a body. The body is not a husk that is broken open to release the soul, or some kind of booster rocket that falls away when the soul leaves earth behind. The separation of soul and body is unnatural; it is in fact what we mean by *death*. Since Christ has destroyed death by his Resurrection, the eternal life God offers us is not simply the immortality of the soul, but a fully human life that includes some kind of bodily existence. And whatever the nature of this spiritual body, it will be *my* body, related to my unique personal identity just as my physical body is now. This conviction about human integrity is central to Catholic life. Our religion is marked by a strongly sacramental emphasis; Catholic worship treats the senses as gateways to the soul. Our reverence for the bodies of the dead, our veneration for the relics of the saints, even what many consider to be our preoccupation with sexual morality, all manifest the Catholic conviction that the body is a temple of the Holy Spirit and is destined to share, in a way unimaginable to us now, in our eternal destiny. It also follows that reincarnation is incompatible with belief in the resurrection of the body, since reincarnation denies the integrity of the body and soul. The Resurrection of Christ reveals that the only "re-incarnation" that awaits us is the celestial body we will each receive in the general resurrection at the end of time.

We can perceive how our resurrection is related to Christ's only when we realize how intimate the union is between Christ and his followers. For us, Jesus is not simply a great teacher or a model to be admired and imitated—he lives in us and we live in him. Jesus spoke about this union at the Last Supper: "I am the vine, you are the branches. He who abides in me, and I in him, he it is that bears much fruit, for apart from me you can do nothing" (Jn 15:5). This mutual indwelling is brought about by the Holy Spirit, sent from the Father by the risen Christ. It would have been a great gift if the risen Christ had continued to appear to the disciples. But God wanted to give us an even greater gift: his Son would not simply live *among* us—he would live *in* us. Saint Paul was deeply aware of this personal union: "I have been crucified with Christ; it is no longer I who live, but Christ who lives in me; and the life I now live in the flesh I live by faith in the Son of God, who loved me and gave himself for me" (Gal 2:20). Here is what Saint Augustine says about this great mystery:

> Let us rejoice then and give thanks that we have become not only Christians, but Christ himself. Do you understand and grasp, brethren, God's grace toward us? Marvel and rejoice: we have become Christ. For if he is the head, we are the members; he and we together are the whole man.... The fullness of Christ then is the head and the members.[2]

The Church: Mystical Body and Bride of the Risen Christ

As Augustine notes, our union with Christ is intensely personal, but it is also profoundly communal: we can be one with Christ only with others. Saint Paul had met the risen Lord himself, but he had to receive the baptism that joined him to the community of believers. In fact, it was on the road to Damascus that Paul learned that the Church is Christ's Body on earth. The risen Lord asked him, "Saul, Saul, why do you persecute me?" When Paul asked who he was, Christ responded, "I am Jesus, whom you are persecuting" (Acts 9:4, 5). To harass the disciples was to attack Jesus himself. This insight into the Church as

---

[2] St. Augustine, *In evangelium Johannis tractatus*, 21, 8: *PL* 35, 1568, quoted in *CCC*, no. 795.

Christ's Mystical Body became an important part of Saint Paul's teaching. On the one hand, he used it to remind his followers that all the members of the Body are united to one another and need one another; we cannot "go it alone" in our discipleship (1 Cor 12; Rom 12). On the other hand, when the members of the Body of Christ endured persecution, the awareness of their union with their glorified Head, who had suffered before them, could give them hope (Col 1; Eph 1 and 4).

This communal aspect of our union with the risen Christ involves all of mankind. We turn again to the fifteenth chapter of First Corinthians, where Saint Paul writes: "'The first man Adam became a living soul'; the last Adam became a life-giving spirit.... The first man was from the earth, a man of dust; the second man is from heaven.... Just as we have borne the image of the man of dust, we shall also bear the image of the man of heaven" (1 Cor 15:45–49). This theme of Christ as the New Adam highlights the unity of mankind: just as we all have received a common human nature from our first parents, so the whole human race is part of the new creation brought about by the Resurrection of Christ. The risen Christ is the Adam of the new age who has received the Spirit in his glorified human nature, and through him, all mankind is raised to a new level of existence.

Christ as the New Adam suggests another biblical image for the Church: the Bride of Christ (Eph 5:25–32; Rev 21:2). The early Fathers pictured the Church as the New Eve drawn from the pierced side of Christ as he slept in death on the Cross. Like the Mystical Body, this image expresses the union between Christ and the Church, but here there is a note of distinctness. The Church (and the individual believer as a member of the Church) is truly one with Christ, but this union does not annihilate difference. In marriage, the two become one flesh without loss of individuality; in fact, the two partners find their deepest identity in relation to one another. This dynamic of unity grounded in mutual relationship points to the greatest Christian mystery, the Holy Trinity.

The Risen Christ Breaks the Reign of Sin

Saint Paul drew another insight from the Adam/Christ relationship that influenced later Christian thought, especially in the West. Through

Adam's disobedience, sin came into the world, and with sin, death. By his obedience, Christ has healed the injury inflicted on mankind in the Fall: "As one man's trespass led to condemnation for all men, so one man's act of righteousness leads to acquittal and life for all men" (Rom 5:18). Our human nature was wounded by Adam's transgression: while preserving its fundamental goodness, it is subject to suffering and death, and it is prone to evil. Tradition calls this condition of alienation "original sin", although the term *sin* here does not mean a personal fault. The *Catechism* notes that the doctrine of original sin is the reverse side of the Good News that Christ is the Savior of all people (*CCC*, no. 389). In light of the Resurrection, we know Christ as the source of grace for all men, and this truth is linked to the mystery of human solidarity in Adam's sin.

While we often think of sin as a matter of transgressing a law, more fundamentally, it is the violation of a relationship. When we read the story of the Fall in that light, we can see better how the Resurrection represents not only a victory over death, but a victory over sin as well. The Bible opens with an idyllic description of a harmonious world: God had created Paradise as a garden to be enjoyed and tended by Adam and Eve, who love each other and freely do the will of their Creator. They are tempted to usurp the place of God, claiming to determine for themselves what is good and what is evil. This revolt disrupts the whole spiritual ecology of Eden. First, their relationship with God: from friends who enjoyed God's companionship in the cool of the evening, Adam and Eve are reduced to skulking truants attempting to hide from the One who knows them better than they know themselves. Second, their relationship to one another is damaged: joint revolt gives way to mutual recrimination, and the desire for dominance replaces reciprocal harmony. Finally, their relationship to the world around them is poisoned: nature now resists Adam and Eve; the joy of gardening becomes the labor of farming. And through sin, death enters the world.

Saint Paul teaches that the wages of sin is death, but we should not understand this as an arbitrary punishment administered by a petulant overlord; it is the unavoidable result of the rejection of God, who is the source of life. God will not force himself upon his creatures, but neither does he leave mankind in this hopeless position. Saint Paul's complete statement is "For the wages of sin is death, but the free gift of God is eternal life in Christ Jesus our Lord" (Rom 6:23). The imagery of the Genesis story may seem naïve to some, but it certainly describes what we see when we look around us, and more importantly, within us: alienation from God, competition and conflict between people, plundering of the natural environment.

How this tragedy was undone by Christ's death on the Cross will be treated in the next chapter. For now, it is sufficient to say that where the pathology was pride, the remedy was humility. In the Second Adam risen from the dead, we see that the relationships that had been wounded by sin are healed by love. First, man's relation to God: the risen Jesus invites us to share the new life that restores us to God's grace. By the gift of the Holy Spirit, we become the sisters and brothers of Christ, able to call the heavenly Father *Abba* with the filial affection of the Son himself. Next, our relationships with one another: the risen Christ forgives the disciples who had abandoned him and scattered; now they are reunited in his love. In the New Testament era, the great sign of human reconciliation was the invitation for the Gentiles to enter the People of God. For centuries, the Jews had kept themselves apart from the nations around them in order to safeguard their unique relationship with God. Now, through the death and Resurrection of Christ, the wall dividing Jew and Gentile is torn down. Finally, all creation is renewed by the Resurrection of Christ, who confidently proclaims: "Behold, I make all things new" (Rev 21:5). God's plan, made known in the fullness of time, was "to unite all things in him, things in heaven and things on earth" (Eph 1:10). It is fitting that on Easter morning Mary Magdalen mistook the risen Jesus for the gardener, for that is who he is: the New Adam in the new Garden of Eden.

The Risen Christ and the Eucharist

We are born into this new creation by faith in Christ and the sacraments that unite us with him in his death and Resurrection. Our union with the risen Lord is nurtured especially in the Sunday celebration of the Eucharist. The Second Vatican Council in *Sacrosanctum Concilium* (*SC*) recalls that this weekly gathering has its roots in Easter: "By a tradition handed down from the apostles which took its origin from the very day of Christ's resurrection, the Church celebrates the paschal mystery every eighth day; with good reason this, then, bears the name of the Lord's day or Sunday" (no. 106). The first day of the week is holy for us because it was the day of the Lord's Resurrection after his Sabbath rest in the tomb. It is the "eighth day", the first day of the new creation, a day that knows no sunset. We keep holy the Lord's Day by celebrating the Eucharist because the Lord himself commanded us to do this. In the same Letter in which Saint Paul reminded the Corinthians of the tradition he had received about the Lord's Resurrection, he also recalled the tradition of the Last Supper. Paul reminds the Corinthians that when Jesus gave his disciples the cup he commanded them: "Do this, as often as you drink it, in remembrance of me" (1 Cor 11:25). Paul then warns them that anyone who eats and drinks without discerning the Body eats and drinks judgment upon himself. What does he mean by this?

The apostle is concerned with divisions and selfishness in the community. His readers must discern that the Church is the Mystical Body of Christ: rivalries and distinctions between rich and poor violate the truth that all in the community are members of the Body of the risen Lord. But since he speaks of eating or drinking unworthily, Saint Paul also means discerning that the Eucharist is the Body and Blood of Christ. This idea resonates with a statement he had made in the previous chapter: "The cup of blessing which we bless, is it not a participation in the blood of Christ? The bread which we break, is it not a participation in the body of Christ?" (1 Cor 10:16). On the basis of the words spoken by Jesus at the Last Supper, and this clear teaching of Saint Paul, the Catholic Church has always discerned that the Eucharist is truly the Body and Blood of Christ. This is the Body and Blood of the *risen* Christ: unlike the relic of a saint, which is a part of the saint's material, earthly body, what we are privileged to receive in Holy Communion is the glorified, resurrected Body of Christ.

As I conclude this chapter, I invite you to see our Sunday Eucharistic celebration in the light of Easter. The account of the appearance of the risen Christ to the two disciples on the road to Emmaus is the pattern of our weekly assembly (Lk 24:13–35). As the story opens, the disciples are walking away from Jerusalem, preoccupied and saddened by the tragedy of the crucifixion; the risen Jesus joins them and enters into their conversation. Each Sunday, we make our way to church with our own concerns, struggles, and distractions, but we gather as

Jesus' followers, and he is in our midst. The disciples in the Gospel are confused: the horrendous death of their Teacher has been traumatic, but they have heard stories of angels insisting that Jesus is alive. This is so like us! We believe, or we want to believe, but sadness, injustice, misunderstanding weigh us down and confuse us.

After Jesus has walked with his followers for a time, he begins to interpret the Scriptures for them, to show them how it was through his suffering that the Messiah was to enter into his glory. This is the Liturgy of the Word: as a community of disciples we listen to the word of God in faith, and the risen Christ himself instructs us through the Holy Spirit. The two disciples invite Jesus to stay with them. Saint Luke relates in a precise way what happened then: "When he was at table with them, he took the bread and blessed, and broke it, and gave it to them" (Lk 24:30). Luke's description evokes the Last Supper and our Liturgy of the Eucharist. We who have been enlightened by God's word in the Scripture are now nourished by the Body and Blood of Christ. We know him in the breaking of the bread.

At this point in the Gospel story, Jesus vanishes. What do the two disciples do? They hurry back to Jerusalem to tell others of their meeting with the risen Christ. The Resurrection appearances in the New Testament always involve a mission: the risen Christ is not a treasure to be jealously hoarded; rather, he is a gift to be generously shared. This final scene in the story corresponds to the dismissal at the end of our Sunday celebration. We are sent out to proclaim by generous service and confident witness that Christ is risen, that God's love is stronger than death. The most common name in the West for the Eucharistic celebration is the "Mass", from the Latin *missa*, a word that means "to be sent" (see *CCC*, no. 1332). Like the women hurrying away breathless from the tomb, like the two disciples rushing back to Jerusalem, like Saint Peter on that first Pentecost morning, we too are entrusted with Good News to share: "This Jesus God raised up, and of that we all are witnesses!" (Acts 2:32).

Chapter Two

Christ's Redemptive Death

Crucifixion was the cruelest form of capital punishment in the Roman Empire. It was meted out to traitors and slaves and was considered so degrading that it could not be inflicted on Roman citizens. The Jews abhorred crucifixion as the ultimate mark of subjugation, and on the basis of a text in Deuteronomy, "cursed be every one who hangs on a tree" (Gal 3:13; cf. Deut 21:23), they did not honor as martyrs their compatriots who were executed in this way. The two disciples on the road to Emmaus had good reason to be disheartened: not only had their Master died, but he had been put to death in the most shameful manner. And yet, within thirty years of Jesus' death, Saint Paul could write: "We preach Christ crucified, a stumbling block to Jews and folly to Gentiles, but to those who are called, both Jews and Greeks, Christ the power of God and the wisdom of God" (1 Cor 1:23–24). The Resurrection of Christ had transformed the badge of shame into a trophy.

What We Believe

Ever since the Fall, mankind has been estranged from God; this inherited state of alienation is ratified by our own sins. We could not repair the breach, but by his own free initiative, God sent his Son to lay down his life for us. Christ embraced his Passion and death in obedience to the Father's will and out of love for each and every man. By this one definitive sacrifice, we have been redeemed: we are freed from sin, delivered from the tyranny of death, and sanctified by the grace that makes us adopted daughters and sons of God. Christ attained this justification for the whole human race; each individual has the opportunity to appropriate this salvation by accepting God's offer of life in

23

Christ. Jesus Christ alone is the Savior, and the one Mediator between God and man.

Some History

Christ's Resurrection prompted his disciples to reflect on the meaning of his death: his crucifixion, such a catastrophic event in itself, clearly must have had a deeper meaning. Saint Paul expressed the fundamental conviction of the first believers very simply: "Christ died for our sins in accordance with the Scriptures" (1 Cor 15:3). How does the death of this one man bring salvation to the whole human race?

The story of Jesus' Passion is familiar to most of us. It has inspired drama, music, art, and literature for centuries. In the Creed, we profess simply that Christ suffered under Pontius Pilate, was crucified, died, and was buried. The mention of Pilate shows that Jesus' death was not a mythical event: it happened at a certain time and place. What about the details of that drama—how reliable are the accounts of Jesus' death in the Gospels? A couple of points should be made here. First, the basic narrative of the last week of Jesus' life, from his triumphant entry into Jerusalem to his crucifixion and burial, was composed very early. The four Evangelists show a great deal of flexibility when recounting the events of Jesus' ministry and his Resurrection appearances, but they are much more similar in their accounts of the final days of Jesus. It is as if the lens is adjusted a bit, and their description comes into clearer focus. The narrative of the Passion was well known by the time the Evangelists wrote. Second, each Evangelist tells the story in his own way. The sacred authors are not writing the life story of Jesus of Nazareth; they and their communities are asking, "What is the meaning of his life?" and more importantly, "What is the meaning of his *death*?"

The Passion of Jesus in the Four Gospels

I cannot attempt anything like a thorough presentation of what the Gospels say about the death of Jesus, but I would like to highlight a few characteristic elements in each account. Throughout the Gospel according to Saint Mark, the shortest of the four, Jesus experiences misunderstanding (even by his disciples) and rejection. A turning point comes halfway through the story when Peter proclaims that Jesus is the Messiah (Mk 8:27–30). In the wake of this profession, Jesus makes the first of three predictions of his Passion and death (Mk 8:31; 9:31; 10:33–34). Christ points to the redemptive significance of his death when he says, "The Son of man also came not to be served but to serve, and to give his life as a ransom for many" (Mk 10:45), and again at the Last Supper, when he tells the disciples: "This is my blood of the covenant, which is poured out for many" (Mk 14:24). Mark describes the death of Christ in stark terms: Jesus prays, "My God, my God, why have you forsaken me?" and dies uttering a loud cry (Mk 15:34, 37). Yet immediately after this scene of dereliction, the veil of the Temple is torn in two and a Roman soldier exclaims, "Truly this man was the Son of God!" (Mk 15:38–39).

Saint Matthew's Gospel is much longer than Mark's. Whereas Mark begins with the baptism of Jesus, Matthew includes an infancy narrative that, in the story of King Herod, provides a preview to the hostility that will bring Jesus to his death. In Matthew's Last Supper account, the redemptive meaning of Jesus' death is stated even more explicitly than in Mark's. Jesus says about the cup: "Drink of it, all of you; for this is my blood of the covenant, which is poured out for many for the forgiveness of sins" (Mt 26:27–28). While Matthew's Passion narrative is similar to Mark's, he adds suggestions of divine power at work: Jesus could, if he chose to, summon legions of angels to free him, and cosmic upheavals (earthquake, split rocks, opened tombs) occur at the moment of his death (Mt 26:53; 27:51–53).

Saint Luke's Gospel also contains an infancy narrative, and the shadow of the Cross appears when Simeon warns Mary that her child is a sign that will be opposed (Lk 2:34). Luke gives a more detailed description of the way of the Cross than the other Gospels; as Jesus is nailed to the Cross, he prays, "Father, forgive them; for they know not what they do" (Lk 23:34). Rather than a uttering a cry at the moment of death, Jesus says: "Father, into your hands I commit my spirit!" (Lk 23:46). This confident expression is preceded by Jesus' assurance to one of the criminals that this very day he will be with Jesus in Paradise. Luke underscores that Jesus' suffering is undeserved: one of the criminals, a soldier, Pilate, and Herod all proclaim Jesus' innocence. Luke wrote a sequel to his Gospel, the Acts of the Apostles, in which he shows that the Passion of Jesus is repeated in the life of the Church.

The Gospel according to Saint John differs significantly from the other three.[1] One fundamental theme in this Gospel is that the humiliation of the Cross and the glory of Christ's triumph are two sides of the same coin. We do not find in John the threefold Passion predictions by Christ, but there are three predictions that the Son of Man will be "lifted up"—and for John this means both lifted up on the Cross and lifted up in the Resurrection/Ascension (Jn 3:14; 8:28; 12:32). From start to finish, Jesus directs the drama: "For this reason the Father loves me, because I lay down my life, that I may take it again. No one takes it from me, but I lay it down of my own accord. I have power to lay it down, and I have power to take it again; this charge I have from my Father" (Jn 10:17–18). Jesus is always in control: he can be arrested only when he allows it, he engages Pilate in a lengthy conversation as his equal (if not his superior), he carries his own Cross without assistance. His dying words are, "It is finished", after which he bows his head and gives up his spirit. John signals the salvific meaning of Jesus' death in several ways: at the beginning of Jesus' public ministry, John the Baptist points him out as the Lamb of God who takes away the sins of the world; at his death, the Evangelist links the piercing of the side of Christ with the lambs that have just been sacrificed for the Passover feast; when Caiaphas suggests that it would be better to sacrifice one man rather than risk Roman reprisals, John comments: "He did not say this of his own accord, but being high priest that year he prophesied that Jesus should die for the nation, and not for the nation only, but to gather into one the children of God who are scattered abroad" (Jn 11:51–52).

The four Evangelists remain faithful to the basic narrative of Christ's Passion, yet each gives it a particular expression. Just as great artists over the centuries have painted the same biblical scenes in different ways, so each sacred author highlights aspects of the story that reflect the concerns of his audience. There are several shared convictions underlying these four different accounts: the death of Jesus was the culmination of his mission and something that he freely chose to undergo; he understood this to be God's will for him; Jesus was innocent and

---

[1] Because the Gospels of Matthew, Mark, and Luke have so many similarities, they are referred to as the synoptic Gospels (from a Greek word meaning "seeing with the same eyes"). Many scholars hold that Mark was written first and that Matthew and Luke used material from his Gospel, but the issue is far from settled.

did not deserve the punishment he received; and he shed his Blood to bring forgiveness of sin and liberation for all people. "Christ died for our sins" is one of the central assertions of the New Testament. How does it "work"?

How Jesus Has Saved Us by His Death

A key biblical concept here is redemption. In the ancient world, someone could buy a slave to free him, and Saint Paul uses this idea to explain how Christ's death liberates us. We are ransomed by the blood of Christ: "Since all have sinned and fall short of the glory of God, they are justified by his grace as a gift, through the redemption which is in Christ Jesus, whom God put forward as an expiation by his blood, to be received by faith" (Rom 3:24–25). To whom or what are we enslaved? Subjectively, to our selfish desires and sins; objectively, to the condition of alienation from God and the tyranny of death. A variation on this idea of redemption is substitution: the innocent Jesus freely paid the penalty for those who were guilty, as we read in the First Letter of Saint Peter: "For Christ also died for sins once for all, the righteous for the unrighteous, that he might bring us to God, being put to death in the flesh but made alive in the spirit" (1 Pet 3:18). These ideas offer some insight into the way Christ's death saves us from our sins. However, if the ideas of redemption or substitution are pushed too far they create a distorted picture of God as some kind of bloodthirsty tyrant. Over the centuries, many theories have been advanced to answer such questions as: To whom is the ransom paid? How can an innocent person's death avail the guilty? Does redemption require the death of Jesus? If so, why? The dogmatic teaching of the Church does not canonize any of these explanations; it simply professes that by his life, death, and Resurrection, Jesus saved mankind. Our understanding of redemption can go off track when we neglect two important truths about Jesus Christ: (1) that he is truly man, and as such in solidarity with the whole human race, and (2) that he is the Son of God, and as such always in intimate communion with the Father.

Christ's solidarity with us helps to clarify the meaning of *for* in the phrase "Christ died for us." Saint Paul taught that Christ did not die instead of us; rather, "we are convinced that one has died for all; therefore all have died" (2 Cor 5:14). Christ identified himself with us, not by a legal fiction, but by a real union. This is why he can act as our representative. As such, he is able to take our guilt upon himself; Paul could even say: "For our sake he [God] made him to be sin who knew no sin" (2 Cor 5:21). Although innocent himself, Jesus unites himself with sinners and lays down his life for them. He can act on our behalf because he truly is our Brother.

Christ's union with the Father means that all he endured in his Passion was willed by the Father. Rather than being a victim delivered up to God's wrath, Christ is the Son handed over by the Father to *our* wrath, handed over to show the depth of God's love for us.[2] When we recall that Jesus accepted death in obedience to the Father's will, we learn something of the depth of God's mercy. Saint John tells us, "God so loved the world that he gave his only-begotten Son" (Jn 3:16)—and God did not simply give him in the sense of sending him into the world; he gave him up to the ignominious death on the Cross. Saint Paul proclaimed the death of Jesus as the great sign of the Father's love for us in his Letter to the Romans: "He who did not spare his own Son but gave him up for us all, will he not also give us all things with him?" (8:32).

The Cross shows God's love for us, but it also shows our love for God, because Jesus gives completely to the Father the filial love and obedience that is his due, the love Adam and his descendants have refused to give. The *Catechism* describes this twofold love succinctly:

> This sacrifice of Christ is unique; it completes and surpasses all other sacrifices [cf. Heb 10:10]. First, it is a gift from God the Father himself, for the Father handed his Son over to sinners in order to reconcile us with himself. At the same time it is the offering of the Son of God made man, who in freedom and love offered his life to his Father through the Holy Spirit in reparation for our disobedience.[3]

We return once again to the theme of the "New Adam": what distinguishes Christ from the first Adam is his *loving obedience*. Saint

---

[2] See *CCC*, nos. 599–600. The reference to "our wrath" touches on the question of who was responsible for the death of Jesus, and the tragic history of anti-Semitism that has laid the blame upon the Jewish people. We must acknowledge that this prejudice has been a very real one among Christians over the centuries, but the teaching of the Church, articulated at least as far back as the *Roman Catechism* four centuries ago, is that all sinners are responsible for the death of Jesus, and that we who claim to know Jesus and yet persist in sin are more culpable than the Jews. See *CCC*, no. 598.

[3] *CCC*, no. 614; cf. Jn 10:17–18; 15:13; Heb 9:14; 1 Jn 4:10.

Paul has a beautiful passage in his Letter to the Philippians that is very likely the citation of a very early hymn:

> Have this mind among yourselves, which was in Christ Jesus, who, though he was in the form of God, did not count equality with God a thing to be grasped, but emptied himself, taking the form of a servant, being born in the likeness of men. And being found in human form he humbled himself and became obedient unto death, even death on a cross. Therefore God has highly exalted him and bestowed on him the name which is above every name, that at the name of Jesus every knee should bow, in heaven and on earth and under the earth, and every tongue confess that Jesus Christ is Lord, to the glory of God the Father. (Phil 2:5–11)

Adam's desire to snatch at divine status led to disobedience and death; Christ's humble embrace of death on the Cross gives us divine life. He restores the spiritual ecology by reversing Adam's revolt.

Christ Freely Laid Down His Life for All People

References to Christ as a sacrificial Lamb appear several times in the New Testament, associated primarily with the Passover lamb, whose blood was instrumental in freeing the Jewish people from slavery in Egypt. The Letter to the Hebrews combines this idea of Christ as sacrificial offering with the conviction that he acts on his own volition. Christ is Victim and Priest on Calvary: he is both one who has been tested, who has offered loud cries and supplications, who can sympathize with us in our weakness; and the holy, blameless, undefiled high priest, separated from sinners and exalted to the heavens, who has offered the one perfect sacrifice that brings about our reconciliation (Heb 4:14–16; 5:7; 9:26–27). Once a year, on the Day of Atonement, the Jewish high priest entered the Holy of Holies with the blood of animals to expiate the sins of the people. Jesus, the Priest of the New Covenant, "entered once for all into the Holy Place [Heaven], taking not the blood of goats and calves but his own blood, thus securing an eternal redemption" (Heb 9:12). This offering took place once, on Calvary, but there is an eternal quality to it: Christ is High Priest forever, as well as forever the Lamb who was slain. Our Catholic tradition sees this eternal priestly sacrifice in Heaven mirrored on earth in the Eucharist. Saint Paul teaches: "For as often as you eat this bread and drink the chalice, you proclaim the Lord's death until he comes" (1 Cor 11:26). In the Eucharistic celebration, the one perfect sacrifice of the crucified and risen Christ becomes present in our midst.

Jesus offered the perfect sacrifice "once and for all". We can understand this to mean "for all time": the Roman Canon describes Christ's sacrifice as the fulfillment of all the sacrifices offered before him, reaching all the way back to Abel; by extension, we could say it is the fulfillment of every human effort to attain reconciliation with God. But we also understand "for all" to refer to all people, to the whole human race and each individual member of it without exception. In the First Letter of Saint John we read: "He is the expiation for our sins, and not for ours only but also for the sins of the whole world" (1 Jn 2:2). For this reason, the Catholic Church has always rejected the idea that Christ died only for some; on the contrary, we affirm: "There is not, never has been, and never will be a single human being for whom Christ did not suffer." [4]

A striking expression of the universality of Christ's redemptive death is his descent among the dead. The phrase in the Apostles' Creed "he descended into Hell" (*descendit ad inferos*) may create confusion because we associate Hell with the place of eternal punishment. In this context, however, the term *inferos* refers to the abode of the dead: we affirm that Christ truly died, and his soul was separated from his body. But there is a deeper mystery at work here, hinted at by an admittedly obscure phrase in the First Letter of Saint Peter: "For this is why the gospel was preached even to the dead, that though judged in the flesh like men, they might live in the spirit like God" (1 Pet 4:6). By his presence among the dead, Jesus associates them with his victory over the grave. Christ himself spoke of this: "Truly, truly, I say to you, the hour is coming, and now is, when the dead will hear the voice of the Son of God, and those who hear will live" (Jn 5:25). Christ's saving power embraces all the righteous dead who lived before him, a truth captured in icons that show the risen Christ leading Adam, Eve, and their descendants out of the dark prison of death. An ancient homily for Holy Saturday expresses this same truth: "He has gone to search for Adam, our first father, as for a lost sheep. Greatly desiring to visit

---

[4] Council of Quiercy (853): DS 624, quoted in *CCC*, no. 605; cf. 2 Cor 5:15; 1 Jn 2:2.

those who live in darkness and the shadow of death, he has gone to free from sorrow Adam in his bonds and Eve, captive with him—He who is both their God and the son of Eve."[5]

God's plan of salvation is universal, but it is unique as well. God "desires all men to be saved and to come to the knowledge of the truth. For there is one God, and there is one mediator between God and men, the man Christ Jesus, who gave himself as a ransom for all" (1 Tim 2:4–6). At the heart of the Gospel stands the conviction that Christ alone is the Savior. As Jesus told his disciples at the Last Supper, "I am the way, and the truth, and the life; no one comes to the Father, but by me" (Jn 14:6). We will take up the implications of this statement for non-Christians in the chapter on the Church; the point here is that God has accomplished the redemption of the whole human race through Christ's sacrifice on the Cross. But the heart of redemption is love, and love presumes freedom; we have a part to play in our redemption. We are free to associate ourselves or not with Christ's filial obedience to his Father. We accept the offer of salvation by seeking union with Christ, by believing in him, obeying him, and striving to live like him.

Implications

Christ restores our relationship with God, as Saint Paul tells us: "And you, who once were estranged and hostile in mind, doing evil deeds, he has now reconciled in his body of flesh by his death, in order to present you holy and blameless and irreproachable before him" (Col 1:21–22). We may think Saint Paul exaggerates when he calls us "hostile" to God; part of the blindness caused by sin is that we minimize its effects. Jesus himself warns us that we cannot serve two masters, that we end up hating one of them (Mt 6:24). We glimpse something of the enormity of sin in the horror of Christ's scourging and crucifixion. In a meditation for the Stations of the Cross, Cardinal Newman has Jesus say, "I am suffering now, but I shall triumph; and, when I triumph, those souls for whom I am dying will either be my dearest friends or my deadliest enemies."[6] We cannot be mere "acquaintances" of God—we

---

[5] An Ancient Homily for Holy Saturday: PG 43, 440A, 452C (Liturgy of the Hours, Office of Readings, Holy Saturday), quoted in CCC, no. 635.

[6] John Henry Newman, Prayers, Verses, and Devotions (San Francisco: Ignatius Press, 1989), p. 230.

are either friends or enemies. The depth of God's love for us is shown in the body of his beloved Son nailed to the Cross. What more could the Father do for us than this? Meditation on Christ crucified is an antidote to both presumption and despair: when we think lightly of our sins, we should recall what those sins cost him; when we are overwhelmed by our sins, we should remember that where sin abounds, grace abounds all the more (Rom 5:20).

Christ Heals Our Relationship to One Another and Creation

The sacrifice that restores our communion with God also drains the poison infecting our relations with one another. The pride that exalts self at the expense of others and divides the world into "us" and "them" is brought low by the humility of Christ, who was driven out of the city and condemned to death with "them", the outcasts. In his death, Jesus was "reckoned with transgressors" (Lk 22:37) to demolish the barriers erected by ambition, fear, and self-righteousness. Human harmony was wrecked by a tree, and it is restored by one—the Cross. Saint John brings this point home when he describes the Mother of Jesus and the beloved disciple standing beneath the Cross. One of the key moments in the drama of the crucifixion comes when Jesus says to Mary, "Woman, behold, your son!" and to the disciple, "Behold, your mother!" (Jn 19:26, 27). The Evangelist tells us that after he said this, Jesus knew that all was now finished—he had completed his mission. A new kind of human bond had come into being, stronger than kinship, treaties, or contracts: the bond of faith. Christ reconciles us to the Father by his death, and in the power of that love, our human ties are transformed.

Why is this? Because Christ lives in us through the gift of the Holy Spirit; we no longer love others solely with our limited human abilities, but with the love of Christ himself. His love is not self-seeking or calculating, but generous and sacrificial. Cut off from God, we are left to our own resources—and when we are honest with ourselves, we recognize how meager those resources are. The new family of believers at the foot of the Cross is quickened by the breath of the Holy Spirit and nourished by the blood and water flowing from the pierced side of the Second Adam. The *new* commandment of Christ, "Love one another; even *as I have loved you*" (Jn 13:34, emphasis added), seems impossible for us to fulfill until we recall that he also said, "As the Father has loved me, so have I loved you; abide in my love" (Jn 15:9). This is the miracle of Cana: the water of human love, essential to our survival, is transformed into the wine of divine love, the source of our joy.

There is another way in which the Cross of Christ heals our human relations: not only in our ability to love, but in our desire to be loved as well. Deep within each of us, there is a tremendous hunger to be cherished, to feel that someone loves us totally, unconditionally, and without limit. No man can give us this love; how much misery is created when we expect that kind of love from another creature who is, like ourselves, weak and limited! The problem lies, not in the desire itself, but in the expectation that anyone other than God can meet it. When our communion with God is restored, we no longer expect a friend, a spouse, a parent, or a child to give us the kind of love that only God can bestow.

Finally, just as human greed marred the whole of creation, so the generous self-sacrifice of Christ graces the whole universe. We profess in the Creed that "through him all things were made", and all creation— earthly and heavenly—is reconciled through the blood of his Cross (see Col 1:20). In the liturgy of Good Friday, we venerate the Cross of Christ, proclaiming: "This is the wood of the Cross, on which hung the Savior of the world." Jesus did not save the world through some celestial combat; he was "crucified under Pontius Pilate" in our earthly creation. He not only endured bodily suffering, but he also taught us to control our desires when using the goods of this world. At the outset of his ministry, Jesus fasted forty days in the wilderness. To the temptation to turn the stones around him into bread, he answered, "It is written, 'Man shall not live by bread alone, but by every word that proceeds from the mouth of God'" (Mt 4:4). Another time his disciples brought him food, but he refused it, saying, "My food is to do the will of him who sent me, and to accomplish his work" (Jn 4:34). By his self-denial, Jesus teaches us to curb our appetite for consumption. We are to use the goods of this world as stewards obedient to God, not as proprietors who plunder the environment for our own selfish ends.

Christ's self-denial found its greatest expression on the Cross. He experienced the indignity many people endure when the end of life becomes a second infancy, a time of utter helplessness. The dying Christ refused to exercise his miraculous power; he would not come down from the Cross. Jesus did not deliver a sermon—he made a plea: "I thirst" (Jn 19:28). It is a thirst both human and divine that is quenched, not only with the prostration of worship, but also with the embrace of love.

Christ's Answer to the Problem of Suffering

The Cross helps us deal with the mystery of suffering. Every philosophy and religion grapples with this problem. Christ does not offer an explanation; he gives an example. We find a paradox at the core of Jesus' life: he devoted himself tirelessly to alleviating the sufferings of others, yet he welcomed the Cross for himself. Saint Luke describes a turning point in the mission of Jesus: "When the days drew near for him to be received up, he set his face to go to Jerusalem" (Lk 9:51). Jesus is like a general launching his campaign: he advances on Jerusalem because that is the city where prophets must die. Christ could have avoided arrest, but once it was clear to him that this was the Father's will, he marched forward to Calvary.

The saints have followed his example: over the centuries, holy people have poured out their lives in generous service to others while welcoming a share in the Passion of Christ in their own lives. The traditional paintings of ascetics gazing on a crucifix strike some people as morbid, but perhaps the saints see a butterfly where we see only a worm. In Christ crucified, the saints contemplate at leisure the brightly colored hues of divine mercy that could only be glimpsed on the wing in Jesus' ministry. That mercy fuels the charity of the saints. To welcome the Cross for oneself while striving to lift it from others is the antithesis of worldly wisdom, which tells us to pursue our advantage no matter the cost to others.

As Jesus took leave of his disciples at the Last Supper, he told them, "You know the way where I am going." In response, Thomas said, "Lord, we do not know where you are going; how can we know the way?" (Jn 14:4–5). A few days later, the Easter light of the Resurrection dispelled the mists of confusion and revealed to the disciples the goal of the Master's journey: life without end, and the Cross as its way. What our Lord said was true: the disciples knew the way—for who does not know suffering and death?—but they did not know it was *the* way until Jesus himself had traveled it and come through it victorious. Before Easter, suffering did not appear to be a way at all, but a dead-end, with futility adding to its cruelty. Christ does not offer a way around suffering, but a path through it: "In the world you have tribulation; but be of good cheer, I have overcome the world" (Jn 16:33).

Our suffering, and, what is much harder to bear, the sufferings of those we love, will always be part of the tribulation of this world, which, for all its beauty, is not our true home. When we are afflicted with illness, humbled by waning strength, embarrassed that we have become a burden to others, the Cross stands as a reminder that Jesus did not save the world through miracles or preaching, but by embracing his death in obedient love. The hands that had reached out to bless, to heal, even to raise the dead, were pinned to the Cross. The feet that had carried him from village to village to proclaim the Good News could no longer move. And yet it was on the Cross that Jesus accomplished his greatest work.

He who made the blind see and the lame walk does not call us to be masochists. Christ shrank from the cup of suffering when it drew near—until he realized that this was now the Father's will. As such, this cup was lovingly accepted by the Son who trusted that the Father who had led him *to* death would lead him *through* it. The Cross, so horrible in itself, was transformed into the royal standard of Christ's love for the Father and for us. And as Saint Paul teaches, the Cross can make suffering redemptive: "Now I rejoice in my sufferings for your sake, and in my flesh I complete what is lacking in Christ's afflictions for the sake of his body, that is, the church" (Col 1:24). This is a mystery of divine condescension: Christ's death was the one perfect sacrifice that redeemed the world, yet he associates our sufferings with his. No human experience is wasted or meaningless.

When Jesus first foretold his Passion and death, Saint Peter would hear none of it: "God forbid, Lord! This shall never happen to you" (Mt 16:22). When the drama of the Passion began to unfold in the Garden of Gethsemane, the leader of the Twelve first resisted it with the sword and then fled from it in terror. Only after the Resurrection, in the strength of the Holy Spirit, was Saint Peter able to stretch out his hands to welcome a martyr's death for the glory of God. He had learned the intimate connection between Good Friday and Easter Sunday. His companion in martyrdom, Saint Paul, wrote from prison:

> Indeed I count everything as loss because of the surpassing worth of knowing Christ Jesus my Lord. For his sake I have suffered the loss of all things, and count them as refuse ... that I may know him and the power of his resurrection, and may share his sufferings, becoming like him in his death, that if possible I may attain the resurrection from the dead. (Phil 3:8–11)

The Cross alone can bear us to Easter; Easter alone can make the Cross bearable.

Chapter Three

The Incarnation of the Son of God

"Who do you say that I am?" (Mk 8:29). The question that Jesus put to his disciples at Caesarea Philippi became more significant after his death and Resurrection. Many answers have been given to that question over the past twenty centuries. What is the response of Catholic faith?

What We Believe

From all eternity, God the Father begets God the Son, who fully shares his divine nature. At a certain moment in history, this eternal Son took on a human nature and was born of the Virgin Mary. As the Son of God, Jesus Christ possesses all of the divine attributes (uncreated, eternal, all-powerful, all-knowing, etc.). As the Son of Mary, he has all the qualities proper to a human nature (created, body, soul, human intellect and will). While the natures themselves remain distinct (Christ is fully human and fully divine, not a mixture of the two), they are related to one another by virtue of their union to the Person of the eternal Son. Jesus Christ is true God and true man.

Some History

I have stated very simply the core meaning of the dogma of the Incarnation; it can be summed up even more succinctly in the words of the Apostles' Creed: "I believe in Jesus Christ, his only Son, our Lord. He was conceived by the power of the Holy Spirit and born of the Virgin Mary." The *Catechism* calls belief in the Incarnation the distinctive sign of Christian faith (no. 463). This doctrine is the key to the riddle of Jesus' identity and the gateway to the most profound mystery of our faith, the Trinity. Although the dogma can be summed up in a

few phrases, it took centuries for some kind of clarity to emerge about
the Incarnation, and there is much we will never comprehend. The
greatest theologians in the early Church struggled to find expressions
and formulas that would do some justice to the identity of Christ; the
first several ecumenical councils met to deal with the deceptively simple question, "Who do you say that I am?" We might picture the
Church during the first seven centuries as a ship navigating a channel.
The strait is fairly wide; the ship tacks first toward one shore, then
toward the other. The dogmatic definitions are like buoys set out as
warnings against shoals: to sail too close to one shore or the other is to
risk shipwreck. Some dismiss these ancient debates as arid philoso-
phizing, but the contenders knew that at the heart of the arguments
stood a very practical question: How does God save us?

What the Bible Tells Us about Jesus

Our starting place is Scripture. Two cautions are in order as we open
the Bible to answer Jesus' question: "Who do you say that I am?"
First, we need to be on guard against reading later insights back into
the New Testament (which is very different from seeing later understandings rooted in the New Testament). Take for example the two
titles "Son of God" and "Son of Man". These titles have been used
for centuries to refer to Christ's divine and human natures, respectively; they meant something different, almost contrary, in the first
century. "Son of God" was a title used in the Old Testament for angels,
the chosen people as a whole, and their kings (*CCC*, no. 441). The
title suggested a close relationship with God, but it did not mean that
the one so designated was divine. "Son of Man" could simply mean a
"man", but the title was also used to refer to an exalted heavenly
figure (see Dan 7:13). Scholars debate what implications can be drawn
about Jesus from the use of these titles in the New Testament; the
point here is that we should not assume that the terms of the title
have the same meanings in Scripture that they came to have later.

   Another caution to keep in mind, especially when reading the Gospels, is that the authors are interpreting the life of Jesus in light of his
death and Resurrection. The title "Christ" (a Greek translation of the
Hebrew *Messiah*) was rarely used of Jesus in his lifetime, but was
employed so frequently after the Resurrection that it soon became

part of his name. Looking back on the career of Jesus in light of Easter, the disciples realized that he was "the Christ", but that what it meant for him to be the Messiah was not what people expected.

Our exploration of Jesus' identity begins with what his followers said about him; we have no other access to the "historical Jesus". Let us consider the New Testament as a whole and ask, "What did the first followers of Jesus believe about him? How did they answer the question, 'Who do you say that I am?'"

We have seen that the disciples were convinced that Jesus had risen from the dead and was now seated in glory at the Father's right hand. There are several allusions as well in the New Testament to belief in some kind of preexistence of Christ before his coming into the world. Jesus makes remarkable assertions in the Gospels: he considers himself superior to the prophets and kings of the Old Testament; he is greater than the Temple and Lord of the Sabbath; he existed before Abraham and King David, who called him "Lord"; angels are his servants; he is superior to Moses and interprets the Law on his own authority; he refers to himself as the "Bridegroom" (a title for God in the Old Testament) and accepts veneration from people; he performs miracles, including the raising of the dead, and he forgives sins; he claims the authority to judge; he is described as the Word who was with the Father before anything was made. On the other hand, Jesus spent most of his life as an ordinary laborer in an obscure village; he grew tired and thirsty; he was gentle and humble, refusing any kind of political power over others; he allowed himself to be handed over to his enemies, experienced terrible mental and physical sufferings, and endured a brutal death. The paradoxes leap out at us from every page of the Gospels, although familiarity may dull their edge: Jesus makes audacious claims about himself, yet washes the feet of his disciples; he weeps at the tomb of Lazarus, then raises him back to life; he claims authority to interpret the Law, but submits to lawful authorities when they condemn him unjustly; he accepts the worship of the man born blind, but rejects the adulation of the crowds; he walks on water, yet asks the Samaritan woman to give him a drink; he forgives sins, but dies with outcasts.

The key to these paradoxes is Jesus' relationship to God, whom he called "Father". The title is used rarely of God in the Old Testament, perhaps fifteen times altogether. The word fills the pages of the New

Testament, and whenever Jesus uses the term, he always distinguishes between "my Father" and "your Father". In Matthew, "your Father" and "my Father" each appear twenty times; in John, Jesus refers to "your Father" only once, and to "the Father" or "my Father" 122 times. In one parable, Jesus describes the owner of a vineyard (an Old Testament image of God, with Israel understood to be the vineyard) sending out messengers to the wicked tenants; his hearers understood that these were the prophets. But Jesus adds a novel twist: "He had still one other, a beloved son; finally he sent him to them, saying, 'They will respect my son'" (Mk 12:6). Far from respecting the son, the tenants kill him. Mark comments that Jesus' opponents knew that he was speaking about them; by implication, Jesus is claiming to be greater than the prophets, to be in fact "the Son". In another place, Jesus gives thanks to the Father, saying: "All things have been delivered to me by my Father; and no one knows the Son except the Father; and no one knows the Father except the Son and any one to whom the Son chooses to reveal him" (Mt 11:27). The unique relationship between Jesus and the Father is presented most extensively in John's Gospel, where the implication of his claim is spelled out: "This was why the Jews sought all the more to kill him, because he not only broke the sabbath but also called God his Father, making himself equal with God" (Jn 5:18). To speak of God as Jesus did would be blasphemy—unless it was true. For the followers of Jesus, his Resurrection was the vindication of his claim to be the Father's Son.

Saint Mark opens his account with the words: "The beginning of the gospel of Jesus Christ, the Son of God" (Mk 1:1); he describes the Spirit descending on Jesus at his baptism and a voice from Heaven declaring, "You are my beloved Son; with you I am well pleased" (Mk 1:11); and at the climax of his narrative, Jesus dies and a Gentile soldier professes, "Truly this man was the Son of God!" (Mk 15:39). The Gospels of Matthew and Luke each include infancy narratives that tell of Mary's virginal conception. Jesus has no human father; God alone is his Father. In the fourth Gospel, John writes that Christ was in the Father's presence "in the beginning", before anything was made, and he possesses "glory as of the only-begotten Son from the Father" (Jn 1:14). The affirmation resounds all through the New Testament that Christ Jesus is, in some unique and preeminent way, *the* Son of the Father.

The Bible gives many answers to the question, "Who do you say that I am?" But these answers raise new questions, principally two: How is Jesus Christ related to God? How is Jesus Christ related to us? In answering these questions, later generations of his followers continued to study the Scriptures, the Old Testament as well as the New, and they mined the riches of Greek philosophy. They knew that they were dealing with profound mysteries, mysteries whose depths would always elude them, but they recognized that the Gospel message of salvation was tied to Jesus' relationships to God and to us. We must also bear in mind that they were not simply exploring the identity of a figure in the past: they sensed that the same Christ who preached, performed miracles, and gave his life on the Cross was risen, living, and active in their midst.

Jesus Is Truly God

Let us consider first the relationship between Jesus and God. There is a trajectory running through the New Testament that increasingly identified Christ as "Son of God" to such an extent that the title implied some kind of equality with God. This raised a pivotal question: How was it possible to claim this, and yet still profess that there is only one God? For Jews, it was blasphemous for anyone to claim equality with God; for Greeks, the idea that God could become a frail, mortal creature was absurd. To safeguard monotheism, some suggested that Jesus was merely a man who at some moment (such as his baptism or Resurrection) received some kind of divine power that made him a "Son of God" by adoption. This did not square with the scriptural testimony that pushed Christ's Sonship back to the beginning of his human life, and further still to the time before anything was created, nor with the fact that in the Gospels Jesus exercised divine prerogatives (such as raising the dead, forgiving sins, judging) in his own name. An alternative explanation held that the one God is at work throughout salvation history, but playing three different roles: Creator, Redeemer, and Sanctifier. This explanation had the advantage of accounting for Jesus' divine power and its ongoing influence in the community of believers. However, it implied that the distinction between the Father and the Son is only apparent; and yet, while Jesus spoke of himself as being one with the Father, he also spoke clearly of him as "*my* Father", which presumed a real distinction between the Father and the Son.

A more fruitful avenue was found in the concept of the "Word", or *Logos*. The foundation for this approach was laid in John's Gospel, which described Christ as the Word who was with God in the beginning, and through whom all things were made (Jn 1:1–3). The term *Logos* resonated with both Jewish and Greek thought. For the Jews, the Word was the agent of God's creative and saving power, as well as divine Wisdom; for the Greeks, the *Logos* was "Reason", the source of order in the world. Christian apologists drew on these traditions to propose a gradual unfolding of the *Logos*: as thought, or mind, the Word was immanent in God from all eternity; in the act of creation, it was generated or expressed outside the mind of God (and here it became distinct, "the Son"); in the Old Testament, it became the revelation of God in the Law, Wisdom, and the biblical theophanies (appearances of God); and finally, the Word became flesh in Christ in order that through his teaching, death, and Resurrection we could receive divine life.

The theology of the *Logos* had much to recommend it. It preserved God's transcendence in relation to creation; it expressed both unity and distinctiveness between God and the Word; and it demonstrated that Christ's mission as universal Savior had been prepared for both by the sacred history of the Jews and the wisdom of pagan philosophy. Christians affirmed that Christ was the Word incarnate, but a crucial question had to be answered: on which side of the line did the *Logos* stand—Creator or creature? Was the Word "God" in the same way the Father was?

Early in the fourth century, a priest in Alexandria named Arius taught that God the Son was a creature. Arius held that the Father had first created the *Logos* and then through him brought everything else into being. The Son enjoyed a unique relationship with God, but, in the words of an Arian slogan, "There was a time when he was not." Arius' explanation was very attractive, and it spread quickly. The doctrine appealed to philosophers and theologians because it preserved God's transcendence by providing a way to distance the full divinity of God from the limitations involved in the Incarnation of the *Logos*. It also had great political appeal, because the emphasis on one God with one earthly representative dovetailed with Constantine's ambitions to use the Christian religion to unify the Roman Empire. But many resisted this teaching because it did not do justice to the fundamental Christian conviction that it is God himself whom we encounter in Christ. The champion of this view was Saint Athanasius, who urged that when the Scripture calls Jesus *Emmanuel* (God with us), it means literally what it says. We are saved only because Christ is truly God.

The religion Constantine had hoped would hold his empire together was threatening to split it apart. Recognizing the need for a unified Christian front, he summoned the bishops to Nicaea in the year 325, to what was to be the first ecumenical council in the history of the Church. The overwhelming majority of bishops agreed with Athanasius and condemned the Arian doctrine that the *Logos* was created. They found it necessary to express more exactly the relationship between the Father and the Son, and they accepted the term *homoousios*, meaning "of the same nature or essence", to be an apt expression of that relationship. The word was translated into Latin as *consubstantialis* (consubstantial). The word *ousia* in Greek meant simply "being" or "substance", but the Fathers at Nicaea gave it a precise connotation: by *homoousios*, they meant that the Father and the Son possess the same divine nature. Since God is by nature without beginning (eternal), the Son must be eternal; he is not in any way a creature. Some objected that this definition risked blurring the distinction between the Father and the Son. In response, the defenders of *homoousios* argued that there is a very real distinction: the Father gives the divine nature, the Son receives it. Just as we pass on human nature to our children, and cats have kittens, so the Father "begets" the Son. (We should recognize that we are in the realm of deep mystery here. First, there is no gender in God, so the language of "Father" and "Son" is analogous, although it is the language used by Christ himself. Second, every example of "begetting" in our experience entails "before" and "after", but God is eternal, so there is no moment when the Son is begotten; if there were, he would not possess the divine attribute of being eternal.) Although it took a long time for the decision of Nicaea to be accepted everywhere, the dogma itself is simple: Christ is truly God. Every time we recite the Nicene Creed, we profess that we believe "in one Lord Jesus Christ, the Only Begotten Son of God, born of the Father before all ages, God from God, Light from Light, true God from true God, consubstantial with the Father".

Jesus Is Truly Man

What about Christ's relation to us? The Nicene Creed goes on to state: "For us men and for our salvation, he came down from heaven, and by the power of the Holy Spirit was incarnate of the Virgin Mary, and became man."[1] Given that the Son is truly God, in what sense can we say that he is truly man? Two responses to this question emerged. One approach emphasized that "he came down from heaven": Jesus was God himself in our midst. The temptation here was to emphasize the divinity of Christ so much that his real humanity was compromised. The alternative approach underscored the truth that "he was made man". The disadvantage here was that, in the interest of safeguarding the full humanity of Jesus, it might seem that there was no intrinsic union between his divine and human natures: Christ would be a human Person and a divine Person living parallel lives. The first approach was favored in Alexandria, which had been the home of Saint Athanasius. Alexandria was a great center of speculative philosophy, and given that their bishop had championed the divinity of Christ in the Arian controversy, the Alexandrians naturally supported the position that highlighted Christ as "God with us". The second view was favored at Antioch in Syria, another great intellectual center, but one less prone to speculative theology than Alexandria.

Such questions might seem rather arcane, but a combination of politics and piety brought the two approaches into heated conflict. Alexandria and Antioch had long been the principal Christian churches of the East, but the ecclesiastical landscape changed when Christianity became the religion of the Roman Empire. Jerusalem, the location of the great events of salvation history, became very prominent; Constantinople, the new imperial capital, likewise enjoyed great prestige.

In the year 428, a priest from Antioch named Nestorius was appointed Bishop of Constantinople. Formed in a tradition that emphasized the humanity of Jesus as distinct from his divinity, he was shocked to hear people in the capital addressing Mary as *"Theotokos"*, the one who gave birth to God. Nestorius considered this title erroneous: he argued

---

[1] This quotation and the preceding are taken from the new English translation of the Ordinary of the Mass, promulgated in the fall of 2011. This version is a more literal translation of the Latin original than the translation that was in use for the preceding forty years.

that she should be called *"Christotokos"*, the one who gave birth to Christ. From the Alexandrian point of view, this seemed to deny that Christ was truly the Son of God, and the Ecumenical Council of Ephesus in 431 affirmed that Mary's Son was, from the first moment of conception, the Son of God, and that for this reason the title *Theotokos* was appropriate. We will explore the teaching of Ephesus in a later chapter, but the events surrounding that council demonstrated the need for greater clarity concerning the relationship between the divine and human natures of Christ, and just "who" Christ is.

A solution was proposed in a letter sent from Pope Leo I to the Patriarch of Constantinople in about the year 449. His way of expressing the matter was adopted by the Ecumenical Council of Chalcedon (451). The pope and the council taught that there is one "subject" in Christ, and that subject is the eternally begotten Son of God. (Saint Leo used the Latin word *persona* and the fathers of Chalcedon used the Greek word *hypostasis*. We will explore the meaning of those terms in the next chapter; for now it is sufficient to know that they answer the question of *who* Christ is: he is God the Son.) This personal subject is unique because he has two natures, divine and human. He possesses the former from all eternity, since the Son receives the divine nature eternally from the Father. The eternal Son of God took on a human nature in the mystery of the Incarnation, but in such a way that each nature maintains its integrity. In the beautiful words of Saint Leo:

> Lowliness was taken up by majesty, weakness by strength, mortality by eternity.... Thus was true God born in the undiminished and perfect nature of a true man, complete in what is his and complete in what is ours.... He took on the form of a servant without the defilement of sin, thereby enhancing the human and not diminishing the divine. For that self-emptying ... spelled no failure of power: it was an act of merciful favour.[2]

The two natures remain distinct, but they are inseparable because the Person of the Son possesses both of them. The Council of Chalcedon formulated the dogma in this way:

[2] Letter of Pope Leo to Flavian, *Decrees of the Ecumenical Councils*, vol. 1, trans. by Norman Tanner (Washington, D.C.: Sheed & Ward and Georgetown University Press, 1990), p. 77.

> We confess that one and the same Christ, Lord, and only-begotten
> Son, is to be acknowledged in two natures without confusion, change,
> division, or separation. The distinction between the natures was never
> abolished by their union, but rather the character proper to each of the
> two natures was preserved as they came together in one person (*pros-
> opon*) and one hypostasis.[3]

This sounds very abstract, but the language was intended to safeguard
a core affirmation of our faith: the Son of God himself was born,
died, and rose from the dead to save us. Because Christ is truly God,
he can perform miracles and free us from sin and death; because he is
truly man, he can give us an example of courage, patience, and humility, and his humanity means that his sacrifice redeems all of mankind.

The Chalcedonian settlement represented a compromise, and it was
not completely successful. It took two centuries to work out some of
its implications, and it was rejected by many Christians in Syria, Egypt,
Ethiopia, and Armenia.[4] Definitions are helpful, even necessary, but
they never fully express the mystery of the Christian faith. The dogmatic teachings that we have inherited from the controversies of distant centuries are best understood as clarifying what Christians must
not say: we must not deny that Christ is truly the eternally begotten
Son of God incarnate; we must not deny that as the Son of God he
possesses a divine nature, with all the attributes proper to that nature;
and we must not deny that by virtue of his Incarnation he has a human
nature that is the same as ours.

Implications

Jesus Is Fully Human and Fully Divine

To say that the Son of God has taken on our human nature means
that he has a body and a rational human soul, with its faculties of
intellect and will. Each of these elements has raised questions. Regarding the body, while many people today find it difficult to believe that
Christ is divine, the stumbling block when the Gospel was first preached

---

[3] Council of Chalcedon (451): DS 302, quoted in *CCC*, no. 467.
[4] These churches preserved many of the apostolic traditions and produced some remarkable mystical theologians. They also carried the Gospel far and wide; for example, missionaries from the Assyrian church of the East traveled as far as China and Korea.

was the claim that he was truly human. The idea that a divine being could suffer and die seemed foolish especially to the Gnostics, who rejected the idea that a spiritual being could be connected with this material, corrupt world.[5] In answer to this view, the First Letter of Saint John emphasizes Christ's bodily reality: "That which was from the beginning, which we have heard, which we have seen with our eyes, which we have looked upon and touched with our hands, concerning the word of life—the life was made manifest, and we saw it" (1 Jn 1:1–2). John's Second Letter states quite frankly: "For many deceivers have gone out into the world, men who will not acknowledge the coming of Jesus Christ in the flesh; such a one is the deceiver and the antichrist" (2 Jn 7). Although Jesus was conceived miraculously, he went through all of the normal stages of bodily growth from conception to death.

Others believed that Christ had a physical body, but that he did not have a human soul; the *Logos* took its place. But if that were true, Jesus would not have been truly man, because men are composed of body and soul. He would not have *been* one of us; he would have just *looked like* one of us—a divine being moving a human body like a puppet. The Fathers of the Church recognized that here again the question of our salvation was at stake. A basic principle they taught was that whatever was not taken up by the Son of God in the Incarnation was not healed or saved: if Christ did not have a human soul, his gift of salvation extended to the body only.

Finally, the faculties of Christ's human intellect and will have prompted much speculation over the centuries, because it is impossible for us to imagine how they function in relation to his divine intellect and will. If God knows everything, and Jesus is God, did Jesus know everything? If he did, does that not contradict the truth of his humanity, since part of human nature is to be limited and to grow in knowledge? And if the Son of God came to do the Father's will, what role did Jesus' human will play? Theologians have proposed various solutions to these quandaries. The Church has never defined *how* Christ's human intellect and will operate in relation to his divine nature and

---

[5] *Gnosticism* is a name given to a variety of philosophical and religious movements that were particularly strong in the first and second centuries. Many Gnostics viewed the material world as corrupt or evil, the spiritual world as good, and held that knowledge (*gnosis*), often imparted by esoteric teachings, offered the way back to the spiritual world.

Person. The dogma of the Church simply asserts that, whatever explanation is put forward, it must respect the full humanity and the full divinity of Christ. As a man, Jesus grew in understanding and he possessed a human will; as the Son of God, he is omniscient. We affirm each of those statements, although we will never fathom how they "worked" in the life of Jesus.

Some corollaries follow from the fact that Christ is the Son of God. For one thing, this means that Christ is free from all sin, original and personal. Looked at from the perspective of his divine nature, this statement presents no difficulty. But what about from the perspective of his humanity? Original sin is passed on by natural generation, and since Jesus was conceived miraculously he was not subject to original sin. Because Christ's human nature is united to the Person of the Son of God, Jesus did not commit personal sins, either. The Son always freely does the Father's will. Would he not be closer to us if he had sinned? Is it "natural" for a man to be sinless? After all, an excuse we often hear (or make) when wrong has been done is, "Well, I'm only human." Here we should distinguish between something being widespread and something being normal. What is normal is for something to function according to its intended purpose: since we are made in the image and likeness of God, it is normal for us to be good. Sin is widespread in mankind as a result of the Fall—but that does not make it normal. In our fallen condition, we think freedom means the liberty to do as we please, but true freedom is to be found in living virtuously, because this means acting according to our nature as God intended it. Human freedom is a created image of the freedom of God, who always freely does the good because he is Goodness itself and acts according to his nature. Although Jesus did not sin, he, like every man, experienced temptation. For this reason, the Letter to the Hebrews tells us that Christ can sympathize with us in our weakness, because "in every respect [he] has been tempted as we are, yet without sinning" (Heb 4:15).

Throughout his earthly life, the incarnate Son of God acted through his divine and human natures. This helps us understand the paradox that Jesus was able to perform miracles, but also experienced hunger and fatigue. It is also the key to puzzling scriptural statements by and about Jesus. For example, Jesus said, "Truly, truly, I say to you, before Abraham was, I am" (Jn 8:58). Now, Jesus was born many centuries after Abraham, but he is the eternal Son of God, and it is as the Son of God that he can say this. Saint Peter told the people in Jerusalem that they had "killed the Author of life" (Acts 3:15). How had they killed the Author of life? By crucifying the man Jesus, who is also God, the Author of life.[6] The fathers of the Second Vatican Council, in *Gaudium et Spes*, expressed the meaning of the Incarnation in this way: "For by His incarnation the Son of God has united Himself in some fashion with every man. He worked with human hands, He thought with a human mind, acted by human choice and loved with a human heart" (*GS*, no. 22). The Sacred Heart of Jesus is thus, in the words of Pope Pius XII, "quite rightly considered the chief sign and symbol of that ... love with which the divine Redeemer continually loves the eternal Father and all human beings".[7] The incarnate Son of God still acts through his divine and human natures, although that human nature has been transformed by his Resurrection. We come into contact with the Word incarnate in many ways, principally through the sacramental life of the Church, a subject that will be addressed in a later chapter. But also noteworthy are the invocation of his holy name, the veneration of his sacred image, and the adoration of Christ present in the Eucharist.

To know the name of another is to have a relationship with that person; to call a name to mind is to make the other present in some way. (Devout Jews are so conscious of the power of God's name that out of reverence they do not even pronounce it.) The name *Jesus*, which means "God saves", expresses the identity and mission of the incarnate Son of God. This name was given to him by the angel (Lk 1:31; Mt 1:21), and it has always been revered by his followers. As the early Christians sang, "... at the name of Jesus every knee should bow, in heaven and on earth and under the earth, and every tongue

---

[6] The unity of the two natures in the one Person of Christ has from the time of the New Testament on prompted bold theological statements; for example, Ignatius of Antioch spoke of "the blood of God" (*Letter to the Ephesians* 1, 1). By virtue of the union of the divine and human natures in the Person of the Word incarnate, attributes of both natures can be predicated of Christ. For this reason, it is true to say, "God died on the Cross", because Christ is God, and Christ truly died on the Cross. Or, "Jesus created the world", because God created the world and Jesus is God incarnate. However, attributes of one nature cannot be predicated of the other. For example, it would wrong to say, "Christ was born *as God* of Mary", or, "Jesus *as man* created the world."

[7] Pius XII, *Haurietis aquas* (1956): DS 3924; cf. DS 3812; quoted in *CCC*, no. 478.

confess that Jesus Christ is Lord, to the glory of God the Father" (Phil 2:10–11). The invocation of the name of Jesus makes present the one who is both our Brother and the Son of God. In the words of the *Catechism*:

> The name "Jesus" contains all: God and man and the whole economy of creation and salvation. To pray "Jesus" is to invoke him and to call him within us. His name is the only one that contains the presence it signifies. Jesus is the Risen One, and whoever invokes the name of Jesus is welcoming the Son of God who loved him and gave himself up for him.[8]

As God, Jesus Is Worthy of Adoration

The dogma that Christ is truly God has had a marked effect on Christian worship. Although most Catholic liturgical prayers are addressed to the Father through the Son, we also address prayers directly to Christ. According to Saint Augustine: "He prays for us as our priest, prays in us as our Head, and is prayed to by us as our God."[9] One traditional expression of the worship of God the Son is the veneration given to icons or statues of Christ. In the eighth and ninth centuries, the Middle East was wracked by a violent conflict about whether it was permissible to make and pay honor to sacred images. Those who opposed the practice considered them idols and held that the Old Testament forbade the making of such objects. The theological defense for icons was tied to the dogma of the Incarnation: once the Word has become flesh, it was not only permissible but praiseworthy to portray him in images. The Second Council of Nicaea taught: "Indeed, the honour paid to an image traverses it, reaching the model; and he who venerates the image, venerates the person represented in that image."[10] While the veneration of images is a hallmark of Roman Catholic life, the iconoclast controversy led Eastern Christians to formulate a more highly developed theology of sacred images.

Western Catholic spirituality was influenced by a different controversy. In the eleventh century and again at the Reformation, disputes

---

[8] *CCC*, no. 2666; cf. Rom 10:13; Acts 2:21; 3:15–16; Gal 2:20.

[9] St. Augustine, *Enarrationes in Psalmos*, 85, 1: *PL* 37, 1081, quoted in *CCC*, no. 2616.

[10] Decree of the Second Council of Nicaea, *Decrees of the Ecumenical Councils*, vol. 1, p. 137. See *CCC*, no. 477. The principle cited by the council is taken from Saint Basil, *On the Holy Spirit*, 18, 45.

arose regarding the presence of Christ in the Eucharist. These debates led to a deeper appreciation of the truth that the Eucharist is the Body and Blood of Christ. Since Christ's Body and Blood are united to his divine Person,

> the Catholic Church has always displayed and still displays this latria [adoration] that ought to be paid to the Sacrament of the Eucharist, both during Mass and outside of it, by taking the greatest possible care of consecrated Hosts, by exposing them to the solemn veneration of the faithful, and by carrying them about in processions to the joy of great numbers of the people.[11]

Why God the Son Became Our Brother

Clearly, it is the faith of the Church that Jesus Christ is the eternal Son of God who was born as man from the Virgin Mary. But *why* did the Word become flesh and dwell among us? The *Catechism* presents several reasons, and I will conclude this chapter by reflecting briefly on them (see nos. 456–60). First, the Son became incarnate to save us by reconciling us with God. Saint Gregory of Nyssa expressed our need for salvation in these words: "Sick, our nature demanded to be healed; fallen, to be raised up; dead, to rise again. We had lost the possession of the good; it was necessary for it to be given back to us. Closed in the darkness, it was necessary to bring us light; captives, we awaited a Savior; prisoners, help; slaves, a liberator." [12] To appreciate the surprising way God accomplished our salvation, let us recall the parable of the wicked tenants. The owner of the vineyard sent servants to receive his share of the harvest, and the tenants beat them and chased them off, or killed them. Finally, the owner sent one more envoy, his son. But the tenants, recognizing him as the heir, instead killed him, hoping to gain his inheritance (Mk 12:7–8). This story has come true in a remarkable way: we killed the Son—and received his inheritance! God showed the depth of his love by sending us a Savior, not a prophet or an angel, but his own Son, and he sent him to die so that we could receive the inheritance of eternal life.

---

[11] Pope Paul VI, *Mysterium Fidei*, no. 56 (English translation from the Vatican website). See *CCC*, no. 1378.

[12] St. Gregory of Nyssa, *Oratio catechetica*, 15: PG 45, 48B, quoted in *CCC*, no. 457.

This points to the second reason for the Incarnation: that we might know the depth of God's love for us. As the ancient hymn from the Easter Vigil, the *Exsultet*, proclaims: "O wonder of your humble care for us! O love, O charity beyond all telling, to ransom a slave you gave away your Son!" The vineyard owner's son laid down his life for those who murdered him: "But God shows his love for us in that while we were yet sinners Christ died for us" (Rom 5:8).

Because the Son of God is truly our Brother, he is our model of holiness. If the Son simply appeared to be human, he might be a sign of God's love for us, but he could never be a pattern for our lives. But because Christ is truly man, we see in him perfect love for God and neighbor expressed in human terms. In the words of the *Catechism*: "In humbling himself, he has given us an example to imitate, through his prayer he draws us to pray, and by his poverty he calls us to accept freely the privation and persecutions that may come our way." [13] Jesus knows our weakness; he has been tempted as we are. We need only meditate on the agony in the garden to see how human Jesus is. It is not enough to know *about* Jesus—we need to know Jesus himself. The "imitation of Christ" is possible only because he truly shares our nature, and our imitation must be inspired by continual, prayerful reading of the Gospels.

We might object, "How can I presume to imitate Christ? He is the Son of God." This brings us to the final reason for the Incarnation: to make us partakers in the divine nature. We become by grace what Jesus Christ is by his very being, sons and daughters of God. It is true that we can be considered God's sons and daughters because he created us; we owe our very existence to God. But Jesus spoke repeatedly of God as *his* Father in a distinctive way, with a unique sense of intimacy. By virtue of the Resurrection, Christ shares this unique relationship with the members of his Body. He gives us everything he can, which means all that he possesses as God the Son apart from the uncreated divine nature itself, since this is incommunicable outside of the three Persons of the Holy Trinity. We are "deified" by our union with Christ. As the Fathers of the Church frequently said, "God became man so that man might become God" (see *CCC*, no. 460).

How do we receive this gift? Through the outpouring of the Holy Spirit. Saint Athanasius, the resolute defender of the divinity of Christ,

---

[13] *CCC*, no. 520; cf. Jn 13:15; Lk 11:1; Mt 5:11–12.

also proclaimed the sanctifying power of the Spirit: "[God] gave himself to us through his Spirit. By the participation of the Spirit, we become communicants in the divine nature.... For this reason, those in whom the Spirit dwells are divinized." [14] This great Church Father's doctrine is rooted in the teaching of Saint Paul:

> But when the time had fully come, God sent forth his Son, born of a woman, born under the law, to redeem those who were under the law, so that we might receive adoption as sons. And because you are sons, God has sent the Spirit of his Son into our hearts, crying, "Abba! Father!" So through God you are no longer a slave but a son, and if a son then an heir. (Gal 4:4–7)

This passage directs our attention to the sending of the Holy Spirit and the revelation of the mystery of the Holy Trinity. We began this chapter by hearing Jesus ask the question, "Who do you say that I am?" We will end it by putting a question to God: "Who do you say that we are?" Thanks to the Incarnation of his Son, and our union with him by the indwelling of the Holy Spirit, God says to us: "You are my beloved son; with you I am well pleased" (see Lk 3:22).

---

[14] St. Athanasius, *Epistulae ad Serapionem*, 1, 24: PG 26, 585 and 588, quoted in *CCC*, no. 1988.

Chapter Four

The Most Holy Trinity

The risen Christ gave the great commission: "Go therefore and make disciples of all nations, baptizing them in the name of the Father and of the Son and of the Holy Spirit, teaching them to observe all that I have commanded you; and behold, I am with you always, to the close of the age" (Mt 28:19–20). This is the most explicit biblical reference to the Holy Trinity, although the mystery runs through the entire New Testament. The risen Christ assured his apostles that he would be with them always; he also had told them that he was going away, but that "another Counselor" would come. How can he be gone and still remain with them? The Holy Spirit is the key to this puzzle, and it is with the sending of the Holy Spirit that the mystery of the Trinity is revealed.

What We Believe

We believe in one God, who is eternal, infinite, and all-powerful. God alone *is* his very being, and everything else receives existence from him. God does not simply possess the attributes of goodness, truth, beauty, and so on: his very nature *is* Goodness, Truth, and Beauty. The coming of Christ and of the Holy Spirit have revealed that this one God is the Holy Trinity: three Persons inseparable and equal in dignity and power as regards their divine nature, but distinct in terms of their relations to one another. God the Father is the absolute origin, God the Son is eternally begotten from the Father, and God the Holy Spirit proceeds eternally from the Father and the Son. Because of their identical divine nature, all activities of God in creation are common to the three Persons. Thus the one God (Father, Son, and Holy Spirit) creates, sanctifies, redeems, forgives, protects, and enlightens.

Some History

The dogma of the Incarnation challenges our imagination, but the mystery of the Trinity frankly mystifies most people, including many Christians. It is "mystery" in the most profound sense of the word: a reality about which we would know nothing if God had not revealed it, and about which we know very little even after he has. As with the Incarnation, it took centuries for the trinitarian dogma to find explicit formulation, although the doctrine emerges from the experience of the first disciples and subsequent believers. We saw in the previous chapter how Christ revealed the mystery of God as Father; now we will open the Bible again and see how the Holy Spirit reveals both the Son and the Father.

We find allusions to the Trinity throughout the New Testament. Saint Paul bids farewell to the Corinthians in these words: "The grace of the Lord Jesus Christ and the love of God and the fellowship of the Holy Spirit be with you all" (2 Cor 13:14). In his first Letter to that community he reminds them: "Now there are varieties of gifts, but the same Spirit; and there are varieties of service, but the same Lord; and there are varieties of working, but it is the same God who inspires them all in every one" (1 Cor 12:4–6). In the life of Jesus, the mystery of the Trinity was foreshadowed at the Annunciation, when the angel Gabriel told Mary: "The Holy Spirit will come upon you, and the power of the Most High will overshadow you; therefore the child to be born will be called holy, the Son of God" (Lk 1:35). The Trinity was manifested at Jesus' baptism, when the Spirit of God descended upon him like a dove and a voice from Heaven proclaimed, "This is my beloved Son" (Mt 3:16–17). But it was at Pentecost, when the same Holy Spirit descended upon the community of believers, that the mystery of the Trinity was revealed to the disciples, and it is in the light of that Gift that they came to understand the meaning of Christ's mission. Viewing the New Testament as a whole, we can say that Christ came so that we could receive the Holy Spirit, and that the Holy Spirit reveals Christ to us and unites us to him.

Christ Gives Us the Holy Spirit

The Gospel of Saint John teaches that Christ came so that we could receive the Holy Spirit. It opens with the proclamation that the Word became flesh and reaches its climax on Easter night when, in the glory of the Resurrection, the Word-made-flesh breathes on his disciples and says, "Receive the Holy Spirit" (Jn 20:22). How do we move from "flesh" to "Spirit"?

The fourth Gospel's account of Jesus' life begins with his baptism by John, who testified that he saw the Spirit as a dove descend from Heaven upon Jesus, remaining with him (Jn 1:32). Later, John the Baptist spoke again about the Spirit in connection with the mission of Jesus: "For he whom God has sent utters the words of God, for it is not by measure that he gives the Spirit; the Father loves the Son, and has given all things into his hand" (Jn 3:34–35). This Evangelist's love of multiple meanings tantalizes us: Is "he" who gives the Spirit the Father, who gives everything over to the Son? Or is "he" the Son, who has been sent to speak the words of God? In either case, whether the Spirit is given by the Father to the Son, or by the Son to us, one hallmark of the gift is that the Spirit is poured out lavishly, without measure.

Jesus speaks about the Spirit to Nicodemus and to the Samaritan woman at the well, but it is in the seventh chapter of John that the promise of the Spirit is renewed in dramatic circumstances: not to a stealthy inquirer under cover of darkness, nor to a lone woman in hostile Samaria, but in the Temple precincts on one of the greatest feasts of the year. Jesus had come up to Jerusalem for the autumn feast of Tabernacles, which included a daily procession to pray for the gift of rain. John tells us:

> On the last day of the feast, the great day, Jesus stood up and pro-claimed, "If any one thirst, let him come to me and drink. He who believes in me, as the Scripture has said, 'Out of his heart shall flow rivers of living water'." Now this he said about the Spirit, which those who believed in him were to receive; for as yet the Spirit had not been given, because Jesus was not yet glorified. (Jn 7:37–39)

Does the verse quoted by Jesus ("Out of his heart shall flow rivers of living water") refer to himself or to the believer? Again, John's word-ing is alluringly ambiguous.

"The Spirit had not been given, because Jesus was not yet glori-fied." We have seen that the Spirit had been given—to Jesus at his baptism. John means that the Spirit had not yet been given to *us*. That gift would come with the glorification of Jesus, which for John embraces both his death and Resurrection. As Jesus was dying on the Cross, he, who had promised rivers of living water, cried out, "I thirst." Then, having tasted the wine offered him, Jesus announced, "'It is finished'; and he bowed his head and gave up his spirit" (Jn 19:28–30). On the surface level, John is simply saying that Jesus breathed his last. But the symbolic import of Christ's words and deeds is particularly pronounced in the fourth Gospel, so we may be certain that this, the climactic moment of the Passion narrative, conveys a profound theological truth. Jesus bowed his head and gave over his spirit, anticipating the gift of the Spirit after his Resurrection. The meaning of this event is reinforced by what happened next: a soldier pierced the side of Christ, and at once there flowed out blood and water. The bold promise made by Jesus in the Temple is fulfilled in a striking way: a river of living water flows from the pierced heart of the dead Christ, and the Spirit of life is bestowed on the believers. In the First Letter of John we are told: "There are three witnesses, the Spirit, the water, and the blood; and these three agree" (1 Jn 5:8).

On Easter night, Christ appeared to his disciples in the upper room and told them, "As the Father has sent me, even so I send you." Then he breathed upon them and said, "Receive the Holy Spirit. If you forgive the sins of any, they are forgiven; if you retain the sins of any, they are retained" (Jn 20:21–23). The same Spirit who came to rest on the Word-made-flesh is now given to his disciples. They are sent out by Christ, just as Christ was sent from the Father. The hearts of believers become living fountains through the Spirit, given by the resurrected Lord. Saint Ignatius of Antioch, writing to the Ephesians not long after the Gospel of John was composed, may have been alluding to this scene in the upper room: "For the Lord received anointing on his head in order that he might breathe incorruptibility on the Church."[1]

Throughout the New Testament, the first Christians affirmed that the Holy Spirit came from Christ. He is called the *Spirit of Christ* (Rom 8:9), the *Spirit of Jesus* (Acts 16:7), the *Spirit of Jesus Christ* (Phil 1:19), and the *Spirit of his Son* (Gal 4:6). On the other hand, the One

---

[1] Ignatius of Antioch, *Letter to the Ephesians*, 17.1 (Office of Readings, Monday of the Second Week in Ordinary Time).

sent by Christ is the *promise of my Father* (Lk 24:49), whom the Son
can send only because he has received the Spirit—as he has received
everything—from the Father (Jn 16:15). Thus the Father gives the
Holy Spirit (Lk 11:13), who is *the Spirit of your Father* (Mt 10:20), the
Holy Spirit (1 Thess 4:8), the *Spirit of him who raised Jesus from the dead*
(Rom 8:11). In a remarkable analogy, Saint Paul likens the Holy Spirit
of God to our own deepest self: "For the Spirit searches everything,
even the depths of God. For what person knows a man's thoughts
except the spirit of the man which is in him? So also no one com-
prehends the thoughts of God except the Spirit of God. Now we
have received not the spirit of the world, but the Spirit which is from
God ..." (1 Cor 2:10–12). This image of the Spirit as "God's deepest
Self" underscores that the Holy Spirit is profoundly *personal*.

The Holy Spirit Gives Us Christ

Christ gives us the Holy Spirit. But it is also true that the Holy Spirit
gives us Christ. Mary conceived her child through the power of the
Holy Spirit, and Jesus' teaching and healing mission was carried out
in the power of the Holy Spirit, who came to rest upon him at his
baptism. All that Jesus did in his ministry he did as "the Christ", the
One anointed by the Holy Spirit. Furthermore, the Spirit reveals the
identity of Jesus; it was through the descent of the Holy Spirit that
John the Baptist recognized Jesus as the Son of God (Jn 1:32–34).
After Christ's exaltation at the Father's right hand, it is the mission of
the Holy Spirit to bear witness to Christ (Jn 15:26), to remind his
disciples of what Jesus told them (Jn 14:26), even to teach them what
Jesus himself could not (Jn 16:12–13). In the words of Saint Paul: "No
one can say, 'Jesus is Lord' except by the Holy Spirit" (1 Cor 12:3).
Saint Luke emphasizes the pivotal role of the Holy Spirit in the plan
of salvation. Taken together, his Gospel and Acts present a two-act
drama directed by the Holy Spirit. In the overture to the first act, the
infancy narrative, Luke presents the leitmotif of his whole production,
the bestowal of the Holy Spirit: Mary conceives by the power of the
Holy Spirit and the other characters are filled with or guided by the
Spirit. Jesus is the central character in Act One, but his actions are
directed by the Spirit. The second act opens with a reprise of the first:
the Holy Spirit comes upon the disciples together with Mary, just as

he did upon her alone at the beginning of the Gospel. This is the birth of the Church as the Body of Christ, and the rest of Acts recounts how the Holy Spirit reproduces in this Body the pattern of the life, death, and Resurrection of Christ, its Head.

When we look at the Son and the Holy Spirit as the first Christians describe them, their missions are strikingly similar: Jesus and the Spirit are each described in John's Gospel as coming from the Father; dwelling with and in disciples; bearing witness, teaching, and guiding into truth; speaking only what he hears; confounding the world that cannot receive him. They are as inseparable yet distinct as word and breath. The Holy Spirit does the work of Christ, Christ does the work of the Holy Spirit, and both do the work of the Father.

As was the case with Christ, it became necessary for believers to articulate the relationship of the Holy Spirit to God and us. This presented a greater challenge than the question of Christ for two reasons. First, the names *Father* and *Son* are relational and indicate both union and distinction, whereas the term *Holy Spirit* seems less precise; it is not easy to distinguish the Spirit from the Father and the Son. Secondly, the earthly mission of the Son ended with his Ascension, so that it could be seen as a whole. The mission of the Spirit continues, and we are living in the heart of it. The intimacy of the Holy Spirit makes it more difficult for us to focus on him.

How Is the Holy Spirit Related to the Father and the Son?

The historic debates about Christ's identity raised questions about the Spirit as well. While affirming that the Son was a divine Person, some denied that the same could be said of the Holy Spirit. Saint Athanasius, the great champion of Christ's divinity, also defended the divinity of the Holy Spirit, and after his death, the cause was taken up by others, notably, Saint Basil the Great, who authored a treatise on the Holy Spirit. The Fathers argued that the Spirit cannot be a creature because creation was brought into existence out of nothing, whereas the Spirit comes from the Father. More importantly, since it is the Holy Spirit who makes us partakers of divinity, the Spirit must possess the eternal divine nature. As was true for Athanasius' defense of the divinity of Christ, the crucial issue here was how we are saved: God himself sanctifies us by the indwelling of his Holy Spirit. But this raises a difficult question: granted that the Holy Spirit comes from the Father and is involved in our salvation, how does the Spirit differ from the Son? That he *is* different is clear from the fact that Jesus had spoken of "another" Counselor who could come only if Christ returned to the Father.

In the last chapter, we saw that the Greek Fathers used the word *ousia* to speak of the divine nature common to the Father and the Son. They took another word, which had been more or less a synonym for *ousia* and gave it, too, a specific connotation. That word is *hypostasis*, and they linked it to the idea of *Person*, meaning "a being-in-relation". *What* the Son is, is God (*ousia*); he possesses the divine nature with all its attributes. *Who* the Son is, is the Person (*hypostasis*) eternally begotten of the Father; he has every attribute of the Father except Fatherhood. What distinguishes the Father from the Son is their relation: the Father is God begetting, the Son is God begotten.

The distinguishing characteristic of the Holy Spirit presented a greater challenge. Saint Basil taught that the relation between the Spirit and the Father was ineffable; the only thing we could say with certainty was that the Spirit was not begotten, since that is the Son's relation to the Father, and the Holy Spirit is not the Son. Saint Gregory Nazianzen drew upon the words of Jesus, "But when the Counselor comes, whom I shall send to you from the Father, even the Spirit of truth, who proceeds from the Father, he will bear witness to me" (Jn 15:26), and suggested that the Spirit "proceeds" from the Father, although he acknowledged that we do not know what the word means in this context.

The Nicene Creed had professed the divinity of both the Son and the Holy Spirit, but it had emphasized the Son's divinity in opposition to the doctrine of Arius. At the Council of Constantinople (381), this Creed was expanded to affirm more explicitly our faith in the divinity of the Holy Spirit: he is the Lord and giver of life, and with the Father and the Son he is worshipped and glorified. The Holy Spirit is truly God because he possesses, like the Father and the Son, the divine *ousia* (nature). He has received this nature because he proceeds from the Father. This is his relation to the Father, and it distinguishes him from the Son, who is begotten. The three Persons are one in nature, but three in terms of their origin: the Father is the unoriginated source, the Son is begotten, the Spirit proceeds. For the Greek Fathers, the fact that the Father is the source of unity among the three Persons underscores the profoundly interpersonal reality of God's nature. But how is the Spirit related to the Son? Some of the Greek Fathers suggested that the Holy Spirit proceeds from the Father through the Son, but they came to no definite conclusions on this point. Thus, the Creed adopted at the First Council of Constantinople simply states that "the Spirit proceeds from the Father".

The question of the relation of the Spirit to the Son was taken up in the West, which held that the Spirit proceeds from the Father and the Son. The division between East and West on this issue is one of the most challenging theological obstacles to the restoration of full unity between the Orthodox and Catholic communions.

The Council of Constantinople was a regional meeting of Eastern bishops; no Western bishops took part. Its decrees and Creed were adopted by the Council of Chalcedon in 451, and the Council of Constantinople attained ecumenical status when recognized as such by the West in the sixth century. The seed of Eastern theology was planted in Western soil, whose great theologians—Saint Hilary, Saint Ambrose, Saint Augustine, and Saint Leo the Great—had all taught that the Holy Spirit proceeds from the Father and the Son. Their reasoning was this: the Son possesses every attribute of God except Fatherhood; the Father is the origin, but not the Father, of the Holy Spirit; therefore, as the Spirit proceeds from the Father, he must also proceed from the Son. The Father is immediately the origin of the Spirit ("he proceeds from the Father"), and he is the origin of the procession of the Spirit from the Son as well, because the Father is the source of all that the Son has ("he proceeds from the Father and the Son"). The Latin Fathers also held that to say that the Spirit proceeds from the Son resonates with Scripture, because Jesus speaks of sending the Spirit, and the Spirit is described as the Spirit of Christ.

Saint Augustine found this "double procession" from the Father and the Son useful in developing his trinitarian theology. Since the distinction among the Persons of the Trinity is found in their mutual relationships, he was puzzled by the term *Holy Spirit*, which, unlike *Father* and *Son*, is not relational. Both the Father and the Son are holy, and both are spirit; what differentiates the Holy Spirit? Augustine found the word *gift* to be apt, since it suggests a donor and a recipient: the Holy Spirit proceeds from the Father as his gift of love for the Son, and in turn from the Son as his love for the Father. As Augustine put it in his magisterial work on the Trinity, "The Holy Spirit proceeds from the Father as the first principle and, by the eternal gift of this to the Son, from the communion of both the Father and the Son."[2] The Holy Spirit is the bond of mutual love between the Father and the Son. Subsequent Western trinitarian theology is built on this understanding of the relationship between the Son and the Holy Spirit.

The ecumenical problem arose because some Western communities added the words "and the Son" (*Filioque*) to the phrase "The Holy Spirit proceeds from Father" in the Creed. This was done to combat Arianism, which had appeared in areas of Spain and Gaul in the sixth century. To assert that the Holy Spirit proceeds from the Father and the Son was an effective way to safeguard the full divinity of the Son. Since the double procession of the Spirit had long been the traditional teaching in the West, many assumed that the East held the doctrine, too. For example, a Creed that included the *Filioque* was attributed (erroneously) to Saint Athanasius. In fact, when the Greeks accused the Franks of adding the phrase to the Creed, the Franks retorted that the Greeks had removed it! For over a thousand years, controversy has surrounded two questions: the legitimacy of inserting the clause into the Creed, and the dogma itself. The position of the Catholic Church on the first point is that, while the doctrine is true, it need not be included in the Greek version of the Creed: Eastern churches in communion with Rome may omit the phrase, and the pope has professed the Creed in Greek without the *Filioque*. Either form of the Creed is legitimate. Some have suggested that the West drop the clause as an ecumenical gesture; in this way, we would again have one profession of faith proclaimed by Christians of East and West. Others hold that the Greek and Latin theologies of the Trinity are complementary and that the variant wordings express an acceptable diversity. The doctrinal question presents a more challenging obstacle, since it is one thing to assert that different creedal formulas about the Trinity can both be true, and it is another to hold that one is true and the other is false. The challenge for Orthodox and Catholic leaders and theologians is to find a way to express the Church's faith that does justice to the beliefs of both traditions about the most fundamental mystery (the Trinity) of the Christian faith.

---

[2] St. Augustine, *De Trinitate*, 15, 26, 47: *PL* 42:1095, quoted in *CCC*, no. 264.

Implications

For many Christians, the dogma of the Trinity seems quite remote from the realities of daily life. Is it not enough to concede that the mystery of God is beyond our limited creaturely minds, and leave the matter at that? Here we need to recall that dogma is *saving* truth: the faith of the Church concerns the Gospel, the Good News that Christ sent his followers to preach to the ends of the earth. The trinitarian doctrines defend the essential truth that it is God himself whom we encounter in Christ and the Holy Spirit. The mystery of the Trinity was revealed to us through the events of salvation history: God invites us into communion with him, and in reaching out to us he reveals something of himself to us. When we fall in love, we want to know everything we can about our beloved, even though we can never know another person completely. If this is true of our understanding of creatures, it is much more so with God. Still, to know something is better than to know nothing, especially when the mystery of truth is also a mystery of love.

To those who object that the theology of the Trinity is abstruse, and who plead for a simpler Gospel, I would respond: Could there be a more basic expression of the Christian religion than to say that it teaches us that God is love, and that we are to love God with all our heart, and to love our neighbor as ourselves? Yet those statements, so liable to be mere platitudes, take on profound meaning when we see them in light of the mystery of the Trinity.

The Trinitarian Meaning of "God Is Love"

Let us consider first the deceptively simple statement "God is love" (1 Jn 4:8). When Moses stood before the burning bush, God revealed his name: "I AM WHO I AM" (Ex 3:14).[3] The name is mysterious—as the *Catechism* teaches, it is at once a name revealed and something like the refusal of a name (no. 206)—and thus expresses how God is infinitely

---

[3] The Revised Standard Version adds a note: "Or I AM WHAT I AM or I WILL BE WHAT I WILL BE." The revelation of God's name defies easy translation. Out of respect for the holiness of God, the Jewish people do not pronounce his name. In reading the Scriptures, the revealed name is replaced by the divine title "LORD" (in Greek, *Kyrios*). For this reason, the use of the title "Lord" for Jesus in the New Testament can be read as an affirmation of his divinity. See *CCC*, nos. 209, 446.

beyond our understanding, and yet draws near to us. The revelation to Moses affirms the truth that God alone IS: that is, being is God's very nature. Everything that exists is contingent upon God; creatures receive their being from God; he alone *is* his very being. (Understood in the light of the name revealed to Moses on Sinai, the frequent "I am" assertions made by Jesus in John's Gospel are audacious and, were he not the Son of God, would be blasphemous.)

God also described himself in another way in this theophany: "I am the God of your father, the God of Abraham, the God of Isaac, and the God of Jacob" (Ex 3:6). God speaks of himself in relation to Moses and his ancestors: he is not only the God who *is*; he is the God who *loves*. The purpose of his revelation was not to give Moses a lesson in metaphysics, but to send him to free the Israelites from slavery. Throughout the Old Testament, God reveals himself as loving, faithful, steadfast, and just. It is on the basis of these attributes that God enters into covenants with his people. However, to profess that "God is love" means much more than "God is loving"—but it is only with the revelation of the mystery of the Trinity that we begin to comprehend the deeper significance of the assertion that God *is* love.

Like the Jewish faith from which it grew, Christianity affirms that God is one. But, in the words of an early Creed, "God is one but not solitary." [4] The oneness of God is a communion of love. The sending of the Son and the Holy Spirit have revealed to us that God's very being is relational—the eternal love between the Father, the Son, and the Holy Spirit.

It is customary to associate different aspects of God's work with specific Persons of the Trinity (e.g., creation to the Father, redemption to the Son, sanctification to the Holy Spirit). This is known as "appropriation". However, it is essential to bear in mind a point made in the *Catechism*: "The whole divine economy is the common work of the three divine persons. For as the Trinity has only one and the same nature, so too does it have only one and the same operation: 'The Father, the Son, and the Holy Spirit are not three principles of creation but one principle.' " [5] Saint Gregory of Nyssa affirmed that

---

[4] *Fides Damasi*: DS 71, quoted in *CCC*, no. 254.

[5] Council of Florence (1442): DS 1331, quoted in *CCC*, no. 258; cf. Council of Constantinople II (553): DS 421.

no divine actions are attributable to one divine Person alone; Augustine's teaching in this regard found expression in a medieval axiom that became central to subsequent Catholic theology: "All the actions of the Trinity outside itself [ad extra] are not divisible."[6]

Love never exists in the abstract: it is always love *for* someone or something. We love many things, but we recognize that there is mutuality in the love shared between men because of our common nature. The second creation account in Genesis captures this reality in an imaginative way: God creates Adam and then makes all kinds of birds and beasts, but none of them is a fitting companion for the man. Then God creates Eve from the side of Adam, who exclaims: "This at last is bone of my bones and flesh of my flesh" (Gen 2:23). Like nature is the foundation of mutual love. What is true for creatures is true for the Creator: since God the Father is infinite in his perfections, the only fitting recipient of his love is a Person who shares those divine perfections. The Son receives infinite love from the Father, and returns infinite love to the Father; and this love is the Holy Spirit. God's very nature is relational: for God, *to be* is to be *in communion*.

The revelation that the one God is a communion of love underscores the freedom of his creative power. God did not bring the universe into existence because he needed an object for his affections. God freely created to share his love and goodness, so that creatures could share in the divine life. In the poetic image of Saint Thomas Aquinas, "Creatures came into existence when the key of love opened his hand."[7] Creation is marked by its trinitarian origin. The opening verses of the Bible tell us that when God made the heavens and the earth the Spirit of God was moving over the waters and that it was by his Word that God created. As it was through his Word and his Spirit that the Father brought the universe into being, so it is through the

---

[6] The Fathers taught this doctrine to safeguard the equality of the three Persons of the Trinity in answer to those who denied that the Son and/or the Holy Spirit were truly God. The reference to "ad extra" points to a very important distinction made by the Fathers between *theology* and *economy*. "Theology" in this context refers to the mystery of God's inner life (*ad intra*), while "economy" refers to works by which God reveals himself to us and shares with us his divine life. By the sending of the Son and the Holy Spirit, God has revealed *something* of who he is in himself; the events of salvation history afford us a glimpse of the mystery of the Trinity, but the reality itself is far beyond our comprehension. See *CCC*, no. 236.

[7] St. Thomas Aquinas, *In libros sententiarum*, 2, Prol, quoted in *CCC*, no. 293.

Spirit and the Son that creation returns to the Father. When we say "God is love", we are proclaiming that the very nature of God's being is to give and receive love, and that we who have become "partakers of the divine nature" (2 Pet 1:4) are invited into that communion of love.

Our Love of God and Neighbor in the Trinity

Now let us consider the twofold commandment—love of God and love of neighbor—in light of the trinitarian mystery. Here we need to recall that the union between the believer and Christ is not figurative; our union with him is real. At the end of the Last Supper, Jesus prayed to his Father: "The glory which you have given me I have given to them, that they may be one even as we are one, I in them and you in me, that they may become perfectly one, so that the world may know that you have sent me and have loved them even as you have loved me" (Jn 17:22–23). The glory that the Father gives the Son is the Holy Spirit, the personal love who unites them. This same Spirit unites every Christian to Christ and to the Father. Jesus claims that it is only this union that enables us to accomplish anything: "I am the vine, you are the branches. He who abides in me, and I in him, he it is that bears much fruit, for apart from me you can do nothing" (Jn 15:5). The fruit disciples bear is divine love; our union with Christ transforms our ability to love God and one another. This transformation begins in baptism, but it is the project of a lifetime—and more—to truly attain "the mind of Christ" (1 Cor 2:16). Who of us would dare to claim, as Saint Paul did, "It is no longer I who live, but Christ who lives in me" (Gal 2:20)? Yet what Paul describes is the program of Christian discipleship.

How does our union with Christ affect our love for God? The heart of the Jewish faith is expressed by the great commandment in Deuteronomy: "Hear, O Israel: The LORD our God is one LORD; and you shall love the LORD your God with all your heart, and with all your soul, and with all your might" (Deut 6:4). God alone deserves our adoration and has a claim on the "first fruits" of our love. Jesus called this "the great and first commandment" (Mt 22:38). Given our creaturely condition, our love for God is always limited and imperfect. But by virtue of the indwelling of the Holy Spirit, we become the brothers and sisters of Christ, and we can love the Father with the love of the Son himself. This is why, in the words with which the Roman Mass introduces the Lord's Prayer, "we *dare* to say 'Our Father'". As Saint Paul wrote: "God has sent the Spirit of his Son into our hearts, crying, 'Abba! Father!' So through God you are no longer a slave but a son, and if a son then an heir" (Gal 4:6–7). The Son loves us with the infinite, ineffable love that the Father lavishes upon him. We in turn can unite our human love with the infinite, ineffable love with which the Son loves the Father—the Holy Spirit, who cries out "Abba!" in our hearts.

But it is not only God whom we can love in this way—we can also share this divine love with one another. The new commandment of Jesus was not, "Love one another"; many religions teach love of neighbor. Rather, he taught: "This is my commandment, that you love one another as I have loved you" (Jn 15:12). He gave this commandment on the night before he died. In Christ crucified, we see divine love expressed in human terms: unstinting, unselfish, prodigal in its generosity. In our more honest moments, we admit how short of that ideal our love falls. Indeed, the commandment to love as Jesus has loved us would be an intolerable burden were it not accompanied by the promise, "As the Father has loved me, so have I loved you; abide in my love" (Jn 15:9). The gift of the Holy Spirit plunges us into the furnace of love that is the Holy Trinity. We allow the Son to love others through us, and we love the Son in them. Ever since the Incarnation, the twofold commandment is truly one: God has become our neighbor. As Saint John teaches, "If any one says, 'I love God,' and hates his brother, he is a liar; for he who does not love his brother whom he has seen, cannot love God whom he has not seen" (1 Jn 4:20).

To say that we are made for love sounds like a trite maxim until we view reality in light of the Holy Trinity. If God's very being is communion, then we should not be surprised to find love at the heart of all God's handiwork. Among earthly creatures, this is especially true of men, who are made in the image and likeness of God. Genesis tells us: "So God created man in his own image, in the image of God he created him; male and female he created them" (Gen 1:27). Mankind is made in the image of God as male and female: the shared nature and complementarity of man and woman is a kind of created echo of the God who is one in nature and distinct in relations. There is also the suggestion that the whole human race, which shares the same nature, is one ("he created him") and intended by God to live in communion ("he created them"). This harmony was ruined in the Fall, but through the sending of Christ and the Spirit, the Father restores human solidarity. In the words of Saint Cyril of Alexandria:

> All of us who have received one and the same Spirit, that is, the Holy Spirit, are in a sense blended together with one another and with God. For if Christ, together with the Father's and his own Spirit, comes to dwell in each of us, though we are many, still the Spirit is one and undivided. He binds together the spirits of each and every one of us, . . . and makes all appear as one in him. For just as the power of Christ's sacred flesh unites those in whom it dwells into one body, I think that in the same way the one and undivided Spirit of God, who dwells in all, leads all into spiritual unity.[8]

The image and beginning of this communion is the Church, the sacrament of our inner union with God and the unity of the whole human race. Made up as it is of sinners, the Church on earth is an imperfect expression of this solidarity. Yet her very imperfections remind us that this communion is the fruit, not of human accomplishment, but of the power of divine love.

Let us return to the great commission with which this chapter opened. The risen Christ sends out his disciples. Why? Because he first had been sent from the Father to heal the wound inflicted by the Fall and restore the Father's communion of love in this world. The members of Christ's Body continue his mission: "As the Father has sent me, even so I send you" (Jn 20:21). This is the mission of the Holy Spirit, who invites into this communion of love, not just one people, but all mankind: "But you shall receive power when the Holy Spirit has come upon you; and you shall be my witnesses in Jerusalem and in all Judea and Samaria and to the end of the earth" (Acts 1:8). The disciples are instructed to baptize "in the name of the Father and of the Son and of the Holy Spirit" (Mt 28:19)—not in the *names*, but in the *name* of the one God, who is Father, Son, and Holy Spirit. Converts are to be baptized, because this is how they are plunged into the mystery of Christ's death and Resurrection and receive the Holy Spirit, who makes

---

[8] St. Cyril of Alexandria, *Commentarius in johannem*, 11, 11: PG 74, 561, quoted in *CCC*, no. 738.

them the sisters and brothers of the only begotten Son of God. The disciples are to teach them to observe all that Christ has commanded them, that is, the new commandment to "love one another as I have loved you" (Jn 15:12). They can fulfill this command only because of Christ's promise: "I am with you always, to the close of the age" (Mt 28:20). We remain in his love because the Holy Spirit of love dwells in us, uniting us to the Son and so bringing us into communion with the Father.

When we picture the risen Christ commissioning his disciples, it can seem so long ago and far away. And yet we can bring that event to mind every time we bless ourselves with holy water. The water recalls our baptism into the crucible of love signified by the Cross, and we invoke the name of the one God who is Father, Son, and Holy Spirit. It is a gracious custom, as they enter church, for one person to offer the holy water to another on the tips of his fingers. This simple gesture proclaims that we have received God's love and we are to share God's love. The risen Christ sends *us* out to carry the divine love of the Trinity to the ends of the earth.

Conclusion to Part One

I have called the first part of this book "*To* the mystery of the Trinity" because in it I have described how this, the central belief of the Christian faith, came to be revealed gradually by the events of salvation history and reflection on those events. Even the most brilliant Fathers of the Church acknowledged that the mystery of the Triune God is far beyond our mortal understanding. Saint Gregory of Nazianzus exclaimed to his catechumens: "I have not even begun to think of the unity when the Trinity bathes me in its splendor. I have not even begun to think of the Trinity when the unity grasps me."[1] Saint Augustine devoted twenty years to writing his magisterial *De Trinitate*, but he concluded the enterprise with a prayer that was a frank admission that words cannot do justice to the reality:

> A certain wise man, when he spoke of You in his book which is now called by the special name of Ecclesiasticus, declared: "We say many things, and fall short, and the sum of our words is, 'He is all.'" But when we shall come to You, these "many things" which we say "and fall short" shall cease; and You as One shall remain, You who are all in all; and without ceasing we shall say one thing, praising You in the one, we who have also been made one in You. O Lord, the One God, God the Trinity, whatever I have said in these books as coming from You, may they acknowledge who are Yours; but if anything as coming from myself, may You and they who are Yours forgive me. Amen.[2]

[1] St. Gregory of Nazianzus, *Orationes* 40, 41: *PG* 36, 417, quoted in *CCC*, no. 256.
[2] Saint Augustine, *The Trinity*, trans. Stephen McKenna (Washington, D.C.: Catholic University of America Press, 1963), pp. 524–25. There is an old legend that Augustine was walking on the beach and came across a boy who had dug a hole in the sand and was using a shell to pour seawater into it. When Augustine asked what he was doing, the boy explained that he planned to empty the ocean into the hole. Augustine pointed out that it was impossible for the hole to contain the whole ocean, and the boy responded that his effort was no more futile than trying to contain the mystery of the Trinity in the human mind. When Joseph Ratzinger became a bishop, he included a scallop shell on his coat of arms as a reminder of the humility with which we should approach the mysteries of God; it appears also on his papal coat of arms.

Would it not be enough to say of God, with the Old Testament sage, "He is the all" (Sir 43:27)? But the dogma of the Trinity is not merely a matter for philosophical speculation—it is, as dogma, saving truth; in fact it is *the* saving truth. Why is this so?

The Letter to the Hebrews presents the simplest biblical description of what is necessary for salvation: "For whoever would draw near to God must believe that he exists and that he rewards those who seek him" (Heb 11:6). First, we must believe that God exists. But he does not exist like you or I do, or like a tree or an angel. His very nature *is* to be, and everything else depends on God for its existence. The revelation of the mystery of the Trinity shows us that it is God's very nature to be *in communion*. The God of philosophy may be the ground of being, the reason why we (or anything) exist at all, but the fundamental Christian affirmation is not "God is all"—it is "God is love." The revelation of the mystery of the Trinity teaches us that "love" is not simply an attribute of God: rather, the one God is the Father, the Son, and the Holy Spirit.

That is why we can seek God, and why we should want to seek him. We do not need to seek a relationship with the ground of being; we have that simply because we exist. The God of Christian revelation is personal, and the dogma of the Trinity suggests that this God is "personal" with an intensity and depth that will forever elude our comprehension. The reward given by this God to those who seek him is not continued existence—it is eternal life. What is the difference between existence and life? Quite simply, it is love. This is why in his prayer at the conclusion of the Last Supper, Jesus said: "And this is eternal life, that they know you the only true God, and Jesus Christ whom you have sent" (Jn 17:3). This does not mean simply that we should know that there is a God, or that he has sent his Son and Spirit; rather, we are invited to know by participation the love of the Father, the Son, and the Holy Spirit. Now that we have come *to* the Trinity, how do we live *in* the Trinity?

PART TWO

IN THE MYSTERY OF THE TRINITY

Chapter Five

The Church

In the English translation of the Nicene Creed used at Mass we say: "I believe in one, holy, catholic, and apostolic Church." But the words "I believe in" do not appear in the original Latin and Greek; after professing faith in the Holy Spirit, the text simply adds: ". . . and one, holy, catholic and apostolic Church". Is the omission significant? Yes: we do not believe in the Church the way that we believe in God. As one Father of the Church expressed it, "We believe the Church as the mother of our new birth, and not *in* the Church as if she were the author of our salvation." [1] To capture this distinction, it might help to punctuate the Apostles' Creed in this way: "I believe in the Holy Spirit: the holy, catholic Church; the communion of saints; the forgiveness of sins; the resurrection of the body; and life everlasting." The colon following "Holy Spirit" shows that we believe in God, who brings the Church into being and sustains her.

What We Believe

God's saving work began with the call of Abraham and the subsequent history of the Jewish people. In the fullness of time, he sent his Son, born of the chosen people, to save us and share divine life with us by the gift of the Holy Spirit. God's covenant with Israel was extended to the whole human race; all are invited to enter the People of God, which is the Body of Christ and the Temple of the Holy Spirit. The Church was founded by Christ as a visible community and possesses certain distinguishing characteristics: she is one, holy, catholic, and apostolic. Objectively speaking, these marks are found in a preeminent

[1] Faustus of Riez, *De Spiritu Sancto* 1, 2: PL 62, 11, quoted in *CCC*, no. 169.

75

way in the Catholic Church, but they also exist in varying degrees in
other Christian communities, and there is a real but imperfect communion among all believers. Christ is the unique Savior of mankind,
and the Church, as his Body, is instrumental in the salvation of all
people.

Some History

What we believe about the Church is rooted in the two great dogmas
of the Holy Trinity and the Incarnation. The divine communion of
love, which is the Trinity, is at the heart of salvation, and the trinitarian unity-in-diversity is reflected in the one Church, which is a
communion of churches. Because our salvation has been accomplished through the Incarnation of the Son of God, the Church is
both a visible, human institution and a spiritual, divine reality. It took
faith to recognize that the man Jesus is the Son of God; as Saint Paul
noted, "None of the rulers of this age understood this; for if they had,
they would not have crucified the Lord of glory" (1 Cor 2:8). If such
ignorance was possible regarding the sinless Christ, it is all the more
difficult to see that the Church, a fellowship of sinners, is also a divine
reality. For two thousand years, sinful Christians—ordinary believers
and leaders alike—have been a source of scandal; yet we are the "earthen
vessels" through whom God's saving work is accomplished. The detached
outsider can find much to admire and much to criticize in the Church;
only faith reveals her to be the People of God, the Body of Christ,
and the Temple of the Holy Spirit. We will examine the Church under
each of these three biblical images, as a reality both human and divine.

The Church as the People of God

The Church is a means to an end, that end being God's desire to
bring all creation into the divine life of the Trinity. According to the
Second Vatican Council, "the Church is in Christ like a sacrament or
as a sign and instrument both of a very closely knit union with God
and of the unity of the whole human race" (*Lumen Gentium* [*LG*],
no. 1). Salvation is both personal and social: we enter into communion with God by belonging to his people. The Book of Genesis
presents a rough sketch of God's saving plan. It opens with the image
of a harmonious creation, and then tells the sad story of discord: the

Fall of Adam and Eve, the strife between brothers (Cain and Abel), and the shadow of sin falling across creation (the Flood) and civilization (the tower of Babel). The second half of Genesis describes the healing of these relationships: Abraham's faith restores man's communion with God, and the ongoing fraternal rivalries are resolved at the end of the story of Joseph. The characters do not always act virtuously; the patriarchs display both heroism and wickedness. But through all the lights and shadows, God's plan is carried out. The key to the meaning of the whole book is given at the end, when Joseph says to his brothers, who had sold him into slavery: "And now do not be distressed, or angry with yourselves, because you sold me here; for God sent me before you to preserve life" (Gen 45:5). For Christians, this climactic moment foreshadows the way God will use the betrayal of Jesus by his brothers to bring about our salvation.

The divine plan comes into clearer focus with the Exodus and the covenant on Mount Sinai. Here we encounter the challenging mystery of election: What does it mean to say that the Jews are the "chosen people"? Are other nations not chosen? Since one aspect of salvation is the unity of the human family, God begins to accomplish his plan by intervening in the history of one people. Election also manifests God's sovereign freedom: he can act where and how he chooses. The long history of the Old Testament is the account of God's often surprising choices. Jesus showed the same freedom in calling his disciples; as he reminded them at the Last Supper, "You did not choose me, but I chose you and appointed you that you should go and bear fruit" (Jn 15:16).

Two important points should be made about the mystery of election. First, God's choice is not based on merit, a lesson driven home throughout the Bible. Moses reminded the Jews, "It was not because you were more in number than any other people that the LORD set his love upon you and chose you, for you were the fewest of all peoples" (Deut 7:7). Saint Paul for his part told the Corinthians, "Not many of you were wise according to the flesh, not many were powerful, not many were of noble birth; but God chose what is foolish in the world to shame the wise, God chose what is weak in the world to shame the strong, God chose what is low and despised in the world" (1 Cor 1:26–28). The apostles Christ chose were slow to understand much of what he taught, and they did not distinguish themselves for bravery when the hour of his Passion came. God's choices are unpredictable and can seem capricious or imprudent. Since this is so, we should not be surprised to find weeds growing alongside the wheat in the field of the Church. The beloved disciple stood beneath the Cross—Peter fled; yet Christ's choice of Peter to lead his flock was not revoked because of his failure.

The second point is that the elect always remain related to those who are not chosen. The prophets sometimes described Israel as a sign of the future gathering of all nations. To fulfill their vocation, the Jews were called to be one and holy: united in their covenant loyalty to God and careful not to mix with other nations, since this invariably weakened their unique relationship with God. After Christ's Resurrection, this covenant relationship was extended to the Gentiles. Now, the People of God were to be not only one and holy, but also catholic and apostolic: by the preaching of the Gospel, the Church extends Israel's election to all of mankind. Later in this chapter, we will look at the thorny question of salvation outside the Church, but the fundamental purpose behind both the call of Israel and the mission of the Church must be kept in mind: God "desires all men to be saved and to come to the knowledge of the truth" (1 Tim 2:4). Everyone is invited to belong to the People of God.

The Church as the Body of Christ

The Son of God was born of the chosen people and directed his ministry primarily to "the lost sheep of the house of Israel" (Mt 10:6). The newborn Jesus had been hailed as "a light for revelation to the Gentiles, and for glory to your people Israel" (Lk 2:32), but the mission to the Gentiles began in earnest only after Pentecost. By the outpouring of the Holy Spirit, the apostles and other disciples became something more than witnesses to Jesus: the community of believers formed the Body of Christ. To appreciate the mystery of the Church, we must realize the truth conveyed by this image. As we have seen, Saint Paul learned this when he encountered the risen Christ on his way to Damascus, en route to arrest the followers of Jesus. A voice said to him, "Saul, Saul, why do you persecute me?" And when asked who he was, the Lord answered, "I am Jesus, whom you are persecuting" (Acts 9:4–5). In that revelation of the exalted Lord, Saint Paul discovered that the community of disciples on earth is the Body of Christ.

Several corollaries flow from this relationship. First, Jesus is the Head of the Body, and Head and Body together form the whole Christ. Christ and his Church can never be separated. The vocation of the Body flows from the Head: Jesus continues his priestly, prophetic, and royal mission through the Church, and each member of the Body plays a unique part in that mission. Through the gift of the Holy Spirit, the Body receives from its Head the gifts and assistance necessary to carry out this mission. We read in the Letter to the Ephesians, "We are to grow up in every way into him who is the head, into Christ, from whom the whole body, joined and knit together by every joint with which it is supplied, when each part is working properly, makes bodily growth and upbuilds itself in love" (Eph 4:15–16).

Second, the Body of Christ on earth is a visible community. To speak of a purely spiritual Church contradicts the dynamic of the Incarnation, by which the uncreated, infinite Son of God expressed himself within the limits of finite, created reality of this world. Like any other human society, the People of God is an organized community; this can be seen as far back as the Exodus. More importantly, the fundamental structure of the Church was established by Christ to enable her to fulfill her purpose: as a created reflection of the unity-in-diversity that is the Trinity, the community of disciples requires a structure that preserves real unity and legitimate diversity. The ecclesial Body of Christ on earth must be truly one, with a variety of members. As was true with the Incarnation, so with the mystery of the Church, we need to avoid two extremes. On the one hand, an overly "spiritual" approach that ignores the need for visible structures denies the truth that God brings about our salvation in this world; on the other hand, an excessively "human" approach that equates unity with visible structures denies the centrality of divine love that is the animating principle of the Body of Christ.

It is sometimes suggested that the Church prolongs the mystery of the Incarnation: Christ the Head teaches, heals, forgives, and nourishes through his Body, the Church. As Saint Leo the Great taught, "What was visible in our Savior has passed over into his mysteries." [2] It is true that Christ continues his mission through the Church, but some important qualifications should be noted. For one thing, Jesus

---

[2] St. Leo the Great, *Sermones*, 74, 2: *PL* 54, 398, quoted in *CCC*, no. 1115.

was sinless; he always did the Father's will. The members of Christ's Body are sinners, so the will of God is not carried out perfectly in the Church. Second, we need to recall that the incarnate Christ was not two persons, but one Person, since the Son of God united Jesus' human nature to his own Person. (However, Jesus had a human mind, memory, and will, distinct from those of the Divine Word.) But in our union with Christ, we retain our personal identity. Even when Saint Paul said, "It is no longer I who live, but Christ who lives in me" (Gal 2:20), he did not mean that his unique individuality had been swallowed up by Christ. On the contrary, the apostle's experience was that he discovered his own deepest identity through his union with Christ. And this suggests another way to express the relationship between Christ and his Body: the union of husband and wife, two persons who in marriage become one flesh.

Nuptial imagery flows through the whole Bible, from the Garden of Eden at the beginning of Genesis to the Wedding of the Lamb at the end of Revelation. God's covenant with Israel was depicted as a marriage bond throughout the Old Testament. One of the most beautiful and evocative expressions of this theology is the Song of Songs. This love poem does not even mention God, yet Jews and Christians alike have always interpreted it as a celebration of the mutual love between God and his people. Given this biblical imagery of God as Israel's Bridegroom, it was significant that John the Baptist compared himself to the best man and that Jesus spoke of himself as the Bridegroom. With the Incarnation, the Divine Suitor has come in the flesh to win his Bride, laying down his life for love of her. Drawing on Saint Paul's theology of Christ as the New Adam, the early Fathers saw the Church as the New Eve, born from the pierced side of Christ as he slept in death on the Cross. The distinction between Lover and Beloved is enhanced, not diminished, in the conjugal relationship of husband and wife: in marriage, each partner truly discovers who he or she is in relation to his or her spouse. When applied to Christ and the Church, this dynamic reflects the life of the Trinity, wherein each Person "is" relationship, and each freely glorifies the others.[3]

---

[3] Jesus chose only men to be his apostles, and the apostles did the same when they chose leaders to succeed them in their ministry. The Catholic Church, in common with all churches that predate the Reformation, does not ordain women to the priesthood; in this matter, the Catholic Church is bound by the choice made by Christ himself (see

The Church as the Temple of the Holy Spirit

The indwelling of the Spirit makes the union of the Church to Christ as Bride and Body more than a mere figure of speech. For this reason, the Church and her members are described in the New Testament as the Temple of the Holy Spirit, and in the Creed, the Church is associated with the article about the Holy Spirit, not the Son. It is certainly true that Jesus founded the Church, in the sense that he gathered the community of disciples together and formed its leaders. But this fact must be balanced by attention to the work of the Holy Spirit, who breathes divine life into this community. The Spirit has been described as the soul of the Church, that is, the life principle of the Mystical Body of Christ. A body without a soul is a corpse. Without the Spirit, the Bible is merely an archeological record, the sacraments simply sociological rituals, the Church only a human institution. With the presence of the Spirit, the Bible is the word of God, the sacraments are an encounter with the paschal mystery of Christ's death and Resurrection, and the Church is an earthly foretaste of Kingdom of God, where the human family is gathered together into the mystery of divine life forever.

The Church is rooted in the mystery of the Trinity. In the words of the *Catechism*: "Thus the Church's mission is not an addition to that of Christ and the Holy Spirit, but is its sacrament: in her whole being and in all her members, the Church is sent to announce, to bear witness, make present, and spread the mystery of the communion of the Holy Trinity" (no. 738). God gives the Church certain characteristics, or marks, to enable her to carry out her mission. These are enunciated in the Nicene Creed: the Church is one, holy, catholic, and apostolic. This Creed is professed by Christians of East and West, and the

---

CCC, no. 1577). Reflecting on this constant tradition, the Congregation for the Doctrine of the Faith noted how the theme of nuptial imagery appears throughout the Bible, and then observed: "That is why we can never ignore the fact that Christ is a man. And therefore, unless one is to disregard the importance of this symbolism for the economy of Revelation, it must be admitted that, in actions which demand the character of ordination and in which Christ himself, the author of the Covenant, the Bridegroom and Head of the Church, is represented, exercising his ministry of salvation which is in the highest degree the case of the Eucharist—his role (this is the original sense of the word 'persona') must be taken by a man." Congregation for the Doctrine of the Faith, *Inter Insigniores* (Declaration on the Admission of Women to the Ministerial Priesthood), no. 5.

scandal of Christian disunity presents itself forcefully in the paradox that most Christians agree that the Church of Christ possesses these attributes, and yet we are divided. How do we as Catholics understand these marks of the Church?

One, Holy, Catholic, and Apostolic

As the creation of the one God, and as a kind of sacrament of the unity of the human family which is the goal of God's saving plan, the Church must be *one*. Saint Paul taught the Ephesians: "There is one body and one Spirit, just as you were called to the one hope that belongs to your call, one Lord, one faith, one baptism, one God and Father of us all, who is above all and through all and in all" (Eph 4:4–6). The nucleus of this Church was the community of Jesus' followers gathered around the Twelve, with Peter as its leader. As the Gospel was preached throughout the world, local communities were established. These local churches maintained fellowship with one another, so that the one Church consisted of a communion of local churches. Saint Luke says that the primitive community "held steadfastly to the apostles' teaching and fellowship, to the breaking of the bread and to the prayers" (Acts 2:42). These characteristics continue to be foundational to the Church's unity: the profession of one faith received from the apostles; a common celebration of the sacramental life; and fraternal spiritual communion among churches all over the world.

It would be naïve to imagine some golden age when all was harmony in the community of disciples. Divisions and dissensions are spoken of in the New Testament, and as far back as the third century, Origen observed: "Where there are sins, there are also divisions, schisms, heresies, and disputes." [4] The Church on earth is a pilgrim people, so human sinfulness wounds the Body of Christ. Because the Church's oneness comes from God, and God remains faithful to his promises, it can never be lost. The fathers of the Second Vatican Council, in *Unitatis Redintegratio*, looked forward to the day when the obstacles dividing Christians would be overcome; then,

> all Christians will at last, in a common celebration of the Eucharist, be
> gathered into the one and only Church in that unity which Christ

---

[4] Origen, *Homiliae in Ezechielem*, 9, 1: PG 13, 732, quoted in *CCC*, no. 817.

bestowed on His Church from the beginning. We believe that this unity subsists in the Catholic Church as something she can never lose, and we hope that it will continue to increase until the end of time. (*UR*, no. 4)

Even as the council fathers expressed the hope that the oneness of the Church would grow, they also recognized that all sides bear responsibility for the divisions that have occurred among Christians over the centuries. It is Christ's will that his Body should be one, so the Catholic Church is committed to the work of Christian unity.

Holiness, too, is God's gift to his Church. Indeed, it must be his gift, because holiness is by its very nature an attribute of God alone; in the Scriptures, holiness is bestowed by God. The people, the Temple, the priesthood of the Old Testament become holy when they are set apart from worldly use and made holy by God. This consecration of one people was extended to all nations after Christ's Resurrection. Saint Peter wrote to Gentiles, those who were once "no people": "You are a chosen race, a royal priesthood, a holy nation, God's own people" (1 Pet 2:9). The Church is made holy by her union with Christ: "Christ loved the Church and gave himself up for her, that he might sanctify her, having cleansed her by the washing of water with the word, that he might present the Church to himself in splendor, without spot or wrinkle or any such thing, that she might be holy and without blemish" (Eph 5:25–27). The Holy Spirit sanctifies the Church, imparting divine life to her and her members.

Some of these members, the canonized saints, have practiced heroic virtue and are proposed as models for us. But the Church is not made up solely of saints, and Catholicism has never accepted a definition of the Church that limits her membership to those predestined for eternal life, or even to those in the state of grace. The holiness of the Church comes, not from her members, but from God. For this reason, the elements that allow the Church to serve as an instrument of grace in the world—the Scriptures, the sacraments, the hierarchical structure, and charismatic gifts—convey holiness even though they are placed into the hands of sinners. At the end of her earthly pilgrimage, the Church will appear as the Bride of Christ without stain or wrinkle; here on earth holiness will always be imperfect.

Our understanding of the third attribute of the Church—*catholicity*—can be confused by the fact that "Catholic Church" has come to mean in general parlance the body of believers in communion with the Bishop of Rome, as distinguished from other Christian bodies. Obviously, when Orthodox, Anglican, or Protestant Christians profess faith in "the catholic Church" they do not mean this. How do we as Catholics understand the term? The *Catechism* teaches that the Church is "catholic" in a double sense (nos. 830–31). The first way is that, by virtue of her union with Christ, the Catholic Church possesses the fullness of the means of salvation willed by Christ: a complete profession of faith, a full sacramental life, ordained ministry in apostolic succession, and visible hierarchical communion. Catholicity in this sense does not depend on geographical expansion; the Church was catholic even before the disciples went out from Jerusalem to preach the Good News.

From this first meaning of catholicity, the *Catechism* draws a lesson that might surprise many Catholics: the local community of believers gathered around its bishop is not simply a part of the Catholic Church; it *is* the Catholic Church made present in a particular place. Over the centuries, the West has stressed the unity of the worldwide Catholic Church, but this truth must be complemented by an awareness that this one Church is a communion of local or "particular" churches. We need to recapture a lively sense of our diocesan identity. Most Catholics know their parish church and can picture the pope and St. Peter's Basilica, but relatively few have a sense of connection to their cathedral, and most rarely, if ever, see their bishop. We belong to the Catholic Church by virtue of our membership in the faith community gathered around our bishop, and in that community, the fullness of the Church is found. The Second Vatican Council taught that "individual bishops . . . are the visible principle and foundation of unity in their particular churches" (*LG*, no. 23), a truth proclaimed as far back as the end of the New Testament era by Ignatius of Antioch: "Let no one do anything concerning the Church in separation from the bishop." [5]

The second meaning of catholicity is that the Church has an obligation to preach the Gospel to the whole world. The People of God in the old covenant was not a missionary community; in fact, it was God's will that the Jews avoid foreigners in order to safeguard their

---

[5] St. Ignatius of Antioch, *Epistula ad Smyrnaeos*, 8, 1: *Apostolic Fathers*, II/2, 309, quoted in *CCC*, no. 896.

unique relationship with him. Apart from a few encounters with Gentiles, Jesus observed this restriction throughout his ministry, but after the Resurrection, he sent his disciples out in the power of the Holy Spirit to preach the Gospel to all nations. The missionary mandate is an essential part of the Church's nature because she shares in the mission of the Son and the Holy Spirit, sent from the Father for the salvation of all people. No one is to be excluded from receiving the invitation to enter the People of God: the catholicity of the Church must embrace all nations and cultures, and every element of society.

The fourth attribute of the Church is linked to the third: she is *apostolic*, because the mission to carry the Gospel to the ends of the earth was entrusted by Christ to his apostles, and that mission continues through their successors, the bishops. We will examine this doctrine in the next chapter, but here I would simply note that the Catholic understanding of apostolicity refers to both the content of the faith (the Church has handed on intact the faith she has received from the apostles) and continuity in leadership (the bishops of the Church have received their authority to teach, govern, and sanctify from the apostles, who received it from Christ himself). Although apostolicity pertains to the leadership of the Church in a particular way, the whole Church is apostolic: every believer has the vocation to spread the love of Christ and the knowledge of the saving truth he came to reveal.

Because these attributes are given by God, we believe that the Church can never cease to be one, holy, catholic, and apostolic. At the same time, because the Church is made up of sinners, on earth she will never be perfectly one, holy, catholic, or apostolic. We perceive in faith that the Church is the Bride of Christ, even though here below she will never be "without spot or wrinkle or ... blemish" (Eph 5:27). The Second Vatican Council notes that Christ was sinless, but "the Church, embracing in its bosom sinners, at the same time holy and always in need of being purified, always follows the way of penance and renewal" (*LG*, no. 8).

Implications

Those human failings cause many people to distance themselves from the Church. They admire Jesus, but have no desire to identify with

"organized religion". For some Christians, all that matters is accepting
Jesus as their personal Lord and Savior; Church affiliation is unimpor-
tant, and should not come between Jesus and the individual. Does the
Church really matter? This is not a new question. Saint Augustine
tells the story in his *Confessions* of a contemporary philosopher, Mar-
ius Victorinus, who informed his friends that he had become a Christian. When they said that they did not believe this because he had not
joined the community, Victorinus retorted, "Do the walls make the
Church?"

The Catholic response to Victorinus' question is that the walls do
not make the Church, but the community does. The Church *does*
"come between" Jesus and me—not as a barrier, but as a bridge: everything we know about Jesus has come to us through the community of
believers. But when different communities profess incompatible beliefs
about the mission and identity of Jesus, how can we resolve the contradiction? If God's will is to bring the whole human family together
through Christ in the Holy Spirit, then Christians cannot be indifferent to the divisions within the very community that God has brought
into being for the sake of unity.

Catholics and Other Christians

As noted above, many Christian denominations teach that the Church
is one, holy, catholic, and apostolic, but they interpret those attributes
in different ways. In the past century, the Catholic Church has experienced a notable development in her understanding of these four marks,
and this has altered her approach to the cause of Christian unity. In
1943, Pope Pius XII taught in his Encyclical *Mystici Corporis* that the
Roman Catholic Church, and she alone, is the Mystical Body of Christ;
only Catholics are really members of that Body. Does this mean that
only Catholics can be saved? No, the Holy Father stated that non-
Catholics can be related to the Church by desire—and this may mean
simply the desire to do God's will as one understands it. *Mystici Corporis* presented the traditional Catholic teaching: Christ intended his
Church to be both a spiritual and a visible body; the four marks of
the Church can never be lost, because they are the work of God;
through her rich spiritual life, historical continuity, and worldwide
union, the Catholic Church shows that she is this Mystical Body of

Christ.[6] Christian unity is achieved by individuals entering the Catholic Church. On the other hand, Pius XII articulated a spiritual, organic understanding of the Church. This represented a change from a tendency in Roman documents to describe the Church in juridical terms, and his use of scriptural and patristic sources prepared the ground for new developments at the Second Vatican Council.

One of the principal reasons Pope John XXIII convened that council was to promote Christian unity. At this gathering, the bishops experienced a monumental shift in their understanding of the relationship of Catholics to other Christians. Where formerly the Mystical Body of Christ was identified exclusively with the Roman Catholic Church, now it was said to "subsist" there; where formerly only Catholics were considered to be members of that Mystical Body, now all baptized Christians were seen to be part of the Church in some way; where formerly Rome had recognized no ecclesial reality beyond the borders of the visible Catholic Church, now there was a recognition that the Holy Spirit uses other Christian churches and communities as means of salvation for their members.

What brought about this change? The organic understanding of the nature of the Church presented in *Mystici Corporis*, together with the biblical and patristic advances of which it was both the fruit and a catalyst, helps to explain this development. Pius XII had urged Catholics to foster a living, spiritual relationship with the Church as members of the Body of Christ; the council echoed this by teaching that in order for Catholics to be "fully incorporated" into the Church it was necessary for them to persevere in charity. If there could be degrees of incorporation in the Church among Catholics, could this not be applied to non-Catholic Christians, who also professed faith in Christ and manifestly possessed charity? Furthermore, Pius XII had spoken not only of the universal Church, but of the Latin and Oriental communities within her gathered around their bishops. If

---

[6] In the previous century, the First Vatican Council had affirmed that the visible attributes of the Catholic Church are signs that speak to human reason: "What is more, the church herself by reason of her astonishing propagation, her outstanding holiness and her inexhaustible fertility in every kind of goodness, by her catholic unity and her unconquerable stability, is a kind of great and perpetual motive of credibility and an incontrovertible evidence of her own divine mission." Constitution *Dei Filius*, no. 3, *Decrees of the Ecumenical Councils*, vol. 2, trans. Norman Tanner (Washington, D.C.: Sheed & Ward and Georgetown University Press, 1990), pp. 807–8; see *CCC*, no. 812.

the one Catholic Church is made up of these communities, might not the unity of the Church be more dynamic than formerly understood?

The bishops gathered in Rome approached the nature of the Church from a fresh perspective. Rather than beginning with the four marks professed in the Creed, they asked: "What are the constitutive elements of the Church?" Many of these were recognized: faith in Christ; the virtues of hope and charity; the life of grace; the Scriptures; baptism, Eucharist, and other sacraments; the gifts of the Holy Spirit; prayer; the historic creeds; veneration of the Mother of God and other saints; bishops in apostolic succession; visible communion among those bishops with one another and with the successor of Saint Peter, the head of the college of bishops. Some, indeed many, of these elements are present to a greater or lesser degree in various denominations. If the one Church is a communion of churches, was there not a real, although imperfect, unity among all Christians? The council fathers answered that question affirmatively, and the Catholic Church adopted a new approach to ecumenism. Certainly individual Christians who recognize the Catholic Church as the fullest ecclesial expression of God's salvific will should enter into "full communion" with her (the language of "conversion" being deemed more appropriate for those coming to faith in Christ), but the path to Christian unity would now entail dialogue among the various churches and Christian communities.

The question the bishops asked is a central issue for the ecumenical movement: "What are the constitutive elements of the Church? What structures, practices, and traditions are necessary for the Church to carry out her mission?" Reviewing the elements listed by the bishops of the Catholic Church, various communions would respond in different ways. The Orthodox churches affirm all of the elements in the previous paragraph save the last, communion with the successor of Saint Peter; communities emerging from the Reformation hold fewer elements to be essential. From the Catholic perspective, all of the elements enunciated by the council are vital, and because they are all found in the Catholic Church, it can be said that the Church of Christ "subsists" in her.

In teaching that the Church of Christ subsists in the Catholic Church, the council fathers were seeking to harmonize two doctrinal positions: (1) that the Church of Christ exists fully only in the Catholic

Church; and (2) that elements of truth and sanctification are to be found in other churches and communities, and that those bodies that have maintained apostolic succession and a valid Eucharist, even though they are not in communion with Rome, are true particular churches.[7] The operative word is *fully*: the shift in Catholic understanding at the Second Vatican Council was the recognition that the defining traits of the Church—one, holy, catholic, apostolic—are dynamic, not static, realities.

This recognition of elements of truth and sanctification beyond the visible community of the Catholic Church is in fact very traditional. For example, while the Donatists re-baptized Catholics who joined them, Saint Augustine observed that this was not the practice of the Catholic Church: "It is because we acknowledge in them that which we do not repeat. By not recognizing our baptism, they deny that we are their brothers; on the other hand, when we do not repeat their baptism but acknowledge it to be our own, we are saying to them: *You are our brothers.*"[8] The ecumenical significance of this ancient Catholic practice was noted at the Second Vatican Council: "Baptism therefore establishes a sacramental bond of unity which links all who have been reborn by it" (*UR*, no. 22). Similarly, the Catholic Church has always recognized that the Orthodox churches have maintained apostolic succession and valid sacramental orders. These communities have preserved all of the constitutive elements of the Church listed by the bishops at the Second Vatican Council *except* visible communion with the See of Peter. The importance of that communion will be examined in the next chapter; here it need only be noted that the bonds uniting the Catholic and Orthodox churches are many.

Objectively speaking, from the Catholic perspective, the traits enumerated at the council—including a visible worldwide unity guaranteed by communion with the successor of Saint Peter—are all integral to the Church's life, and this is why we believe that the Church of Christ exists *fully* only in the Catholic Church. But it is also objectively

---

[7] This is the explanation of "subsists in" given by the Congregation for the Doctrine of the Faith in its declaration *Dominus Iesus*, nos. 16–17.

[8] St. Augustine, *Discourse on Psalm 32* (Office of Readings, Tuesday of the Fourteenth Week in Ordinary Time). The Donatists were a rigorist sect in North Africa who held that they were the only true church, and that the sacraments administered by others were invalid.

true that the Church of Christ is present to varying degrees in other Christian bodies, and, according to the teaching of the Second Vatican Council, "the Spirit of Christ has not refrained from using them as means of salvation which derive their efficacy from the very fullness of grace and truth entrusted to the Church" (*UR*, no. 3). Subjectively speaking, other Christian communities have plumbed the depths of some of these constitutive elements very profoundly, and the Catholic Church can learn from them. The Protestant emphasis on Scripture has opened up the riches of the word of God, and the Orthodox experience of a collegial relationship between particular churches provides a balance to a Catholic ecclesiology that can tend to be monolithic. Dialogue worthy of the name presumes that all the participants have something to contribute.

The search for deeper Christian unity is not a matter of finding the lowest common denominator (or denomination?) and claiming on that minimal basis that Christians are now united. Rather, it entails the demanding work of examining what different communities consider essential and exploring how these elements can be shared with other communities. At times, this can be an exhilarating process: the "genius" of each tradition enriches the dialogue between churches. But it is also very difficult, because often the traditions of one community have been influenced by its opposition to another. True Christian unity must be built on fidelity to truth, and nourished by prayer and mutual charity. The Catholic Church is committed irrevocably to this endeavor, as Pope John Paul II clearly stated in his Encyclical *Ut unum sint*.

Non-Christians

What about non-Christians: Can they be saved? There is an inherent tension in the Christian response to this question, and to understand it we should recall what Saint Paul wrote to Timothy: God our Savior "desires all men to be saved and to come to the knowledge of the truth. For there is one God, and there is one mediator between God and men, the man Christ Jesus, who gave himself as a ransom for all, the testimony to which was given at the proper time" (1 Tim 2:4–6). The fundamental point is that God desires all men to be saved; Christ gave himself as a ransom for all. The second point is that salvation involves knowledge of the truth that Christ Jesus is the one mediator between God and men. The impetus for the Church's missionary efforts, going back to the commission of the risen Lord, is to preach the Gospel to the ends of the earth, and so to bring the offer of salvation to the whole world. Christ emphasized how crucial this mission was: "He who believes and is baptized will be saved; but he who does not believe will be condemned" (Mk 16:16).

For a thousand years, from the fifth to the fifteenth centuries, the vast majority of Christians lived in cultures where the Gospel had been preached throughout the known world, and they interpreted strictly the idea that only those who professed faith in Christ (and were thereby members of his Body, the Church), could be saved. Those who did not were considered to be condemned because they had refused to believe.

This assumption was shaken with the discovery of the New World. The practical response was to send out missionaries to preach the Gospel, but the awareness that vast numbers of people had lived for centuries in complete ignorance of Christ raised a challenging question: If God's will is for all to be saved, what was the fate of these millions of souls? Some answered that if God had intended them to be saved, they would have heard the Gospel; since they had not, it was not his intention to save them. Others argued that since God is just, he would not condemn those who had no chance to accept the Gospel through no fault of their own. By the nineteenth century, the commonly held Catholic position (and one taught by Pope Pius IX) was that while ordinarily it was necessary to belong to the Catholic Church to be saved, those who were unaware of this obligation could be saved because God would not punish people for ignorance.[9] In the century since, the Catholic Church has continued to profess a more positive view of the salvation of non-Christians than was true in the Middle Ages, although we still affirm that Christ alone is the Savior of mankind. At Pentecost, Saint Peter told those who listened to the first proclamation of the Gospel what they must do: "Repent, and be baptized every

---

[9] "We all know that those who suffer from invincible ignorance with regard to our holy religion, if they carefully keep the precepts of the natural law which have been written in the hearts of all persons, if they are prepared to obey God, and if they lead a virtuous and dutiful life, can, by the power of divine light and grace, attain eternal life. For God, who knows completely the minds and souls, the thoughts and habits of all persons, will not permit, in accord with his infinite goodness and mercy, anyone who is not guilty of a voluntary fault to suffer eternal punishment." Pius IX, *Quanto Conficiamur Moerore* (1863), no. 7; DS 2866.

one of you in the name of Jesus Christ for the forgiveness of your sins; and you shall receive the gift of the Holy Spirit" (Acts 2:38). God has established faith in Christ and membership in his Body as the ordinary means by which we are saved, but God is not limited to ordinary means. In the words of the *Catechism*: "*God has bound salvation to the sacrament of Baptism, but he himself is not bound by his sacraments*" (no. 1257; italics in the original).

The Church is the sign and instrument of communion with God and the unity of the human race, because God desires the whole human race to be one People of God, to form one Body of Christ, and to be built up into one living Temple of the Holy Spirit. Yet, while Christ's mandate to preach the Gospel to all creation continues to animate the Church, believers need to avoid the presumption that faith in Christ and membership in the Church guarantee salvation. The same Lord who said, "He who believes and is baptized will be saved" (Mk 16:16), also cautioned, "Not every one who says to me, 'Lord, Lord', shall enter the kingdom of heaven, but he who does the will of my Father who is in heaven" (Mt 7:21).

Chapter Six

The Pope and the Bishops

In 1969, the Bishop of Rome traveled to the cradle of Calvinism, Geneva. Pope Pius XI had cautioned Catholics in 1928 to avoid "pan-Christian" organizations; forty years later, Pope Paul VI was calling at the headquarters of the World Council of Churches. The visit was an irenic ecumenical gesture from both sides. But, important as gestures are, the Holy Father knew that the cause of Christian unity faced serious obstacles, and he touched on one of the most challenging when he introduced himself: "Our name is Peter." The rock upon whom we Catholics believe Christ built his Church is, for non-Catholics, a stumbling block—in fact, for many, *the* stumbling block. What is the Catholic understanding of the role of the pope in the Church? What is his relationship to the other bishops? And what do we mean when we say that the pope is infallible? In the first part of this chapter, we will look at the *pastoral* role of the pope and the bishops in the Church, in the second half, examine their *teaching* office.

Pastoral Role: What We Believe

Jesus gathered together a community of disciples, and from among them, he chose and formed those who were to lead the community after his Resurrection: the twelve apostles, and among the Twelve, Simon Peter. The apostles passed on to others the authority they had received from Christ to be pastors and teachers, and this apostolic leadership is exercised by the bishops, the successors of the apostles. Each bishop is the pastor of his own particular church, and the bishops together form a college that shares responsibility for the worldwide Church. As the successor of Saint Peter, the Bishop of Rome is head of the college of

93

bishops and has pastoral responsibility for the whole flock of Christ on earth.

Some History

Some of the strongest disagreements among Christians concern the structure Christ intended for his community. Advocates of various systems can appeal to scriptural warrants for their positions, but nowhere in the New Testament do we find a clear "blueprint" of Church order. There are several reasons for this: only occasionally do the biblical texts make explicit reference to the organization of Christian communities; structures evolved as the community grew and faced new challenges; governance varied from one place to another. What follows is a Catholic interpretation of the scriptural evidence, made in light of the Church organization that emerged soon after the New Testament.

The Biblical Basis for the Leadership of the Catholic Church

Jesus carried out an informal itinerant ministry for a short period of time, so we presume that the community of his followers was relatively unstructured. As we read the Gospels, we can discern concentric circles surrounding Jesus. The outer group consists of crowds of the curious. Closer in are the disciples who follow his teachings. Some of these disciples left their work and families to follow Jesus (among them women, a cultural novelty in those times); others continued their daily occupations.

From among the disciples, Jesus chose twelve men to be the leaders of the community. Their names are recorded in the Gospels, they are commissioned solemnly by Jesus to be "apostles" (meaning those sent out with his authority), and much of his teaching is directed exclusively to them. We know little about the inner workings of this group—it seems that Judas was responsible for finances, and that Peter, James, and John enjoyed a special relationship with Jesus. Peter held a unique place among the Twelve, and his name always appears first in lists of the apostles in the New Testament. He was, like the rest of the Twelve, one of the apostles, but he also received some kind of authority directly by Christ. After the Ascension, we find the same group: a community of disciples, led by the twelve apostles (the place of Judas having been filled by Matthias), and Peter as a leader within the Twelve and a spokesman for the whole community. The Holy Spirit descended upon these followers at Pentecost, and they set out to be witnesses of Jesus "in Jerusalem and in all Judea and Samaria and to the end of the earth" (Acts 1:8).

The Gospel spread rapidly, and the New Testament reflects its reception in various parts of the Mediterranean world. There was diversity even among Jewish communities in the first century. Jews in Palestine lived in a culture permeated by their religion, while those dwelling in the Diaspora (Jewish communities scattered throughout the known world) came into contact with Gentile cultures. The Good News that the Messiah had come took on a different flavor among these various Jewish groups. One of the challenges facing Christian leaders was how to accommodate these various interpretations of Jesus and keep the community united. This became an even greater challenge when Gentiles began to accept the Gospel. For the first time (but certainly not the last), the Christian community had to wrestle with the challenging question: What is essential to our identity? For some, the fact that Jesus was the Messiah meant that Gentile converts had to follow the whole Jewish law, including circumcision and dietary norms. Others urged that it was not necessary for Gentiles to follow such practices.

In his Acts of the Apostles, Saint Luke relates how the crisis was resolved by a gathering of the apostles and elders in Jerusalem (Acts 15). The solution reached was not as readily accepted as Luke's account suggests—the question of how Jewish the disciples of Jesus should be continued to crop up in various places—but two points are significant. First, the early Christians felt that it was important to maintain fellowship while respecting diverse interpretations of the Gospel. To believe in Christ was not simply to follow a philosophy; it was to be incorporated into the one Body of Christ. Even Saint Paul, who staunchly defended the position that Gentile converts were not bound by the Jewish law, taught that the Gentiles were "wild olive shoot[s]" who were saved by being grafted onto God's "cultivated olive tree", that is, Israel (Rom 11:17–24). Different facets of the mystery of Christ came to light as the Gospel was preached in various settings; at times, these differences created tension and even conflict. But these tensions were not permitted to break the communion among the members of the one Body of Christ. The second point is that there were limits to

how much diversity could be allowed without rupturing the fellowship of believers, and the leaders of the community had to determine
what these limits were. So long as the apostles were alive, they clearly
had the authority to make such determinations, but who could do
this after they were gone?

As the apostles preached the Gospel and formed communities, they
appointed leaders and shared with them the authority they had received
from Christ. Here is how the fathers of the Second Vatican Council
described this process:

> In order that the mission assigned to them might continue after their
> death, they [the apostles] passed on to their immediate cooperators, as
> it were, in the form of a testament, the duty of confirming and fin-
> ishing the work begun by themselves, recommending to them that they
> attend to the whole flock in which the Holy Spirit placed them to
> shepherd the Church of God. They therefore appointed such men, and
> gave them the order that, when they should have died, other approved
> men would take up their ministry. (LG, no. 20)

When the apostles passed from the scene, the leaders of their communities were recognized as their successors *in some ways*: they could
not take the place of the apostles as the foundation of their churches
nor as witnesses to Christ's Resurrection, but they did succeed them
as pastors and teachers.

This very broad sketch should not mask the complexities of the
lived experience of the New Testament. Historians and biblical scholars examine several questions: What was the nature of the relationship
between the Twelve and Paul, called as an apostle by Christ although
he had not been part of the original community of disciples?[1] Did
local congregations have one leader or several? To what extent did the
organization of Christian communities differ from Jewish or Gentile
religious groups, and from one another? But these concerns do not
call into question the bigger picture presented by the New Testament
as a whole: Jesus gathered disciples around him with the intention that

---

[1] Although "the Twelve" were apostles in a unique way, the term *apostle* was also applied
to others. Paul, quoting the list of Resurrection appearances he had learned from the
earliest Christian community, distinguishes between an appearance to "the Twelve" and
one to "all the apostles" (1 Cor 15:7). Barnabas was called an apostle in the New Testament and is commemorated as such in the liturgy.

they continue his mission; he chose certain men to lead the community, whose authority was passed on to others; and, as the Gospel spread, communities grew up that saw themselves as "the church" in their particular locale, but also part of "the Church", which was one organic, worldwide body. The community of disciples was characterized by both diversity and unity.

The One Church: A Communion of Local Churches

It is easy to speak of "diversity" and "unity", but the just demands of each are difficult to balance in practice. Unity can become equated with uniformity, and diversity can lead to disintegration. As the Gospel spread throughout the world, the challenge was to maintain unity in the fundamentals of the faith while allowing legitimate diversity in the expression of that faith. The bonds between Christian communities have always been manifold. First and foremost is charity. Saint Paul assumed that his Gentile converts had an obligation to assist the Jerusalem community, and help in time of need has always been a practical expression of ecclesial unity. But more formal bonds developed as well: an agreed-upon collection of sacred writings; mutually recognized sacramental rites; common creedal statements; and structures uniting local churches and the worldwide communion of believers. It is in this *unifying* role that we can best understand the position of the pope and the other bishops in the Church.

The diversity-unity dialectic is expressed in collegiality and primacy. By *collegiality*, we mean that authority rests with a group, by *primacy* that there is a single leader. Which form of government did Christ will for his Church? The evidence of the New Testament suggests both. Jesus commissioned the Twelve to lead his community, and he commissioned one of the Twelve, Peter, to lead his community.[2] This arrangement carries a built-in tension. It seems that this tension was intentional, because Christ could have arranged things differently.

[2] Jesus commissioned the Twelve to preach the Gospel (Mt 28:19; Mk 16:15), baptize (Mt 28:19), bind and loose (Mt 18:18), celebrate the Eucharist (Lk 22:19), and forgive sins (Jn 20:23). He declared that Peter is the rock upon which he would build his Church, and commissioned him to bind and loose (Mt 16:18), prayed for him individually so that he could strengthen his brethren (Lk 22:32), and commended the care of his flock to him (Jn 21:15–17).

He could have appointed the Twelve and then have them choose one of their number to preside; in this case, it would have been clear that Peter (had he been the one chosen!) was simply a spokesman for the group. Or, Jesus could have appointed Peter and then had him choose the other Eleven; in this way, it would have been clear that there was one leader, and the others were his deputies. But Jesus gave authority to *both* the Twelve as a group *and* to one of its members individually. This structure of leadership reflects the nature of the Church: as one community, she has one visible head with pastoral responsibility for the whole Church; as a communion of churches, the leaders of each of those churches exercise authority in their own right, and all of them together share responsibility for the whole Church.

Even under the best of circumstances the inherent tensions between collegiality and primacy would create conflict, and in our imperfect world, we are not living in the best of circumstances. Broadly speaking, it could be said that over the past two thousand years the East has tended to favor collegiality and the West to favor primacy. While the history is long and complex, it might be helpful to sketch it briefly, because it provides the context for our understanding of the role of the pope and the bishops in the Church today.

The East is the cradle of Christianity. While Rome was "the Apostolic See" of the West, many communities in the East claimed apostolic foundation. Two of these, Alexandria and Antioch, became the major theological centers in the early Church, and with the adoption of Christianity as the religion of the Roman Empire, two more major sees emerged: Jerusalem and Constantinople. Theological disagreements were dealt with regionally; if a major conflict threatened the unity of the Church, the solution was to hold a meeting of bishops representing the whole Church, an ecumenical council. These were convened by the emperor, so the state played a role in safeguarding the unity of the Church.

How did Eastern Christians view Rome? As the city where the two greatest apostles, Peter and Paul, had shed their blood, and as the historic center of the empire, Rome was accorded precedence in lists of the major sees, and her interventions were received with respect—as one view to be seriously considered. Since most of the early theological debates took place in the East, Rome occasionally arbitrated disagreements between Eastern churches. In the fifth and sixth centuries, the system of patriarchates emerged: five regional centers (Rome, Constantinople, Alexandria, Antioch, and Jerusalem) shared responsibility for maintaining the unity of the Church. The presumption in the East was that matters touching the Church as a whole should be dealt with collegially—through discussions among the five patriarchs or ecumenical councils. Rome was accorded a certain undefined primacy and sometimes served as a court of appeal.

The West presents a very different picture. Rome was *the* Apostolic See, and the fact that it was the capital and, more importantly, the city of Peter and Paul, gave it great prestige. Its influence varied—stronger in Italy, resisted at times in North Africa and elsewhere—but the Roman church and her bishop felt the "anxiety for all the churches" that had motivated Saint Paul (2 Cor 11:28). Christ had designated Peter as the rock upon which he would build his Church and had solemnly commended the care of his flock to him; on the basis of that commission, the successor of Saint Peter assumed he had a responsibility to act wherever he perceived the flock to be in danger—and not just in the West. These interventions were not always either welcome or successful, but it is significant that they were made at all; primacy was taken for granted in Rome.

The collapse of the Empire in the West, the barbarian invasions, and the rise of the Holy Roman Empire of Charlemagne enhanced the importance of the Roman church in the West. One has only to think of the use of the Latin language in the liturgy, universal in the Western rites of the Catholic Church until fifty years ago, to sense how central Rome and its bishop have been in the life of the Church in the West. Much of this influence flows from the *patriarchal* role of Rome; the patriarchate of Constantinople exercised a similar influence in Russia and other churches in the East that adopted the Byzantine liturgy. With the division between the East and the West in the eleventh century, the Roman patriarchate and the Church came to be experienced *de facto* as identical in the West. Some prerogatives we have come to associate with the pope really pertain to his role as a patriarch rather than to his Petrine ministry of primacy, and the untangling of these functions could provide a promising avenue for ecumenical dialogue with the churches of the East.

Other factors shaped the role of the pope in the West during the second millennium: struggles to free the Church from interference by secular rulers; the scandal of competing claimants to the See of Peter and the effort to break the impasse by appeals to a general council; the upheavals of the Reformation and the French Revolution—all of these encouraged greater centralization of authority in Rome. It was in this context that the First Vatican Council in the late nineteenth century proclaimed as dogmatic truth the primacy of the Bishop of Rome: as Saint Peter received authority from Christ to care for his flock, his successors have pastoral responsibility for the whole Church. The Second Vatican Council reaffirmed this teaching within the framework of the relationship between the pope and his brother bishops. Each bishop is the successor of the apostles and receives his authority as pastor and teacher from Christ himself in episcopal ordination. He is the Vicar of Christ for his particular church (see *CCC*, no. 1560; *LG*, no. 27). As such, the bishop is a visible source and foundation of unity for his community, but he is also a member of the worldwide college of bishops presided over by the Bishop of Rome. The variety and universality of the People of God is expressed by the many members of the episcopal college, the unity of the flock of Christ by the fact that the college is assembled under one head.

Implications

For the past thousand years, the estrangement between East and West has fostered an emphasis on primacy in the West and collegiality in the East. The weakening of collegiality in the West encouraged a process of "Latinization". For example, although the liturgical rites of Eastern churches in communion with Rome were tolerated, for a long time, the presumption was that the Roman way was best and its customs should be adopted because they were more authentically "Catholic". In the East, the absence of primacy on a worldwide level produced an uneasy confederation of national churches, marked by internecine rivalries among various patriarchates, metropolitans, and synods.

Closer ties between Catholics and Orthodox can bring the blessing of greater collegiality to the West and greater unity to the East, but centuries of isolation and mutual mistrust have left a painful legacy. The way forward does not lie in a return to a vague ideal of the "undivided Church" of the first millennium. The Mediterranean world was the cradle of the Church, but the Church has outgrown that cradle:

the five patriarchates did not include Russia, by far the largest Orthodox communion today; and the title "Patriarch of the West" only has
meaning in a world coterminous with the Roman Empire. Furthermore, the churches emerging from the Reformation find both Catholic and Orthodox governance foreign to their experience.

The Communion of the Church in the Mystery of the Trinity

If Church structures should not be determined by attempts to re-create
the past, still less should they be a matter of titles and prerogatives,
concerns which were so contrary to the mind of Christ and are a
source of scandal to many, Christian and non-Christian alike. Rather,
we must begin by asking: Why the Church? When we understand the
purpose of the Church, we can then discern what structures are necessary for her to fulfill her mission. A clear expression of the Catholic
understanding of this mission is given in the *Catechism*: "The Church's
first purpose is to be the sacrament of the *inner union of men with God*.
Because men's communion with one another is rooted in that union
with God, the Church is also the sacrament of the *unity of the human
race*" (no. 775; italics in the original). The Second Vatican Council,
quoting the great, third-century Church Father Saint Cyprian of Car-
thage, expressed the purpose of the Church very succinctly: "Thus,
the Church has been seen as 'a people made one with the unity of the
Father, the Son and the Holy Spirit'" (*LG*, no. 4).

And so we recall that the Church is founded on the mystery of the
Trinity; as such, she is not primarily an institution, but a communion.
"Communion" by its very nature demands both unity and diversity.
Each community of the faithful gathered around its bishop *is* the Church,
and each bishop has a responsibility both for his own community and
for the worldwide communion of the Church. This sense of inter-
dependence is expressed in the ancient practice of having a bishop
ordained by several other bishops. The bishop belongs to that body,
the college of bishops, which succeeds the college of apostles brought
into being by Christ. To safeguard and promote the unity of that body,
Jesus had appointed one of them, Peter, to lead the college. Peter was
one of the Twelve, and each of the other Eleven was his equal as an
apostle. In the same way, the pope is a bishop, and the others are his
equals as bishops. There is no special sacrament or consecration imparted

when a man becomes pope; he becomes pope because he is the bishop of a particular faith community, the church of Rome. As the successor of Saint Peter, the pope holds a unique place, but not a solitary place, in the care of the worldwide Church. Neither primacy nor collegiality can be "honorary": the pope is not merely the spokesman for the bishops, nor are the bishops merely the deputies of the pope. How to be faithful to both collegiality and primacy in practice is a tremendous challenge, but it is ultimately the challenge of striving to reflect in our limited and imperfect human condition the divine mystery of the one God who is a Trinity of Persons.

Obstacles to Unity

The papacy is a source of unity for Catholics and a cause of division for other Christians. In a similar way, the office of bishop creates both unity and division among Christians. Many communions, the Catholic Church among them, hold that the apostolic succession in an unbroken line of bishops is an essential element of ecclesial leadership; the communions that emerged from the Reformation maintain that the New Testament describes several patterns of leadership, and for most Protestants, the historic episcopate is not seen as indispensable. What is the Catholic understanding of "apostolic succession"?

We saw earlier that, as the Gospel spread, Christian leaders had the task of safeguarding the unity of believers while allowing for the diversity of communities that made up the one Church. As the apostles died, the link with them was maintained in two related ways: doctrine and ministry. As regards doctrine, Christians looked to those communities founded by the apostles; the fact that a community could trace its origins to an apostle meant that its doctrine was apostolic. Some variation between these communities was natural (as we see reflected in the diversity of the New Testament writings), so the patrimony of the Christian faith was held to be the fundamental beliefs commonly professed by the churches founded by the apostles.

Apostolic fidelity was guaranteed in another way as well: the leader's authority came from the apostles. Jesus had sent out his apostles to teach, and he had commanded them to baptize, to celebrate the Eucharist, and to forgive sins. They had handed on this commission to the leaders who came after them, and this became a permanent pattern in the life of the Church. When a community chose its pastor, that man had learned his apostolic doctrine from the community—but he could not be made bishop by the community; only those who had received pastoral authority from the apostles and their successors could ordain him. The participation of the bishops of other churches in the ordination of a new leader expressed both the common bond of a shared apostolic faith and continuous leadership reaching back to the apostles.

The great theological controversies of the first millennium concerned the question of whether a particular theological position was faithful to apostolic doctrine, but these debates never called into question the ministry of those who had received their authority through apostolic succession. At the Protestant Reformation, however, a new problem arose: some of the Reformers judged that the Church had become so corrupt that the apostolic ministry of bishops compromised the apostolic faith described in the New Testament. The communities that emerged from the Reformation represent a spectrum on the question of bishops. The Anglican communion maintained that the episcopate was indispensable; Lutherans held that it was beneficial but not essential (the episcopate was retained in Scandinavia, but not in Germany); Calvinists rejected the idea that the office of bishop was necessary for valid pastoral leadership.

Once again we return to challenging ecumenical questions: What is essential to the nature of the Church, and what are the limits of acceptable diversity, if unity in faith is to be maintained? This problem provides a context in which to consider the *teaching office* of the successors of the apostles.

Teaching Office: What We Believe

Christ is the way, the truth, and the life, and he promised his disciples that the Holy Spirit would confirm them in all truth. He commissioned his apostles to preach the Gospel. In order that this saving truth can be passed on to future ages, the Holy Spirit protects the Church from falling into error in matters of faith and morals. This infallibility in such matters pertains to the Church as a whole, and also to those who have succeeded the apostles as teachers—the college of bishops and the successor of Saint Peter—when they give a definitive judgment on a dogmatic question.

Some History

There are few Catholic dogmas so widely misunderstood, by non-Catholics and Catholics alike, as the doctrine of papal infallibility. To grasp its meaning, we must return to a fundamental idea enunciated in the First Letter to Timothy: "God our Savior ... desires all men to be saved and to come to the knowledge of the truth" (1 Tim 2:3–4). The apostle links salvation with knowledge of the truth. This resonates with what Jesus himself had said: he claimed that he had come to bear witness to the truth, indeed that he *was* the truth, and he commissioned the apostles to teach all nations. How could this saving truth be preserved and shared down through the ages? Certainly Scripture plays an important role in this process, since it is the inspired word of God. But even more foundational is the living community of believers from which the Scriptures emerged. Jesus left no writings, but he created a community of disciples to carry on his mission. For this reason, Saint Paul calls the Church "the pillar and bulwark of truth" (1 Tim 3:15).

Bishops as Teachers in the Early Church

The role of bishop as teacher came to the fore in the second century. In order to understand why, we need to return to the New Testament and recall the variety of interpretations of Jesus found there. Broadly speaking, we might picture a spectrum stretching between "Jewish" and "Gentile" poles. The Jerusalem community stood at the Jewish end of the spectrum: Jesus was understood primarily in terms of the fulfillment of Jewish expectations. Paul's mission to the Gentiles stood at the other end of the spectrum: although he certainly believed that Jesus was the Messiah, Paul recognized that the Good News for the Gentiles was not tied up exclusively with Israel's expectations. We know little about the interactions between Christian communities in the first century, but the evidence of the New Testament suggests that the various views on this spectrum came into contact with each other, sometimes in combination and at other times in conflict. The task of the apostles, and the leaders who followed them, was to maintain unity in the fellowship of believers while respecting the diversity of interpretations of Christ.

The spectrum was not infinitely elastic; there were positions at one extreme or the other that were untenable if unity was to be maintained. Some on the Jewish end of the spectrum believed that Jesus was the Messiah, but only human, and in order to be his disciple, one must observe the whole Jewish law. On the Gentile end were Gnostics who taught that Christ was a purely divine being and that he had nothing to do with the Old Testament. These alternatives, though contradictory, were similar in that they claimed to give *the* meaning of Jesus' life and teaching, and to reject all other positions on the spectrum. Gnostics purported to possess the secret meaning of apostolic doctrine accessible only to initiates. In response to their claim, Saint Irenaeus pointed out that none of the churches founded by the apostles espoused these Gnostic doctrines. The leaders of these communities, not the Gnostic adepts, were the successors of the apostles as teachers in the Church.

Both the communities founded by the apostles and their leaders guaranteed fidelity to apostolic teaching. As we saw above, as far back as the second century, a bishop's apostolic credentials were twofold: he bore witness to the apostolic doctrine he had learned from his community, and as a duly ordained successor of the apostles, he possessed authority to teach his community. The apostles entrusted the Gospel to the whole of the Church, as the Second Vatican Council taught in *Dei Verbum*: "Holding fast to this deposit the entire holy people united with their shepherds remain always steadfast in the teaching of the Apostles, in the common life, in the breaking of the bread and in prayers" (*DV*, no. 10). But the council also noted the unique role of the bishops as teachers in the Church, quoting Saint Irenaeus: "But in order to keep the Gospel forever whole and alive within the Church, the Apostles left bishops as their successors, 'handing over' to them 'the authority to teach in their own place'" (*DV*, no. 7).

The Teaching Authority of the Pope and Bishops

In our Catholic tradition, this teaching authority is called the Magisterium. Each bishop exercises this teaching office in his own diocese, and the college of bishops together with its head, the pope, holds the teaching office for the Church as a whole. The pope and bishops instruct in many ways. Most of the time, this teaching is "ordinary": a bishop preaching in his cathedral, the bishops of a region or country addressing the concerns of Catholics in their area, the pope issuing an encyclical letter—these are some examples of how our pastors carry out their role as successors of the apostles as teachers in their day-to-day ministry. An exceptional manifestation of the Magisterium is an ecumenical council, in which bishops from the whole Church take part.

None of these are necessarily expressions of *infallible* Church teaching, but they are nonetheless authoritative. We believe that the successors of the apostles are guided by the Holy Spirit, and that we should strive to follow their instruction. The Second Vatican Council calls the faithful to adhere with religious assent to the ordinary teaching of the Magisterium in matters of faith and morals. The pope and the bishops hold the place of the apostles in the Church today, and what Jesus said to Peter and the Twelve pertains to them: "He who receives you receives me, and he who receives me receives him who sent me" (Mt 10:40). In a felicitous phrase, the *Catechism* states: "The *ordinary* and universal *Magisterium* of the Pope and the bishops in communion with him teach the faithful the truth to believe, the charity to practice, the beatitude to hope for" (no. 2034; italics in original).

Infallible Teaching

In certain extraordinary circumstances, the Magisterium teaches "the truth to believe" in such a way that the doctrine is held to be infallibly taught as divinely revealed truth. The basis for believing that certain doctrines are infallible is the conviction that the Holy Spirit protects the Church from error and guides her into all truth. According to the Second Vatican Council,

> The entire body of the faithful, anointed as they are by the Holy One, cannot err in matters of belief. They manifest this special property by means of the whole people's supernatural discernment in matters of faith [*sensus fidei*] when "from the Bishops down to the last of the lay faithful" they show universal agreement in matters of faith and morals. (*LG*, no. 12)

A principle taught as far back as Saint Irenaeus in the second century, and reiterated over the centuries since, is that the consensus of the universal Church in her faith is an infallible norm of truth.

But how to determine the consensus of the universal Church? One useful answer to this question was proposed by Vincent of Lérins in the fifth century: whatever has been believed everywhere, always, and by everyone. It should not be thought, however, that Vincent envisioned these beliefs to be static. He asks, "Is there to be no development of religion in the Church of Christ?" and responds: "Certainly, there is to be development and on the largest scale.... But it must truly be development of the faith, not alteration of the faith. Development means that each thing expands to be itself, while alteration means that a thing is changed from one thing into another." [3] The problem, of course, is that one person's development is another's alteration. When contradictory doctrines are put forward, each claiming to be based on Scripture and to reflect the consensus of the universal Church, how is the issue to be settled?

Throughout history, the bishops of a region have met to resolve doctrinal disagreements. If the question could not be settled, an appeal was made to one of the major apostolic sees. But what was to be done when these major sees disagreed? A final decision was sought in the definitive dogmatic judgment of an ecumenical council (representing the collegial leadership of the Church) or the Bishop of Rome (as the successor of Saint Peter and head of the college of bishops). Because the Holy Spirit protects the Church as a whole from error regarding revealed truth, and because the solemn definitions of ecumenical councils and popes have been accepted as definitive judgments of what the faith of the whole Church is, we believe that such decisions are free from error. Infallibility was not an attribute accorded *a priori* to councils or the pope; it was a conclusion drawn from the recognition that their solemn definitions expressed the faith of the Church.

It would be a mistake to limit revealed truth to defined dogmas. Such definitions are exceptional, and frequently have been prompted by a theological dispute. Some of our most basic beliefs, such as the Resurrection of Jesus, have never been solemnly defined because they were never challenged. Infallibility extends as far as the deposit of divine revelation itself, so that basic affirmations of the Church's faith,

---

[3] Saint Vincent of Lérins, *First Instruction*, cap. 23 (Office of Readings, Friday of the Twenty-seventh Week in Ordinary Time).

such as the Creeds, contain dogmatic truths, not all of which have been solemnly defined.

Although some people think that the Catholic Church has a mania for doctrinal definitions, in fact there have been relatively few teachings infallibly defined in the two-thousand-year history of the Church. When the First Vatican Council proclaimed the dogma of papal infallibility in 1870, some Catholics hoped—and others feared—that this would make the pope into a kind of dogmatic oracle issuing infallible decrees. In fact, there has been only one papal dogmatic definition since 1870, regarding the bodily Assumption of the Mother of God.[4] In defining the teaching office of the Bishop of Rome, the First Vatican Council was defending a principle, not establishing a practice.

Solemn definitions are extraordinary expressions of the Church's Magisterium, and there are several requirements to be met in making such a declaration. The issue ordinarily concerns a truth revealed by God for the sake of our salvation. It must be the clear intent of the council or the pope to give a definitive teaching on the matter, calling for the assent of faith. Although the Holy Spirit assists the leaders of the Church in such matters, they are not "inspired" in the sense of receiving some kind of heavenly communication; they need to study the sources of our faith, debate and discuss the matter, and so come to a conclusion.[5] The definitive teaching is infallible, and as such irreversible, but it can be developed further. We have seen that the dogmas concerning the divine and human natures of Jesus emerged in a series of ecumenical councils that affirmed first one, then another, of the truths about Christ. The Second Vatican Council reiterated the doctrines of the previous council on the primacy and teaching authority of the pope, but articulated those doctrines in the context of the

---

[4] And there were very few such definitions before. Scholars disagree about the numbers, but at most there would be about a dozen, from the *Tome* of Leo I in 449 to the definition of the Immaculate Conception in 1854. Of these, seven were censures of certain theological opinions as heretical, not positive definitions of dogma. From a Catholic perspective, ecumenical councils also involve the teaching authority of the pope, since they are an exercise of the college of bishops, of which the pope is the head.

[5] During the First Vatican Council, the wording of the definition was changed from the "infallibility of the Roman Pontiff" to the "infallible magisterium of the Roman Pontiff" to emphasize that infallibility pertained to the teaching office, not to a personal quality of the pope.

relationship between the pope and the rest of the college of bishops. Dogmatic definitions answer certain questions and raise new ones.

These teachings are an important part of the content of our faith, but they do not exhaust it. If there is a danger of according infallibility to every utterance of the pope, there can also be a contrary temptation to hold that *only* teachings that have been solemnly defined as infallible must be accepted by Catholics. This is not consonant with the description of the early community given in Acts: "And they held steadfastly to the apostles' teaching and fellowship, to the breaking of the bread and to the prayers" (Acts 2:42).

Implications

The first Christians devoted themselves to the apostles' teaching— but also to fellowship, the breaking of the bread, and prayers. While the teaching office of the pope and bishops plays a vital role in the life of the Church, we should see it within the broader picture of the living tradition. The truth that makes us free is not simply a catalogue of dogmas, but it is the whole way of life of Jesus and the apostles. The community of believers has lived this life continuously for two thousand years and handed on the Gospel in a variety of ways: through the liturgy, various customs and prayers, art and music, the writings of the Fathers of the Church and other spiritual authors, catechetical texts, the example of the saints, and so on. Among these many forms of handing on tradition, Scripture holds a unique place, because it alone *is* the word of God. As such, we believe that it is the measure and norm of belief and conduct—but Scripture should be interpreted from within the context of the living community that produced it. Our understanding of the meaning of the apostolic faith has deepened over time. When the Council of Nicaea defined the divinity of Christ in the fourth century, this was not an addition to the faith of the New Testament, but an explicit articulation of that faith. The challenge, of course, is to distinguish legitimate development from corruption. An appeal to Scripture alone cannot settle the matter, since, like any text, Scripture needs to be interpreted. The existence of hundreds of denominations professing contradictory beliefs on the basis of what the Bible says testifies to the futility of such an appeal.

We believe that God has entrusted this decisive authority to the successors of the apostles as teachers in the Church. But the pope and the bishops are teachers *in* the Church, not *above* the Church. And, in fact, they learn their doctrine *from* the Church. They do so like everyone else: by taking part in the liturgy, reading the Bible, talking with other believers, studying the artistic and literary records of the Catholic faith. We do not regard these men as charismatic prophets who receive heavenly revelations; they are disciples who have learned the faith of the Church from others, and who have a responsibility to hand on that faith. Nor do we expect them all to be eminent scholars. Over the past two thousand years, there have been some popes and bishops who were great theologians; most were not, by training, theologians at all. They are primarily witnesses to the faith they have received. Critics may deride the pope and the bishops for being conservative—but since it is their responsibility to safeguard the faith as they have received it, it is appropriate for them to be cautious of innovations.

We live in an age that is suspicious of authority and dismissive of any knowledge that cannot be demonstrated scientifically. For these reasons, "hierarchs" (spiritual leaders) fill a particularly demanding office these days. They must speak authoritatively on matters of faith and help God's people apply that faith to a variety of complex issues. And they do so as disciples, ever mindful of their own faults. Here a proper appreciation of the Catholic understanding of the role of the pope and the bishops in the Church can guide us between the extreme of a personality cult that exalts men to superhuman status and the opposite tendency to reject Church teaching because of the human failings of her spokesmen. There have been great saints among our pastors, and notorious sinners as well, but most have been people with ordinary talents and limitations. In this, they are not unlike the first apostles. Saint Paul described himself to the Corinthians, "But we have this treasure in earthen vessels, to show that the transcendent power belongs to God and not to us" (2 Cor 4:7). Our conviction is that the Catholic Church has faithfully handed on the Gospel for two thousand years, not because of the outstanding virtue of her leaders, but because of the unfailing fidelity of God.

Chapter Seven

Sacred Scripture

Every Sunday, Christians all over the world gather to listen to ancient sacred texts. The selections are introduced by a reference to their authors: the prophet Isaiah, Saint Paul, Saint Luke, and so on. At the end of the passage, the reader proclaims that this is the word of God. The introduction and conclusion suggest dual authorship. While we often speak of writers as "inspired", the word has a precise meaning when applied to the Scriptures: although they were written by men, God himself is their author. It is helpful for us to see the Bible in the context of a worshipping assembly: Scripture was written within communities and recognized as the word of God by communities. In this sense, it can be said that the Church gives birth to the Scriptures. On the other hand, because the Bible alone *is* the word of God, it is the standard against which the belief and behavior of the Church is to be measured.

What We Believe

The Sacred Scriptures are the inspired word of God, which means that while human authors wrote them, they are also the revealing and saving word of God himself. This divine inspiration gives a unity and completeness to the collection of books that comprises the Bible. The Scriptures teach without error the truth that God confided to the sacred writings for the sake of our salvation. Individual biblical passages should be interpreted within the context of the whole of Scripture and the living tradition of the Church.

Some History

In the Second Letter to Timothy, we read: "All Scripture is inspired by God and profitable for teaching, for reproof, for correction, and for training in righteousness" (2 Tim 3:16). This simple statement raises some important questions: What constitutes "all Scripture"? What do we mean by "inspired by God"? How does inspiration affect the truth-fulness of Sacred Scripture in such a way as to make it "profitable for teaching ... and for training in righteousness"?

The Canon of Scripture

We think of the Bible as one book, but it is in fact a library of writings composed and compiled over many centuries. Just as God's saving plan gradually unfolded through the long history of his people, so the formation of the canon of Scripture was a lengthy process.[1] Many people are aware that Catholic and Protestant Bibles are not exactly the same, but that disparity can best be understood when we have some idea of how the Bible was put together.

The development of the New Testament canon is fairly straightfor-ward, and most Christian churches accept the same collection of twenty-seven books. Copies of apostolic writings circulated among early Christian communities, and compilations of these writings were made. By the end of the second century, the four Gospels with which we are familiar, and only these four Gospels, were accepted as inspired. Over the next two centuries, the rest of the New Testament canon gradually took shape. The first recorded list of the New Testament books as we know them appears in a letter of Saint Athanasius written in 367; the same canon occurs in the decrees of regional councils in North Africa and Rome at the end of the fourth century, and in a letter of Pope Innocent I in 405.

What determined canonicity? The primary criterion was apostolic origin. This could mean direct authorship, but also attribution to an apostle or some connection with one. The Gospels of Matthew and John were associated with two of the apostles, Luke was a companion of Paul, and an early tradition holds that the Gospel of Mark relied on the preaching of Peter. Another important norm was conformity with "the rule of faith", that is, the basic beliefs professed by Christian communities. On this basis, the second-century Gospel of Peter, although it claimed apostolic authorship, was rejected because of its

---

[1] *Canon* comes from a Greek word meaning a "fixed measure" or "rule". When applied to Scripture, it refers to the list of books recognized as being the inspired word of God.

Gnostic doctrines. Finally, the prominence of churches that had received or preserved writings had a role to play; in response to Gnostic claims that their texts were apostolic, Irenaeus pointed out that none of these writings was recognized as such by the communities founded by the apostles themselves. For several centuries, the canon of the New Testament varied from place to place, and even today, the New Testaments of the Armenian, Ethiopian, and Syrian churches differ somewhat from the set of twenty-seven books accepted by most other Christians.

The formation of the Old Testament canon is more complicated. The Jewish Scriptures consist of the Law, the Prophets, and the Writings. We find an allusion to this threefold collection in the words of Jesus recorded in the Gospel of Saint Luke: "Everything written about me in the law of Moses and the prophets and the psalms must be fulfilled" (Lk 24:44). The Law, or Torah, is contained in the first five books of the Bible, the Pentateuch. This was, and remains, the heart of the Jewish faith. The collection known as the Prophets includes what we call the historical books. The contents of these two parts of the Jewish Scriptures had been determined by the time of Jesus, but the collection known as the Writings was still somewhat fluid. Whenever the New Testament speaks of "the Scriptures", it means these Jewish Scriptures—but we must bear in mind that there was not unanimity about which books among the Writings this included.[2]

In addition to the fact that in the first century the canon of Jewish Scriptures was not firmly established, another factor muddied the waters in determining (for Christians) which books belonged in the Old Testament, and it is here that we find the root of the difference between Catholic and Protestant Bibles. Because many Jews lived outside of the Holy Land and did not know Hebrew, a Greek translation of the Jewish Scriptures was produced in the centuries immediately before Christ. According to tradition, it was made by seventy scholars, and for this reason, it is known as the Septuagint (often abbreviated as "LXX", the Roman numeral for "70"). The problem is that the

---

[2] At the end of the Second Letter of Peter, the author mentions "all the letters" of Saint Paul, and notes: "There are some things in them hard to understand, which the ignorant and unstable twist to their own destruction, *as they do the other Scriptures*" (2 Pet 3:16; emphasis added). This is the first reference to New Testament writings as Scripture. Second Peter was one of the last books to be included in the New Testament canon, and many scholars believe it is one of the last biblical books written.

Septuagint contains several writings not found in the Hebrew Scriptures. Some of these works are translations of Hebrew or Aramaic texts that have been lost, and others are original compositions in Greek. (These writings are designated as "deuterocanonical" by Catholics and "apocrypha" by Protestants.) As the Gospel spread beyond the Holy Land and more converts were Greek-speaking, the Septuagint became the version of the Jewish Scriptures used by most Christians. The question was: Were the books for which there was no extant Hebrew version part of the canon?

There were points to be made on both sides of the issue. No less an authority than Saint Jerome favored the shorter canon (although he included the deuterocanonical books in his Latin translation of the Bible), and he was followed in this by some other Western Fathers and theologians. The East leaned toward the shorter canon as well—in theory. On the other hand, references to the deuterocanonical books appear in the New Testament, and they were read in liturgical celebrations. For the West, the determining factors were that Saint Augustine had included these books in his canon of the Old Testament, as did regional councils in North Africa and Rome in the late fourth century, as well as Pope Innocent I in the early fifth century. In 1442, the Council of Florence reiterated the Catholic acceptance of the longer canon.

The issue flared up when Martin Luther rejected the practice of prayer for the dead as unscriptural. His Catholic opponents responded by citing an incident recorded in the Second Book of Maccabees, when Judas Maccabeus offered expiatory sacrifices for Jews who had been killed in battle (2 Macc 12:38–45). Because Maccabees is one of the deuterocanonical writings, Luther maintained that it was not part of the Bible. He considered the shorter Jewish canon to be more primitive, but his primary criterion for canonicity was the inherent quality of a book, that is, its relationship to the fundamental Gospel of salvation as Luther understood it. Luther and the Reformers held that the deuterocanonical books might be useful for private reading, but they were not the inspired word of God; in Protestant Bibles they are included as an appendix ("with the apocrypha") or omitted. In answer to the Protestant Reformers, the principal Catholic criterion for canonicity invoked by the Council of Trent was continuous use. The deuterocanonical books had been treated as Scripture throughout history—referred to in the New Testament, cited by Fathers of the Church, accepted as canonical by Saint Augustine and Pope Innocent I, held to be inspired by the Council of Florence, and used all through the centuries in the liturgy—and so the Council of Trent defined that they are part of the Old Testament.[3]

Inspiration

While Christians disagree on the exact list of books to be included in the Bible, we all agree that the Scriptures, and they alone, are the inspired word of God. What does the word *inspiration* mean in connection with these writings? Occasionally, we read of a prophet receiving a message or revelation from God, but instances of this direct kind of inspiration are unusual in the pages of Scripture. For the most part, the authors of the various books of the Bible simply employed their human abilities. It is clear that large sections of the Old Testament were produced by the compilation of texts over many centuries; Saint Paul wrote his Letters in response to specific problems in various communities; and Saint Luke states his intention to be to compile an orderly account of testimonies he has gathered from others. The Second Vatican Council spoke of the human authors in this way: "In composing the sacred books, God chose men and while employed by Him they made use of their powers and abilities, so that with Him acting in them and through them, they, as true authors, consigned to writing everything and only those things which He wanted" (*DV*, no. 11).

And yet the council also affirms of their works that, "because written under the inspiration of the Holy Spirit, they have God as their author and have been handed on as such to the Church herself" (*DV*, no. 11). Apart from those rare passages where a writer claims direct inspiration, the Holy Spirit works through ordinary human means to convey the truth to future ages. Saint Paul was convinced that when he preached to the Corinthians his words were affected by the Spirit: "My speech and my message were not in plausible words of wisdom, but in demonstration of the Spirit and of power, that your faith might not rest in the wisdom of men but in the power of God" (1 Cor

---

[3] The matter remains unsettled in the East—some Orthodox churches accept the shorter canon, some the longer canon, and some include a few books not found in the Catholic canon.

2:4–5). When he wrote to that same community, he did so in response to specific concerns that had arisen there, but his written words were inspired by the Holy Spirit so that they could pass on to future generations the truth God wants us to know. We might say that as Saint Paul was composing a Letter to the Corinthians, God was communicating to Christians of all times and places. This charism of inspiration pertains to the foundational events of God's revelation, which reached their fullest expression in the coming of Christ. As the Letter to the Hebrews points out, in previous ages, God spoke to his people through the prophets, but in the last days he has spoken instead through his Son (Heb 1:1–2). For this reason, there are no further inspired writings after the age of the apostles; there is no need for a new revelation after Christ.

In considering the divine and human authorship of Scripture, it might help to recall the relationship between the divine and human natures of Christ: he is totally God and totally man, not a mixture of the two. The Second Vatican Council pointed out how the inspired Scriptures reflect the mystery of the Incarnation: "For the words of God, expressed in human language, have been made like human discourse, just as the word of the eternal Father, when He took to Himself the flesh of human weakness, was in every way made like men" (*DV*, no. 13). The human authors wrote within the cultural context of their time, and with their individual talents and limitations. But to believers, the Scriptures are more than monuments of human genius— they are also divinely inspired. The books in the Bible are not partly human and partly divine; they are entirely human and entirely divine.

Inerrancy

The fundamental effect of divine inspiration on the biblical texts is to make them the revealing and saving word of God. God revealed himself first through the *events* of salvation history, and then by the interpretation of those events preserved in the Bible. We receive that revelation through the written Scriptures that God inspired. This inspiration gives a unity to the whole collection of sacred writings. For this reason, the *Catechism* calls Christ the unique Word of Sacred Scripture, because he is the key to understanding both the New Testament and the Old (nos. 101, 129). Saint John of the Cross spoke eloquently of the unity of God's revelation in Christ: "In giving us his Son, his only Word (for he possesses no other), he spoke everything to us at once in this sole Word—and he has no more to say ... because what he spoke before to the prophets in parts, he has now spoken all at once by giving us the All Who is His Son." [4] Finally, because God cannot deceive, his word teaches the truth without error.

How do we Catholics understand biblical inerrancy? According to the Second Vatican Council: "Since everything asserted by the inspired authors or sacred writers must be held to be asserted by the Holy Spirit, it follows that the books of Scripture must be acknowledged as teaching solidly, faithfully and without error that truth which God wanted put into sacred writings for the sake of salvation" (*DV*, no. 11). The history of this sentence reflects how our understanding of the truth of Scripture has developed over the past century. A preliminary draft stated that since divine inspiration extends to all of Scripture, it necessarily follows that the whole of Scripture is absolutely free of error. Did this assert too much? After all, the human authors were writing within the cultural limitations of their age (as every author does), and there are certainly some historical inaccuracies and discrepancies in the pages of Scripture—as opponents of Christianity have pointed out as far back as the second century. The discussion among the council fathers shifted from "inerrancy" to truth: specifically, the *saving* truth of God's love for us revealed in the events of salvation history. The kind of truth that the Bible teaches "firmly, faithfully and without error" is that truth which God confided to Scripture for the sake of our salvation.

This understanding of biblical inerrancy sheds light on questions regarding the relationship between religion and science. For example, we do not have to understand the account of creation in Genesis as a literal description of *how* the universe was made. Sacred Scripture teaches a different kind of truth, the truth of *why* the universe was made. What God teaches us through the stories of Genesis is that everything was brought into being by God's gracious will, that creation is good, and that we are to use our free will in a way that respects our proper

---

[4] St. John of the Cross, *The Ascent of Mount Carmel*, 2, 22, 3–5, in *The Collected Works*, trans. K. Kavanaugh, OCD, and O. Rodriguez, OCD (Washington, D.C.: Institute of Carmelite Studies, 1979), 179–80 (Office of Readings, Monday of the Second Week of Advent), quoted in *CCC*, no. 65.

relationships with God, others, and the world around us. Rightly understood, scientific truth and sacred truth are not contradictory, because
they answer different questions. While some Christians hold that Genesis contradicts the idea that the earth is billions of years old, from a
Catholic perspective, it is not necessary to assert this to safeguard the
truthfulness of Scripture. On the other hand, when secular writers
claim that science has "proven" that the Bible is wrong, they have
strayed from the proper field of scientific truth. Science examines the
properties of and relationships between existing realities, but it cannot
answer the question of why anything exists at all. Science and religion
are not contradictory, but complementary. The Catholic view is that
truth is one, and that the same God reveals himself in both the book
of nature and the book of salvation history. While divine revelation
goes beyond what human reason alone can discover, it does not contradict the findings of reason. (The complementarity of scientific knowledge and revealed truth was taught explicitly by both the First and
Second Vatican Councils; see *CCC*, no. 159.) In order to understand
the meaning of Scripture, we must ask what kind of truth it conveys.

Implications

When we ask what kind of truth the Bible conveys, we raise the question of the meaning of Scripture. Like any other document, the Bible
must be interpreted, and the human and divine authorship of Scripture must both be taken into account in this process. As regards human
authorship, when we open the pages of Scripture we encounter texts
that were written over many centuries in cultures foreign to our own,
and some familiarity with the biblical world helps us to understand
the meaning of the sacred text. To take a very simple example, we
describe someone who helps a stranger as a "Good Samaritan", but
we grasp the meaning of Jesus' parable better when we know that his
hearers detested the Samaritans. Because the Scriptures are writings
from the distant past, their meaning is not always self-evident. And
because the Scriptures are inspired by the Holy Spirit, individual passages should be read in light of the rest of the Bible and the faith of
the communities that wrote them. The Bible is an inexhaustible foun-
tain, so we should avoid claiming that a particular interpretation is
"the" meaning of a text. Saint Gregory the Great likened the Scriptures

to a river in which a lamb can wade and an elephant can swim. Whether we are wading or swimming, what are the principles we as Catholics follow in interpreting the Bible?

The Literal Sense of Scripture

The first question we must ask is "What did the author mean when he wrote this?" This is part of what we call the *literal* sense, but this must be distinguished from "literalist", i.e., a fundamentalist view that every word in Scripture is literally and historically true. When Jesus told the parable of the Good Samaritan, was he relating an historical event or telling an imaginary story to make a point? While such an incident could happen, it is more likely that this, and the many other parables Jesus told, were stories he devised to teach a lesson. An awareness of the genre of parables helps us to understand the meaning of the text. On the other hand, when the Gospels describe a miracle like the multiplication of the loaves and fishes, it is clear that the authors intend to report an actual event. (Readers in a later age, uncomfortable with the idea of the miraculous, may want to treat the story as a parable about generosity, but they should recognize that this was not the *author's* intent: the Evangelists believed that the miracle took place.)

Over the past century and more, biblical scholarship has concentrated on the literal meaning of the text, that is, what the author(s) meant.[5] Archeological explorations, historical studies of the ancient world, the examination of the meaning of words, literary genres, and the formation of the biblical texts all help to bring alive the original meaning of Scripture. Many modern translations and commentaries make the fruit of this research available to the general reader. The fact that there are diverse translations and shelves of commentaries indicates that this scholarship is to some degree a matter of conjecture, and the warning to be wary of the man of one book applies here as in other areas of life. But if we are serious about understanding the Bible, we should acquaint ourselves with the insights of those who have devoted their lives to the study of Scripture. Whatever else a passage may mean, at least it means what its human author originally intended. Saint Thomas Aquinas was simply reiterating a traditional Catholic

---

[5] We should say "authors", in the plural, because many biblical books are the end result of a process of editing at many hands.

principle of biblical interpretation when he taught: "All other senses of Sacred Scripture are based on the literal." [6]

Because the Scriptures are the inspired word of God, we want to know not just what they meant, but what they mean: What is God saying to us today through his word? We read the Bible for our spiritual nourishment, and we read it as members of a faith community. The Second Vatican Council laid down a fundamental principle in this regard: "Holy Scripture must be read and interpreted in the sacred spirit in which it was written" (DV, no. 12), meaning, according to the Holy Spirit who inspired it. Because the Holy Spirit inspires the whole of Scripture, we can find depths of meaning beyond the human author's intent when we consider a particular passage within the broader framework. What does this mean in practice? The council describes this broader framework on three levels: the contents of the whole Bible, within the living tradition of the Church, and against the backdrop of the plan of God's revelation (CCC, nos. 112–14).

The Unity of the Bible

The first criterion is to attend to the content and unity of the whole of Scripture. The fact that the entire Bible is inspired gives a spiritual unity to texts that were written over many centuries in diverse settings. Taken as a whole, Scripture presents a gradual unfolding of God's revelation. For example, we perceive in the Old Testament a growing awareness that there is one God: early in their history, the Israelites believed that their God was greater than the gods of other nations; later they came to see that there are no other gods. We also see growth in the understanding of the moral law, as in the gradual adoption of monogamy and a more internalized understanding of the Law. We should not reduce this development to a simplistic dichotomy that paints the Old Testament as bloodthirsty and the New Testament as a religion of love. There are descriptions in the Old Testament of God as gentle and merciful, and apocalyptic descriptions of divine judgment in the New, as Michelangelo's magnificent frescoes in the Sistine Chapel illustrate. But development does take place, and one of the keys to biblical interpretation is to distinguish

---

[6] St. Thomas Aquinas, *Summa Theologiae*, I, 1, 10, *ad* 1, quoted in *CCC*, no. 116.

what is passing from what is perennial. This was a subject of debate among the Jews at the time of Jesus, and it became a crucial question for the infant Church in regard to Gentile converts: What elements in the Old Testament have been superseded, and what elements abide?

Another way in which attention to the Bible as a whole can assist our understanding of a particular text is by the recurrence of fundamental themes such as *covenant, exodus,* and *exile*. These pivotal events shaped the Jewish way of thought and worship, and they connect events from the time of Abraham down to the life of Jesus. God's people viewed their history through the lens of these foundational events, and these themes provide a helpful context for our reading of Scripture. For example, in Saint Luke's account of the Transfiguration, Jesus spoke with Moses and Elijah about "his exodus, which he was to accomplish at Jerusalem" (Lk 9:31). The Greek word the Evangelist uses, *exodos*, evokes the central event of Jewish history—and this in a Gospel written by a Gentile for Gentiles! The Bible as a whole presents the panorama of God's saving acts, and this helps explain particular incidents or teachings.

The central events of salvation history for Christians are the life, death, and Resurrection of Christ. While recognizing that the events of the Old Testament have a meaning in their own right and continue to be central to the relationship of the Jewish people with God, we believe that God's saving work is accomplished in the coming of Christ. The New Testament abounds with references to how Jesus fulfilled the Scriptures, so for us, the Old and New Testaments comprise one narrative. They are mutually revelatory: the events and institutions of the Jewish covenants find their fulfillment in Christ and shed light on the meaning of his Person and mission; at the same time, the history of Israel takes on a new meaning beyond the Jewish people as it becomes the spiritual history of Gentile believers as well. This is why, as far back as the second century, the leaders of the Church opposed those who wished to discard the Old Testament. In his commentary on the Psalms, Saint Augustine emphasized how all the Scriptures find their unity in Christ: "You recall that one and the same Word of God extends throughout Scripture, that it is one and the same Utterance that resounds in the mouths of all the sacred writers, since he who was in the beginning God with God has no need of separate syllables; for he is not subject to time."[7] In a sermon on the Transfiguration, Saint Leo the Great suggested that the appearance of Moses and Elijah with Jesus in the presence of three apostles illustrated this unity: "What word could be more firmly established, more securely based, than the word which is proclaimed by the trumpets of both old and new testaments, sounding in harmony, and by the utterances of ancient prophecy and the teaching of the Gospel, in full agreement with each other?"[8]

Scripture and Tradition

The second criterion is to read Scripture within the living tradition of the whole Church. Ever since the Reformation, there has been a tendency to see the authority of the Church and the authority of the Bible in competition, if not in conflict. In reality, Church and Bible are inseparable. In the centuries before Christ, the community of Israel recognized certain writings to be the word of God. This collection of writings was accepted as Scripture by the Church. The New Testament canon gradually took shape over several centuries, and all through that time, the Christian community was preaching and living the Gospel. To return to a point made in the last chapter, it was primarily through the life of the community of the Church that the Gospel was handed on. This is what we as Catholics mean by "tradition": the apostolic faith as it was lived by the first Christians and handed on to those who came after them. This tradition was expressed in many ways: through the liturgical life of the churches, the writings of the Fathers, and the moral and doctrinal teachings that guided the community. Among these many forms of tradition, Scripture holds a unique place, because it alone *is* the word of God in written form.

But if the Scriptures have a unique place, it is not a solitary place. The same Holy Spirit who inspired the sacred authors also sanctifies God's people through the sacramental life of the Church and assists the leaders of the Church in their role as pastors and teachers. Jesus commanded his apostles to baptize, to forgive sins, to celebrate the Eucharist, to teach, to heal, and to expel demons. The New Testament tells us very little about how the first Christians did these things;

---

[7] St. Augustine, *Enarrationes in Psalmos* 103, 4, 1: *PL* 37, 1378, quoted in *CCC*, no. 102; cf. Ps 104; Jn 1:1.

[8] St. Leo the Great, *Sermon* 51, 4 (Office of Readings, Second Sunday of Lent).

they were part of the Gospel life that grew up around the preaching and instruction of the apostles. And the New Testament books themselves took shape in these assemblies. A key to understanding the Scriptures is to read them within the context of the community from which they emerged.

This Gospel, expressed through Scripture and the rest of tradition, has been entrusted to the whole People of God to hand on by living it, teaching it, and sharing it. When conflicting ideas of what is essential to this Gospel arise, the successors of the apostles have the responsibility of deciding the matter. According to the teaching of the Second Vatican Council:

> The task of authentically interpreting the word of God, whether written or handed on, has been entrusted exclusively to the living teaching office of the Church, whose authority is exercised in the name of Jesus Christ. This teaching office is not above the word of God, but serves it, teaching only what has been handed on, listening to it devoutly, guarding it scrupulously and explaining it faithfully in accord with a divine commission and with the help of the Holy Spirit, it draws from this one deposit of faith everything which it presents for belief as divinely revealed. (*DV*, no. 10)

The council clearly states that the teaching office of the pope and bishops is not above the word of God: their role is to help interpret that word in a way that safeguards the unity of faith. This unity concerns the essential beliefs of the Church. In exercising this responsibility, the pastors of the Church teach with the assistance of the Holy Spirit and the authority that Christ gave to his apostles. Theirs is a conservative role: they must listen, guard, preserve, and transmit faithfully the word of God. With the recognition that the Magisterium is not above the word of God, we can better understand what the council fathers meant when they said that the task of *authentically* interpreting the word of God has been entrusted to the teaching office of the Church alone. (Conciliar texts, like biblical texts, require interpretation!) It has been suggested that a better translation of the Latin word *authentice* is "authoritative" rather than "authentic". The opposite of authentic is "inauthentic", which would seem to suggest that *only* the pope and the bishops can interpret Scripture correctly. That is not what we believe. By teaching that the Magisterium is entrusted with giving an *authoritative* interpretation of the word of God, the council fathers are affirming that when disputes arise concerning the essential faith of the Church (which obviously involves the interpretation of Scripture), the successors of the apostles have the authority to decide the matter. As we saw in the last chapter, this has been the practice of the Church all through her history: disagreements regarding fundamental beliefs have been resolved by the decisions of an ecumenical council or the pope.

This more precise understanding of the relationship between the word of God and the teaching office is borne out by the Church's practice. Although the idea has gained currency in some quarters since the Reformation that the Catholic Church imposes interpretations of Scripture on her members, the fact is that definitive pronouncements on the meaning of biblical texts are rare. A handful of such statements were made at the Council of Trent concerning baptism, original sin, the Eucharist, and the priesthood. But even here, the bishops did not define what a scriptural passage meant; they rejected interpretations that denied a traditional understanding of the text. For example, in speaking of baptism, the fathers at Trent declared: "If anyone says that true and natural water is not a necessary element in baptism, and therefore twists those words of our Lord Jesus Christ, 'unless one is born of water and the Holy Spirit', into some form of metaphor: let him be anathema." [9] As with dogmatic statements, so in biblical interpretation, the Church is more reluctant to define than many suppose, and such definitions do not declare what "the" meaning of the text is, but reject interpretations that are contrary to the faith of the Church.

The Bible and the Creed

This brings us to the third criterion for reading Scripture in light of the same Spirit who inspired it: attentiveness to the relationship between various truths of the faith seen within the whole plan of salvation. This is called the "analogy of faith". The term comes from Saint Paul, who instructed those who prophesy to do so "in proportion to our faith" (Rom 12:6). That is, any particular teaching must be consonant

---

[9] Council of Trent, Canons on the Sacrament of Baptism, no. 2, in trans. Norman Tanner, *Decrees of the Ecumenical Councils*, vol. 2 (Washington, D.C.: Sheed & Ward and Georgetown University Press, 1990), p. 685.

with the whole of revelation. By the late second century, Christian communities had developed brief summaries of belief, known as "the rule of faith" or "the norm of truth". At this time, the New Testament canon was still taking shape; one criterion for recognizing a book as Scripture was that it was in accord with these fundamental Christian doctrines. The analogy of faith means that this basic set of beliefs provides a context for a Christian understanding of Scripture.

These three criteria for reading Scripture primarily concern the doctrinal truth to be found in the sacred word. How does this relate to our personal and communal search for what God is saying to us through his word? G. K. Chesterton once described a small island inhabited by children. On all sides, sheer cliffs dropped to the sea far below, and there was a fence around the perimeter of the island. The children played happily and freely on the island until one day some of them decided to tear down the fence. Now, Chesterton says, the children huddle in the middle of the island, scared to venture near the edge of the precipice for fear of falling off. The principle of interpreting Scripture within the context of the whole Bible, read in light of the Church's tradition, and grounded in the fundamental tenets of the apostolic faith acts as a fence to protect us from falling over the cliff and plunging into a sea of idiosyncratic interpretations. But within this broad enclosure, we have the freedom to explore the many meanings of God's word to our heart's content.

The Place of the Bible in Catholic Life

The liturgical celebration is a privileged setting in which we can carry out this exploration. It was just such gatherings that shaped the formation of Scripture in the first place: God's people came together to listen to the Law, to hear the message of the Prophets, and to praise God with Psalms. To these writings, Christians gradually added the Gospels and other apostolic writings. The proclamation of the word of God in the liturgy is an event today, as it was when Jesus proclaimed God's word in the synagogue of Nazareth. In that assembly, he read a passage from the prophet Isaiah: "The Spirit of the Lord is upon me, because he has anointed me to preach good news to the poor. He has sent me to proclaim release to the captives and the recovering of sight to the blind, to set at liberty those who are oppressed, to proclaim the acceptable year of the Lord." Then, with the whole congregation looking at him intently, Jesus announced, "Today this Scripture has been fulfilled in your hearing" (Lk 4:18–21; cf. Is 61:1–2). When we listen in faith, the biblical readings at Mass do not simply remind us of what God once did, or what he might do. The living Christ in the midst of the community fulfills the word of God in our hearing. The prophetic mission of Christ finds its most intense expression when his community listens attentively to his word.

Since the Second Vatican Council, there has been a renewed emphasis on the importance of the Scriptures in Catholic liturgy. This is in fact a profoundly traditional idea, as the council teaches: "The Church has always venerated the divine Scriptures just as she venerates the body of the Lord, since, especially in the sacred liturgy, she unceasingly receives and offers to the faithful the bread of life from the table both of God's word and of Christ's body" (*DV*, no. 21). The three-year Lectionary and the expanded number of readings at Mass have opened up more generously the treasury of the word of God. The choice of readings according to the seasons of the liturgical year helps us understand specific passages in light of the yearly celebration of the paschal mystery of Christ's birth, ministry, death, and Resurrection. As the Old Testament reading is chosen in light of the Gospel selection, we constantly see how the Old Testament and the New are united. In the homily, the preacher helps us to apply the word of God to our present circumstances.

But for the word to penetrate our hearts on Sunday, we must prepare the soil by prayerfully pondering God's word throughout the week. Here we can be grateful for the many resources available for both group and individual Bible study. There have been significant ecumenical advances in this area: several Protestant communions use a Lectionary similar to ours, and scholars of various denominations cooperate to produce translations and commentaries on the Bible. A shared love for the word of God can bring Christians closer together. At the same time, we recognize that the relationship between the Bible and the Church is a source of disagreement between Christians. It is our conviction as Catholics that the Scriptures have a unique authority as the word of God, and the Bible is the mirror into which the Church in every age must gaze to know God's will. But the inspired word was entrusted to a community that has safeguarded it and passed it on for two thousand years. Just as it is misleading to isolate particular Scripture passages and treat them as "proof texts", so it is unsound to divorce the Bible from the community that gathers to listen to it. Sacred Scripture should be understood in light of the Holy Spirit who inspired it, and that same Holy Spirit has shaped the worship, moral teaching, and pastoral leadership of the Catholic Church from the apostolic age to the present.

God's revelation reached its fulfillment in Christ, and the Scriptures are the inspired record of "the faith which was once for all delivered to the saints" (Jude 3). But what was delivered was a living word, and each generation of believers must strive to grasp more fully the truth enshrined in Scripture. Nor will we ever reach the end of that exploration. What the great doctor of the Syrian Church, Saint Ephrem, wrote in the fourth century remains true today:

> Lord, who can comprehend even one of your words? We lose more of it than we grasp, like those who drink from a living spring. For God's word offers different facets according to the capacity of the listener.... And so whenever anyone discovers some part of the treasure, he should not think that he has exhausted God's word. Instead he should feel that this is all that he was able to find of the wealth contained in it ... precisely because he could not capture it all he should give thanks for its riches.[10]

---

[10] St. Ephrem, *A Commentary on the Diatessaron*, I, 18–19 (Office of Readings, Sixth Sunday in Ordinary Time).

Chapter Eight

The Life of Grace

God has revealed himself in history to invite us into a relationship of love. In the fullness of time, the Father sent his Son to share our human condition; by his death and Resurrection, Christ has transformed human nature to enable us to receive divine life by the indwelling of the Holy Spirit. This divine life is what we call "grace". Several cognates of this word touch on different aspects of the mystery: it is *gratuitous*, that is, it is a completely free act of mercy on God's part, and not something we can claim as our right; the effect of the gift is to make us *graced*, that is, God's gift truly changes us and so makes us pleasing to him; finally, this gift prompts a sense of *gratitude* and a desire to express this by loving God and our neighbor.

This seems straightforward enough. And yet the doctrine of grace has raised many vexing questions. Does God offer this divine life to all, or only to some? Does a "chosen people" imply an "unchosen" people? If God knows that some will refuse this offer—and if the refusal entails eternal misery—does God predestine some people for Heaven and others for Hell? Does grace change us, or simply God's estimation of us? If we have lost our original orientation toward God as a result of the Fall, how can this be restored? What is the relationship between grace and free will? If faith is a gift, and if even the ability to respond to this gift depends on grace, do we play any part in the process? Surveying these puzzling problems, we might be tempted to say about grace what Saint Augustine said about time: "I know what it is until someone asks me to explain it."

What We Believe

Grace is our life of communion with God. Through the acceptance in faith of God's gracious mercy offered to us through Christ, we are justified; that is, we are cleansed of sin and become the adopted daughters and sons of God and sharers in his divine life.[1] This justification is accomplished for us by the death and Resurrection of Jesus Christ and is a pure gift; however, we are free to accept or reject it. Once we are justified, we can merit greater sanctification because God desires our cooperation in the life of grace. Still, no good comes to us apart from the grace of God: his grace precedes and accompanies all of our good actions, and the source of our merit is Christ's love.

Some History

On the night before the soldier pierced the heart of Christ with a lance, the Lord himself opened his heart to his disciples at the Last Supper. His "Farewell Discourse" (Jn 13:31–17:26) affords us a glimpse at the living flame of love that is the Holy Trinity and the remarkable gift of our union with God. Jesus assured the Twelve that he alone is the way to the Father; indeed, so close is their union that to see him is to see the Father. Christ promised his disciples that the Father would send the Holy Spirit to dwell in them. He told them, "In that day you will know that I am in my Father, and you in me, and I in you" (Jn 14:20). This infusion of divine life will enable the disciples to live Christ's commandment of love and raise them up to friendship with God. Apart from Christ they can do nothing, but united to him they will bear much fruit: "He who believes in me will also do the works that I do; and greater works than these will he do" (Jn 14:12).

Saint Paul's Teaching on Grace

The gift of divine life makes us sons and daughters of the Father, members of the Body of Christ, and temples of the Holy Spirit; God abides in us, and we abide in God. Saint Paul reflected frequently on this divine indwelling, and his writings are an important resource for the later theological development on the doctrine of grace. Paul uses the word *grace* (in Greek, *charis*) far more than any other New Testament

---

[1] The term *justification* has a different meaning in a theological context than it does in common parlance. The Glossary of the *Catechism* defines justification as "the gracious action of God which frees us from sin and communicates 'the righteousness of God through faith in Jesus Christ' (Rom 3:22). Justification is not only the remission of sins, but also the sanctification and renewal of the interior man" (nos. 1987–89).

writer: two-thirds of the references appear in his Letters. He uses the term in several ways: grace can refer to the whole reality of the salvation brought about by the death and Resurrection of Christ; an individual's incorporation into that reality by faith and baptism; and the expression of this new life through service to the community.

In writing to the Corinthians, Paul is dealing with an exuberant young church prone to factions and rivalry. He admonishes them that extraordinary gifts (*charisms*) such as speaking in tongues or prophecy, far from being a cause of division, ought to be used to build up the whole Body of Christ, and they will be if they are linked to the more fundamental gift of the transforming power of the indwelling Spirit. This is the theme of Paul's famous "hymn to love" (1 Cor 13). His Letter to the Galatians addresses the relationship between faith and freedom. This epistle was provoked by preachers who were telling Paul's Gentile converts that they must observe the Jewish Law. For Paul, this contradicts not only the Gospel he had preached to them, but his own experience of conversion: righteousness comes from faith in Christ, not from fulfilling the requirements of the Law. Finally, in the Letter to the Romans, Saint Paul presents his most developed exposition on grace. These are the main ideas he advances:

1. All have sinned, Jew and Gentile alike, and are in need of God's mercy. Sin means slavery, tyranny, and death, and it has infected all of creation.

2. Through faith in Christ and baptism, we are delivered from the slavery of sin, the curse of death, and the yoke of the Law (by which Paul means both our futile effort to do God's will perfectly and the burden of our past sins).

3. We are not freed by the Law—since it only shows us what we *should* do, but cannot enable us to do it—nor by our works, since we have no claim on God; we are liberated by the salvation offered freely by God in Christ and by our acceptance of that gift, which makes us the adopted children of God.

4. God has allowed a large number of the Jews to reject this offer of salvation so that the Gospel might be preached to the Gentiles; once the full number of Gentiles has accepted this offer, Israel will be saved.

Several aspects of the doctrine of grace make their first appearance in Paul's writings: filial adoption and sharing in divine life; the way we are made righteous; salvation as God's gift and our role in it; the effect of the Fall and our need for healing; the relationship between freedom, sin, and grace; how acceptance or rejection of salvation is foreknown by God.

For the first several centuries, the Fathers of the Church primarily spoke of the power of grace to raise us, mere creatures, to a relationship of communion with God. The classical biblical expression of this doctrine is found in the Second Letter of Peter: "His divine power has granted to us all things that pertain to life and godliness, through the knowledge of him who called us to his own glory and excellence, ... that through these you may escape from the corruption that is in the world because of passion, and become partakers of the divine nature" (2 Pet 1:3–4).

The leitmotif of many patristic writings was presented with bold simplicity by Saint Athanasius: "For the Son of God became man so that we might become God." [2]

Saint Augustine, "Doctor of Grace"

Saint Augustine embraced this doctrine of elevating grace, but his long struggle against sin led him to highlight the healing or medicinal aspect of grace. His celebrated *Confessions* recounts that conflict, his gratitude that grace liberated him from slavery to sin, and his recognition of the need for divine help to accomplish any good. Augustine's experience made him the inveterate foe of a spiritual movement known as Pelagianism, and this controversy shaped much subsequent theology of grace in the West.

We might approach the ancient debate by means of a contemporary question: Is bad behavior, or sin, due to environment or heredity? Those associated with Pelagius (and scholars disagree as to how faithfully they reflected his own thinking) held that sin is primarily a matter of environment. Their position was that human nature was not really wounded in the Fall: Adam's sin had affected him alone, and original sin consists mainly of bad example. In this view, we always

---

[2] St. Athanasius, *De incarnatione*, 54, 3: PG 25, 192B, quoted in *CCC*, no. 460.

have the ability to do what is right and doing so is simply a matter of exercising the will. (The advice to "just say no" to drugs captures the Pelagian position succinctly.) There was a certain logic to the doctrine: if God is to be just in rewarding or punishing us on the basis of our actions, then we must be responsible for them; in order to be responsible for our actions, we must be free; however, if we can only do good with God's help, are we really free?

If the Pelagians gravitated to the "Self Help" corner of the bookstore, Augustine was definitely to be found in the "Twelve Step" section. His experience was that he had been unable to "just say no" to sin, and he needed the help of a higher power. He also had theological objections to Pelagianism, since it seemed to call into question the necessity for redemption by Christ as well as the practice of infant baptism. Augustine believed that sin is primarily due to heredity—the inheritance of a human nature deeply wounded as a result of the Fall. For him, this was a catastrophic event, which rendered us incapable of resisting temptation by our free will alone. He believed, like the Pelagians, that Christ had taught us by word and example what to do, but Augustine emphasized that Christ also gives us the strength we need to follow his teaching. Without this grace, we cannot do what we ought, at least not for very long. We also have our part to play: as Augustine observed, "God created us without us: but he did not will to save us without us." [3] But our cooperation is always aided by grace.

Augustine's view triumphed, but the conflict became rancorous, and at times, he espoused extreme positions on the necessity of grace. On the positive side, Augustine's understanding of grace offered hope to those struggling with sin. Pelagian confidence in innate human capability masked some frightening corollaries: if it is possible for us by our own unaided abilities always to do good, then perfection is not only possible; it is necessary. There are no mitigating circumstances; everyone is called to perfect sanctity. In Augustine's view, man is a mass of mixed motives; the pull of sin is ever-present; we are lifelong invalids. In contrast to the Pelagian idea of individual achievement, Augustine had a vivid sense of the solidarity of the human race: every one of us has fallen in Adam, and every one can be raised up in Christ. He also had a lively awareness of the need for and the effective

---

[3] St. Augustine, *Sermones*, 169, 11, 13: *PL* 38, 923, quoted in *CCC*, no. 1847.

power of the sacraments: baptism did not simply symbolize a break
with conventional worldliness, but it made those who received it a
new creation and strengthened them to do good. Augustine's teaching
provided a theological impetus for infant baptism and the practice,
already fairly common, became universal.

But if there were negative corollaries to the Pelagian position, Augustine's teaching also had its shadow side. In his Letter to the Romans,
Saint Paul had described the human predicament very darkly: "All
have sinned and fall short of the glory of God" (Rom 3:23), but he
did this to highlight the mercy of God: "They are justified by his
grace as a gift, through the redemption which is in Christ Jesus"
(Rom 3:24). Saint Augustine looked out on a world where the Gospel had been preached for centuries, and many had rejected it; on a
civilization that was collapsing in the face of barbarian invasions; and
at the struggle against sin in his own life and the lives of his people;
and from his meditations, there emerged a picture with colors as
dark as any used by Paul, but with a heightened sense of pessimism.
When Jesus was asked, "Lord, will those who are saved be few?"
(Lk 13:23), he did not answer the question directly, but urged his
disciples to strive to enter through the narrow door. Augustine the
pastor encouraged his flock to follow the Lord's advice; Augustine
the theologian surmised that only a minority of people would get
through the door.

Like Paul, Augustine affirmed that salvation was a free gift of God,
totally unmerited, and that our "striving" itself required the help of
God's grace. In fact, at times Augustine underscored the necessity of
grace so insistently that he seemed to deny free will. And, more seriously still, if everything depends upon God's grace, does this mean
that God gives the needed grace to one person and not to another,
and so predestines the former to be saved and the latter to be damned?
In some of his later writings, Augustine seems to have espoused this
doctrine of "double predestination", a teaching rejected by the Church
but adopted by some of the Protestant Reformers.

In the wake of the Pelagian controversy, there were several schools
of thought on the question of how seriously human nature had been
corrupted by the Fall. Some found Augustine's teaching too extreme,
and they posited that it was possible sometimes to attribute a person's
initial movement toward God to unaided free will. The Church defended

the doctrine that grace is essential to the whole process of redemption. God's grace is at work every step of the way: the external gift of the preaching of the Gospel, the internal desire to respond to this offer, the ability to profess faith in Christ, and the final perseverance leading to eternal life.

Does the activity of grace short-circuit human freedom? In his opposition to Pelagianism, Augustine came close to denying free will, and some of the Protestant Reformers did do so. More frequently, Augustine spoke of grace aiding our free will. He suggested that by cooperating with God's grace we can move from the freedom to choose between good and evil to the liberty of freely choosing the good. The dilemma was how to affirm God's sovereign freedom to offer salvation as a pure gift, and yet defend human freedom to accept this gift as an act that is truly our own.

These issues came to a head at the Reformation, but before looking at that drama we should note that, although the healing or medicinal aspect of grace was emphasized in the wake of Pelagianism, the belief in the elevating or adoptive nature of grace was not lost. For example, Saint Thomas Aquinas complemented the Augustinian emphasis on the healing power of grace by also teaching that grace raises us up to supernatural life because of our communion with God. The divine life that we receive from the indwelling of the Holy Spirit is *both* elevating and healing, and in accomplishing these purposes, grace transforms our nature. Justification and initial sanctification are freely given by God without regard to our merits, but once we are justified we can merit an increase of grace by our good acts. Thomas balanced the Augustinian position shaped by the Pelagian controversy with the elevating nature of grace found in Augustine's other writings and the broader patristic tradition.

Protestant Challenge, Catholic Response

Early in the sixteenth century, a German Augustinian friar surveyed the scene around him and judged that, although the Church had consistently condemned Pelagianism for a thousand years in theory, in practice, she had set up a system in which Christians tried to earn salvation by the works they performed. Martin Luther's theological appraisal was tied to a personal spiritual crisis: he had tried hard to do all the right things, but his conscience was still troubled. Luther undertook a thorough study of Scripture on the matter, focusing especially on Saint Paul's Letters to the Romans and Galatians. He read these texts through the lens of Augustine's theology, especially his anti-Pelagian writings. This theology he viewed in the light of a philosophical system known as Nominalism, which stressed the absolute omnipotence of God. Luther's concern was that people seemed to think that God *had* to save those who do good works. If that were true, then God was not free and redemption was not a gift. In opposition to this idea, Luther proclaimed a doctrine that was for him the issue by which the Church either stands or falls: justification by faith alone. By "faith", Luther meant here not belief in revealed truth, but trust in God's promise of mercy and forgiveness in Christ. Luther taught that we are saved by Christ's righteousness, which is imputed to us, not by any righteousness of our own. He denied that justification changed us; human nature had been corrupted by the Fall, and remains so. For this reason, we have no part to play in our salvation other than to accept it. John Calvin followed this doctrine to its logical conclusion: God is absolutely free to save or damn as he chooses; should he choose to save, his grace is irresistible; should he choose to damn, his justice is beyond our scrutiny.

The legacy of four centuries of division between Catholics and Protestants shows how crucial was Luther's concern about justification. His theology was revolutionary, and it had implications for a broad spectrum of issues. Our interest here is limited to the dogmatic teachings of the Council of Trent, which articulated the Catholic understanding of grace in response to the challenge of the Reformation. The two fundamental truths affirmed by the fathers at Trent were that grace really changes our nature and that we freely cooperate in our salvation. Regarding the doctrine of original sin, Trent professed that everyone stands in need of redemption, that we are saved only by the merits of Christ, and that baptism removes all sin, including the guilt of original sin. The council reaffirmed the value of infant baptism, a practice about which the Reformers disagreed among themselves. As to justification, the teaching of Trent was that the initiative always lies with God, who acts externally through the preaching of the Gospel and internally through the promptings of grace, but we act freely in responding to God's invitation, and so have a part to play in our salvation.

Furthermore, the council taught: "Justification is not only the remission of sins, but also the sanctification and renewal of the interior man." [4] As to merit, because God is infinitely greater than we are, we have no strict right to merit salvation; however, God has freely chosen to involve us in the work of our redemption. By virtue of our filial adoption, God freely bestows on us the ability to merit, as the *Catechism* notes, quoting the Council of Trent: "This is our right by grace, the full right of love, making us 'co-heirs' with Christ and worthy of obtaining 'the promised inheritance of eternal life.' The merits of our good works are gifts of the divine goodness." [5] We cannot claim that God "owes" salvation to us, for it is his gift, but once we are united with Christ, our good works are deserving of reward. God's grace precedes and accompanies all the good we do, but eternal life is both a gift *and* a reward.

While Luther accused the Church of Pelagianism, from the Catholic perspective, both Pelagians and Lutherans had driven a wedge between the divine and the human elements in good acts. For the Pelagian, a good act could be attributed to man alone; for Luther, to God alone. The first view exalts human freedom, the second divine omnipotence. The Catholic position is that good acts involve both God *and* man, grace *and* freedom. No good act can happen without God's grace; at the same time, however, God respects our freedom and it is truly *we* who act. The Council of Trent described this synergy in this way: "When God touches man's heart through the illumination of the Holy Spirit, man himself is not inactive while receiving that inspiration, since he could reject it; and yet, without God's grace, he cannot by his own free will move himself toward justice in God's sight." [6]

To affirm that both grace and free will are involved in what we do does not explain how they are related. Dominican and Jesuit theologians clashed on this question in the late sixteenth century. The Jesuits maintained that the Dominicans gave too little scope to the role of human freedom, while the Dominicans held that the Jesuits exaggerated free will to the detriment of the action of God's grace. A heated debate was carried on for twenty years, and it was suspended—not

---

[4] Council of Trent (1547): DS 1528, quoted in *CCC*, no. 1989.
[5] Council of Trent (1547): DS 1546, quoted in *CCC*, no. 2009.
[6] Council of Trent (1547): DS 1525, quoted in *CCC*, no. 1993.

resolved—by a ruling of Pope Paul V in the year 1607 that each side could teach its doctrine, but not condemn the other's position as heretical. He asked the disputants to abstain from harsh words and to wait for a final decision from Rome on the question. The decision has yet to come. The Catholic Church affirms two basic principles on this question: if we are saved, it is due to God's grace; if we are not, it is because of our own free rejection of that grace. Different theological schools propose solutions to the issue of the relationship between grace and free will, but it remains an open question.

While the Council of Trent defined some fundamental positions, a good many Catholic theologians remained sympathetic to a more pessimistic view of the human condition after the Fall. This anthropology surfaced in the seventeenth-century movement known as Jansenism. The Jansenists asserted that on the one hand it is impossible to follow the commandments without a special grace from God, and on the other hand, that when this grace is present, it is irresistible. In effect, they denied free will: we are subject to an internal determinism to do either evil or good. Only those who receive grace are saved, and since redemption comes from the death of Christ, the Jansenists concluded that Christ died only for the elect. The Church condemned these doctrines several times, affirming that Christ died for all people without exception, that God gives sufficient grace to all, but that it is possible for us to resist grace.

The improved ecumenical climate of the twentieth century has allowed Catholics and Lutherans to enter into dialogue on the issue of justification. On October 31, 1999, representatives of both communions signed a "Joint Declaration on the Doctrine of Justification", which affirmed: "Together we confess: By grace alone, in faith in Christ's saving work and not because of any merit on our part, we are accepted by God and receive the Holy Spirit, who renews our hearts while equipping and calling us to good works." [7] It would be naïve to think that this declaration has resolved all the theological issues involved in this difficult question, but it signals a willingness on both sides to examine this divisive issue in a positive way.

---

[7] The World Lutheran Federation and the Catholic Church (Pontifical Council for Promoting Christian Unity), "Joint Declaration on the Doctrine of Justification", no. 15 (text taken from the Vatican website).

Implications

The mystery of grace elicits a sense of gratitude for the goodness of God. First, we are grateful for creation itself. The human mind never tires of exploring the mysteries of the universe, but our searching can only answer questions about how the world works; *why* anything exists at all is due to the goodness and love of God. The effects of the Fall should not blind us to the original goodness in all that God has made. The *Catechism* reminds us of the graced reality of creation: "In the creation of the world and of man, God gave the first and universal witness to his almighty love and his wisdom, the first proclamation of the 'plan of his loving goodness,' which finds its goal in the new creation in Christ" (no. 315). God loves everything he has made, and the universe cannot exist apart from him. The divine presence surrounds and permeates all creatures.

Sanctifying Grace

But in addition to the love God has for everything he has created, there is a special love by which he invites spiritual beings (men and angels) into a communion of love with him. We call this gift "supernatural" since it is an invitation to a relationship beyond the horizons of our limited creaturely nature. Genesis paints a picture of God walking in the cool of the evening with Adam and Eve to suggest an atmosphere of familiarity and mutual love. This is the relationship that Adam and Eve rejected in their revolt. In turning away from God, our first parents severed their friendship with him and forfeited other gifts God had given them that, while beyond our present experience as creatures, are not beyond the nature of created beings as such: infused knowledge in the intellect, loving obedience in the will, absence of suffering and death in the body. As a result of the Fall, our intellect is clouded by ignorance, our will is attracted to selfishness by concupiscence, and our bodies experience suffering and death.

Far from abandoning us in this tragic condition, God invited us to restore our communion with him. Where human pride had sought to grasp at equality with God, divine condescension led the Son of God to empty himself and become a slave: "And being found in human form he humbled himself and became obedient unto death, even death on a cross" (Phil 2:8). We were unable to reach across the chasm to

God, so he reached across the chasm to us. The restoration of this relationship is what we mean by justification, and it has been merited for us by the death and Resurrection of Christ. Our acceptance of this divine invitation removes the state of enmity with God known as original sin, makes us inwardly just, and strengthens our intellect and will with the virtues of faith, hope, and charity. According to the *Catechism*,

> Justification is the *most excellent work of God's love* made manifest in Christ Jesus and granted by the Holy Spirit. It is the opinion of St. Augustine that "the justification of the wicked is a greater work than the creation of heaven and earth," because "heaven and earth will pass away but the salvation and justification of the elect ... will not pass away." [8]

This relationship with God is a permanent condition, and it is what we mean by "the state of grace". Sanctifying grace implants in us the theological virtues of faith, hope, and charity; it strengthens the natural moral virtues; and it bestows on us the gifts of the Holy Spirit. The combination of graces is unique to each of us, depending on our distinctive vocation in the Body of Christ. We can sever our ties with God by committing mortal sin, but conversion and forgiveness are always possible in this life. When we are truly contrite and seek the Lord's forgiveness (ordinarily through the sacrament of penance), we are restored to friendship with God.

Actual Grace

Along with this permanent relationship, Catholic tradition speaks of "actual graces" that are God's interventions that precede, invite, and accompany our good actions. Because we cannot merit justification, the initial invitation to accept it is an actual grace. Since God desires the salvation of all men, he gives everyone sufficient grace to be saved. He never abandons us, nor does he ask more than we are able to do. On the other hand, because God respects our freedom (indeed, love demands freedom), it is possible for us to refuse what he offers. God's universal salvific will stops at the threshold of our consent. The fact that it is possible to reject the gift of salvation raises the troubling

---

[8] *CCC*, no. 1994, citing St. Augustine, *In evangelium Johannis tractatus*, 72, 3: PL 35, 1823.

question of predestination. As far back as the sixth century, the Catholic Church rejected the doctrine of "double predestination" and affirmed that we can speak of divine predestination only as regards the salvation of the elect. The problem is with those who are damned: What role if any does God play in their fate? Different theories have been proposed over the centuries, but none have been adopted as official Church teaching. The basic Catholic conviction is that God desires all to be saved but that he respects human freedom; God will not save someone against his will.

Once we are restored to communion with God, our cooperation with actual graces increases our holiness. Far from short-circuiting our freedom, grace makes us more free. We describe accomplished dancers or athletes as "graceful": their movements seem effortless, and yet that ability is the fruit of a great deal of self-discipline and practice. Similarly, the more we cooperate with the graces God gives, the more inner freedom we experience. Repeated acts of virtue make the virtuous life more natural to us. Our experience of human love provides an analogy for the working of grace, sanctifying and actual, in our lives. At the core of any loving relationship, there exists a permanent bond that unites; we nourish that bond by particular expressions of love, consideration, and self-sacrifice; the relationship deepens and calls forth from us gifts that we may not have known we possessed. Such a relationship, far from constraining us, actually allows us to be more truly who we are. Similarly, divine grace enhances our human freedom.

Gift and Reward

Our cooperation with God's grace is the basis for our understanding of merit. Catholic teaching is very clear that we cannot claim to merit justification: salvation is a free gift of God. However, once we are in communion with him, the good that we do deepens our holiness, assists others, and helps us to attain eternal life. The idea that God compensates us for our good actions runs through the whole New Testament, which speaks of a reward (Mt 5:12; Col 3:24; Heb 10:35), a prize (Phil 3:14), and a crown (Jas 1:12). At the end of the Second Letter to Timothy, Saint Paul states, "I have fought the good fight, I have finished the race, I have kept the faith. From now on there is laid up for me the crown of righteousness, which the Lord, the righteous judge, will award to me on that Day, and not only to me but also to all who have loved his appearing" (2 Tim 4:7–8). Properly understood, our merit cannot be separated from Christ's. The *Catechism* teaches that the charity of Christ is the source of all our merits: "Grace, by uniting us to Christ in active love, ensures the supernatural quality of our acts and consequently their merit before God and before men" (no. 2011). At the Last Supper, Jesus told his disciples quite plainly: "Apart from me you can do nothing." But then he added, "I chose you and appointed you that you should go and bear fruit and that your fruit should abide" (Jn 15:5, 16). We who are the branches bear fruit because of our union with Christ, but it is *our* fruit, too. Quoting Saint Augustine, the Preface for the Saints in the Roman liturgy praises God because "you are glorified in the assembly of your Holy Ones, for in crowning their merits you are crowning your own gifts."[9]

Can we rely on our merits to guarantee our entrance into eternal life? Again, we should not dissociate human effort from divine assistance. But on this point, the Church teaches that the grace of final perseverance is God's gift, and, far from presuming on this gift, we ought to pray for it. The Council of Trent taught that while we should trust in the mercy of God, no one can claim with absolute certitude that he is among those predestined to be saved. When we are exhorted to pray for "a happy death", this does not mean primarily a painless passing from this world—although there is nothing wrong in asking for this—but for the grace of final perseverance: that God will call us to himself at the moment when we are most ready to go to him.

As we come to the end of this chapter, let us return to the scene of the Last Supper. On the very eve of his death, Jesus spoke of himself as the source of true life: "I am the vine, you are the branches. He who abides in me, and I in him, he it is that bears much fruit, for apart from me you can do nothing" (Jn 15:5). What is the nature of this life? It is not some impersonal force like the sap rising in a plant, still less some inanimate energy like electricity. It is spiritual. The only direct experience we have of spiritual creatures—men—is that we are personal beings, and that our spiritual life is tied up with our unique

9 The *Roman Missal*, Prefatio I de Sanctis; *Qui in Sanctorum concilio celebraris, et eorum coronando merita tua dona coronas*, citing the "Doctor of grace", St. Augustine, *Enarrationes in Psalmos*, 102, 7: PL 37, 1321–22, quoted in *CCC*, no. 2006.

personal identity. But the life God gives us is not merely spiritual; it is also divine, and as such it is life that is intensely *interpersonal*: the mutual indwelling of Father, Son, and Holy Spirit poured into our human, limited lives. This grace is given to each of us in a unique way, because God shapes its contours to our deepest self. In his *Confessions*, Saint Augustine professed that he had discovered God to be *intimior intimo meo* (more inward than my innermost self).[10] The mystery of grace is intensely personal, and it is mysterious precisely because it unites two realities beyond our comprehension: God and the human heart.

But while grace is personal, it is never private. How could divine love, which is in its very essence communion, limit its scope to my solitary union with God? In the upper room, Jesus washed the feet of his disciples and gave them the Eucharist to teach them that grace not only makes each of them one *with* him; it also makes all of them one *in* him. At the end of the Supper, Jesus prayed not only for those at table with him, but for all who would come to believe in him "that they may all be one; even as you, Father, are in me, and I in you, that they also may be in us, so that the world may believe that you have sent me" (Jn 17:21). The image of the vine and branches must be complemented by the image of the Mystical Body. All grace comes to us as members of that Body from Christ our Head, and the sacraments are its lifeblood. In addition to the graces that sanctify us, God also gives charisms intended for the common good of the Church. Divine life is the love between the Persons of the Trinity, and that life finds its expression in our communion with God and with one another.

So, we have a stake in the salvation of others. Saint Paul exhorted the Galatians: "Bear one another's burdens, and so fulfil the law of Christ" (Gal 6:2). The Mystical Body is the communion of all who are one in Christ, from Abel to the last of the elect. For the members of the Church on earth, the bond of love with the Triune God and with one another is nourished above all through the sacramental life, and it is to that great mystery that we now turn.

---

[10] St. Augustine, *Confessiones*, 3, 6, 11: PL 32, 688, quoted in *CCC*, no. 30.

Chapter Nine

The Sacraments

When we read about the miracles and teaching of Jesus, it is natural to wish that we had been there to witness them in person. But Christ continues to teach, heal, and sanctify through his sacraments. The love of God became manifest in the Incarnation; similarly, through the visible signs of the sacraments, we receive, in body as well as soul, the invisible grace of divine life.

What We Believe

Christ instituted the seven sacraments to continue his saving mission by giving us divine life through the outpouring of the Holy Spirit. Since Christ himself is the primary minister of the sacraments, they unfailingly bestow the grace they signify. The holiness of the human minister does not affect the validity of the sacraments, but their fruitfulness depends on the dispositions of the recipient. Three of these sacraments (baptism, confirmation, and holy orders) effect a permanent change in those who receive them.

Some History

As devout Jews, Jesus and his disciples observed the religious customs and rituals of God's people. Some of these rites were absolutely essential, such as circumcision to enter into the covenant and the annual celebration of the Passover meal. Other ceremonies included pilgrimage to the Temple for great feasts, weekly gatherings in the synagogue, dietary regulations and lesser practices and customs as well. Jesus criticized the tendency of some observant Jews to fall into ceremonial formalism—a pitfall in any religion—but it is clear from the

Gospels that he loved the Law and followed the religious practices of his people. After the Resurrection, Jesus' disciples continued to frequent the Temple and the synagogue.

Very soon, however, the religious observances of the disciples changed. Baptism became the rite by which one entered the New Covenant, and the Passover meal took on a new meaning in connection with the Last Supper and the sacrifice of Christ, the Lamb of God. The New Testament mentions other rites, such as the imposition of hands to confer ministries and the anointing of the sick with oil. Since Christ had commanded his apostles to forgive sins, there must have been some ritual expression of this, and doubtless Christian communities had other practices as well.

Like other religious societies, the early Christians celebrated certain communal rites. But it is crucial for us to appreciate the profound connection they saw between these rituals and Jesus Christ himself. His Resurrection and the outpouring of the Holy Spirit had shattered the constraints of time and space. These ceremonies did not simply recall what Jesus had done—they were the means by which he continued to save, to teach, to heal, to forgive, and to feed. We recall again the words of Saint Leo the Great: "What was visible in our Savior has passed over into his mysteries." [1] The Latin word Leo uses for "mysteries" is *sacramenta*.

Christ Acts in the Sacraments

In the centuries following the New Testament, the understanding of the Christian rites deepened, often in the context of controversy. Some Gnostics presented the challenge: Why have rites at all? They appealed to the words of Jesus, "God is spirit, and those who worship him must worship in spirit and truth" (Jn 4:24). Underlying this objection was their conviction that material creation is evil. The Fathers of the Church responded by asserting that God's creation is good, that the Incarnation is at the heart of the Christian faith, and that visible sacramental rites are appropriate to our human condition. Another question emerged in the third century: What is required of the recipient of a sacrament? The simple answer is "Faith"; in the case of the baptism

[1] St. Leo the Great, *Sermones*, 74, 2: *PL* 54, 398, quoted in *CCC*, no. 1115.

of infants or small children, this was understood to mean the faith of their families. Tertullian challenged the practice of infant baptism because the child could not make a profession of faith, and because he believed that a newborn child was completely innocent. Origen maintained that the practice had been handed down from the apostles themselves, and Saint Cyprian argued that it was beneficial because of inherited sin. Another question concerned the minister: Who could confer the sacraments? The accepted teaching was that the minister must receive his pastoral authority from the apostles and their successors. But what about duly ordained pastors who had denied the faith during persecutions? Cyprian held that their sacraments were invalid, and that it was necessary to re-baptize or re-ordain in these cases. The position of Rome was that they were valid, because it is Christ himself who acts in the sacraments; the minister simply represents Christ and the Church.

Three fundamental principles emerged during the first millennium, and they are so central to a Catholic understanding of the sacraments that I would like not only to list them, but also to quote the paragraphs of the *Catechism* that speak about them. First, because Christ is the primary minister of sacramental acts, they possess an inherent efficacy:

> Celebrated worthily in faith, the sacraments confer the grace they signify. They are *efficacious* because in them Christ himself is at work: it is he who baptizes, he who acts in the sacraments in order to communicate the grace that each sacrament signifies. The Father always hears the prayer of his Son's Church which, in the epiclesis[2] of each sacrament, expresses her faith in the power of the Spirit.[3]

Second, this efficacy means that sacramental rites actually accomplish what they signify:

> It follows that "the sacrament is not wrought by the righteousness of either the celebrant or the recipient, but by the power of God." From the moment that a sacrament is celebrated in accordance with the intention of the Church, the power of Christ and his Spirit acts in and

---

[2] The *epiclesis* (invocation upon) is the intercessory prayer calling upon the Father to send the Holy Spirit to act in the sacramental celebration. See *CCC*, no. 1105.

[3] *CCC*, no. 1127. Cf. Council of Trent: DS 1605; DS 1606.

through it, independently of the personal holiness of the minister. Nevertheless, the fruits of the sacraments also depend on the disposition of the one who receives them.[4]

Third, baptism, confirmation, and ordination cannot be repeated:

> The three sacraments of Baptism, Confirmation, and Holy Orders confer, in addition to grace, a sacramental *character* or "seal" by which the Christian shares in Christ's priesthood and is made a member of the Church according to different states and functions. This configuration to Christ and to the Church, brought about by the Spirit, is indelible; it remains for ever in the Christian as a positive disposition for grace, a promise and guarantee of divine protection, and as a vocation to divine worship and to the service of the Church.[5]

These three paragraphs from the *Catechism* present fundamental Catholic doctrines concerning the sacraments, and also highlight the trinitarian nature of those doctrines.

During the patristic era, the terms *sacrament* or *mystery* did not have a very precise meaning.[6] For example, Saint Augustine referred to the whole Church as a sacrament (*CCC*, no. 1067), and he applied the term to many things, including the Lord's Prayer and the Creed. In the high Middle Ages, scholastic thinkers developed a more precise definition of the word *sacrament*. Scholasticism sought to bring the data of the world into a coherent system. One Scholastic technique was to ask: What distinctive features does this entity possess? When this question was applied to the liturgical rites of the Church, theologians discerned that seven of them were "efficacious signs". That is, these signs accomplish what they symbolize, like the barrier at a railroad crossing that not only directs us to stop, but also stops us. What do the sacraments accomplish? They impart divine life to those who receive them. This grace cannot come from the minister or from the Church; it can come only from God. The Scholastics reasoned that since these seven actions unfailingly impart the grace of the Holy Spirit, Christ himself acts in them. They did not search the Scriptures for

---

[4] *CCC*, no. 1128 citing St. Thomas Aquinas, *Summa Theologiae*, III, 68, 8.

[5] *CCC*, no. 1121. Cf. Council of Trent (1547): DS 1609.

[6] *Sacramentum* was a Latin term for something sacred or an oath. It was used to translate the Greek *mysterion*, as, for example, in Ephesians 5:32, where Saint Paul describes the union of husband and wife as a "mystery" referring to Christ and the Church.

proof that Jesus instituted this or that sacrament. Rather, their starting place was the Church's experience that the seven sacraments give grace by their very celebration: it is Christ who acts in them, and so it was he who instituted them.[7]

Christ Instituted the Sacraments

Are there scriptural passages that describe the explicit institution of specific sacraments by Christ? The Protestant Reformers insisted that this was essential, but in response, the Council of Trent simply reiterated the teaching of the Second Council of Lyons (1274) that Christ instituted the seven sacraments, without identifying precisely when. Most Christians agree that Jesus told his disciples to baptize and celebrate the Eucharist, but the scriptural testimony even for these fundamental rites is somewhat vague. Christ commanded the apostles to baptize "in the name of the Father, and of the Son, and of the Holy Spirit", but there is evidence to suggest that initially converts were baptized in the name of Jesus alone (e.g., Acts 2:38; 19:5). John's Gospel has no account of the institution of the Eucharist; instead, at the Last Supper Jesus commanded the apostles to wash one another's feet (Jn 13:14); and, while many churches practice a ritual of footwashing, it has not traditionally been considered a sacrament. Jesus told his apostles to forgive sins, but no description is given in Scripture as to how they did this. He authorized the apostles to act in his name, and they commissioned others to carry on their ministry through the imposition of hands, but we are not told that Jesus had laid hands on the apostles or had instructed them that this was how they were to commission other leaders. Much of the liturgical life of the first Christians is not described in the New Testament.

The Catholic approach to the institution of the sacraments is based on our conviction that the whole experience of Jesus and the first disciples is constitutive for the life of the Church. The "mysteries" of

[7] The Eastern churches encountered the Catholic enumeration of seven sacraments at the Councils of Lyons (1274) and Florence (1439), and have always been rather ambivalent on the question of numbering seven sacraments. They recognize that these seven rites hold a special place, and in ecumenical dialogue with Protestants have defended belief in the seven sacraments. The seven sacraments are also commonly presented in Orthodox catechisms. On the other hand, the East finds the broader patristic view of the sacraments more congenial and is less concerned than the West to define sacraments.

the Head have passed into the "mysteries" of the Body. The early Christians celebrated various rites—some received from Judaism, some mandated by Christ himself, some simply part and parcel of what any community does to express its religious life (special feasts, family customs, blessings, and so on). The apostolic faith was handed on by this whole pattern of worship. The life of this community was guided by the Holy Spirit, and over time, the meaning of these rites became more apparent. (There is a parallel here with the development of the Creed and the shaping of the biblical canon over several centuries.) All of these rites and prayers, great and small, have played a part in the sanctification of God's people, but the seven sacraments came to be recognized as distinctive because Christ himself acts through them to give us divine life.

As with other areas of theology, our understanding of the sacraments has been influenced by controversy: debates in the early centuries focused attention on the question of validity; the Scholastic penchant for categorizing encouraged the practice of describing the sacraments in Aristotelian terms; the challenge of the Reformation made it necessary for the Catholic Church to defend the number of the sacraments, their necessity, and the doctrine that they are efficacious signs. All of these factors combined to encourage a tendency in recent centuries for Catholic theologians to speak of the sacraments in legal and philosophical terms. For example, theological manuals examined how the intentions of the minister and recipient, the materials used, and the actions performed affect the validity, lawfulness, and fruitfulness of a sacramental rite. This Scholastic approach should not be seen in isolation, however; Catholics received a broader and richer understanding of the sacraments through spiritual writings, art, and sermons.

Sacraments and Liturgical Renewal

It is often observed that the liturgical life of Catholics changed radically after the Second Vatican Council. The discontinuity can be overstated: a perusal of the footnotes in the council documents and the *Catechism* demonstrates that the council fathers embraced the traditional Catholic understanding of the sacraments, especially as this was articulated by the Council of Trent. The originality of Vatican II consisted in rereading these traditional doctrines in a new context. Beginning in the late nineteenth century, significant advances were made in the understanding of the historical, patristic, and liturgical foundations of Christianity. These studies prompted a liturgical renewal in Catholicism throughout the twentieth century, nourished by the scholarly efforts of monastic communities and encouraged by the popes. The sacraments came to be viewed in their liturgical context, which in turn pointed to the mystery of the Church and Christ. The conciliar document on the liturgy expresses the broader vista in these words:

> The purpose of the sacraments is to sanctify men, to build up the body of Christ, and, finally, to give worship to God; because they are signs they also instruct. They not only presuppose faith, but by words and objects they also nourish, strengthen, and express it; that is why they are called "sacraments of faith." They do indeed impart grace, but, in addition, the very act of celebrating them most effectively disposes the faithful to receive this grace in a fruitful manner, to worship God duly, and to practice charity. It is therefore of the highest importance that the faithful should easily understand the sacramental signs, and should frequent with great eagerness those sacraments which were instituted to nourish the Christian life. (*SC*, no. 59)

Several points should be noted here. First, the Second Vatican Council reiterates the traditional Catholic doctrines that the sacraments presume faith, employ specific words and actions, and confer grace to make people holy. But whereas previously there was a tendency to view sanctification in individualistic terms, here it is connected to the ecclesial dimension of building up the Body of Christ. This communal perspective is balanced by a third stated purpose of the sacraments, the worship of God. I would suggest the word *finally* indicates not simply the last in a series, but the ultimate purpose: the sacraments make individuals holy, they build up the community, and most importantly, they glorify God. Thus the sacraments express our communion with God (they confer grace *and* they express worship), and they are both personal and communal (they make the recipient holy *and* they build up the Body of Christ). Lastly, the *sign* value of the sacraments is underscored. Whereas formerly questions about how the sacraments were celebrated dealt primarily with the requirements for validity, this legitimate concern is broadened to include the power of the elements and gestures to open people up to a more fruitful expression of their relationship with God and the rest of the Church. The words and actions of the liturgy should make their meaning clear to those participating; more importantly, they should encourage people to take part in the sacramental celebrations of the Church often and eagerly.

Implications

It is impossible to do justice to the Catholic understanding of the seven sacraments in a few pages. Part Two of the *Catechism*, "The Celebration of the Christian Mystery", provides a thorough introduction to these rites that are the lifeblood of the Church. I would urge the reader to study this part of the *Catechism*. I will simply highlight some key ideas that appear there.

The part of the *Catechism* that describes the seven sacraments is preceded by a section dealing with "The Sacramental Economy". The term *economy* here refers to the way in which God has revealed himself in salvation history. We might say that this is "the big picture"— the individual sacraments are best understood when seen against the backdrop of the whole drama of salvation. For this reason, the *Catechism* situates each sacrament in salvation history: how it is prepared for in the Old Testament, rooted in the mission of Christ, and expressed in "the age of the Church", in which, by the outpouring of the Holy Spirit, Christ continues his saving work.

Sacraments and the Mystery of the Trinity

This section of the *Catechism* begins with a beautiful meditation on the liturgy as the work of the Trinity (nos. 1077–112). God's saving plan unfolded gradually over the centuries, reaching its climax in the Incarnation of the Son and the sending of the Holy Spirit. This trinitarian pattern is at the heart of the Church's sacramental life:

> In the Church's liturgy the divine blessing is fully revealed and communicated. The Father is acknowledged and adored as the source and end of all the blessings of creation and salvation. In his Word who became incarnate, died, and rose for us, he fills us with his blessings.

Through his Word, he pours into our hearts the Gift that contains all gifts, the Holy Spirit. (*CCC*, no. 1082)

To be sanctified means to have the image of the Holy Trinity increasingly impressed within us.

Our response to God is also trinitarian: because the Holy Spirit dwells in us, we are united to the Son and offer our prayer to the Father through him. Most of the prayers in the Catholic liturgy are addressed to the Father through the Son in the communion of the Holy Spirit. Our prayer ascends in the Spirit through Christ to the Father, and divine life comes to us from the Father, through the Son, in the Holy Spirit. This "dialogue" is ongoing:

> On the one hand, the Church, united with her Lord and "in the Holy Spirit," blesses the Father "for his inexpressible gift" in her adoration, praise, and thanksgiving. On the other hand, until the consummation of God's plan, the Church never ceases to present to the Father the offering of his own gifts and to beg him to send the Holy Spirit upon that offering, upon herself, upon the faithful, and upon the whole world.[8]

Early in John's Gospel, Jesus promised Nathaniel: "Truly, truly, I say to you, you will see heaven opened, and the angels of God ascending and descending upon the Son of man" (Jn 1:51); his image is drawn from Jacob's dream (Gen 28:10–18). We might think of the liturgy as our "Jacob's Ladder" upon which our worship ascends to God, and God's love descends to us.

In a previous chapter we saw that the mystery of the Trinity is reflected in the unity-in-diversity that is the communion of the Church. This reality is expressed in the liturgy. The rich variety of liturgical traditions or rites across the world shows that the mystery of Christ is one, but the forms of its celebration are many. For this reason, the Second Vatican Council taught that "holy Mother Church holds all lawfully acknowledged rites to be of equal right and dignity; that she wishes to preserve them in the future and to foster them in every way" (*SC*, no. 4). Each local church is a communion of smaller communities—parishes, religious communities, families, and so on—united around its bishop. As far back as the beginning of the

---

[8] *CCC*, no. 1083, citing Lk 10:21; 2 Cor 9:15.

second century, Saint Ignatius of Antioch underscored the sacramental unity of the local church: "Let only that Eucharist be regarded as legitimate, which is celebrated under [the presidency of] the bishop or him to whom he has entrusted it." [9]

Every liturgical celebration also manifests the unity-in-diversity of trinitarian life. Many older Catholics will remember the "low Mass" celebrated by an individual priest assisted by one server. Since the council, other ministries have been restored or added to our liturgical celebrations. This change was made to express concretely that the one body of the assembly, made up of a variety of members, celebrates the liturgy. A fundamental principle laid down by the Second Vatican Council was this: "In liturgical celebrations each person, minister or layman, who has an office to perform, should do all of, but only, those parts which pertain to his office by the nature of the rite and the principles of liturgy" (SC, no. 28). The whole community, composed of many members with different responsibilities, celebrates the liturgy.

Another way the liturgy reflects its trinitarian nature is by its structure; it is a holy conversation, a dialogue. The pattern of proclamation and response runs through the entire celebration. The priest greets the community, and the community answers; the reader concludes the Scripture by proclaiming, "The word of the Lord", and the assembly responds, "Thanks be to God"; the choir sings the verse of a psalm, and the people answer with an antiphon. This pattern shapes the Mass as a whole: in the Liturgy of the Word, we hear the proclamation of God's saving deeds, and in the Liturgy of the Eucharist, we offer our response of thanksgiving. Our earthly liturgy mirrors in some small way the ongoing exchange of love between the Father, the Son, and the Holy Spirit.

What has been said thus far pertains to the whole "sacramental economy". As the Catechism then goes on to examine each of the sacraments individually, we also perceive a unity-in-diversity linking the seven sacraments. The Catechism presents its treatment of the sacraments under three headings: sacraments of initiation (baptism, confirmation, and Eucharist), sacraments of healing (penance and anointing of the sick), and sacraments in the service of communion (holy orders

---

[9] St. Ignatius of Antioch, *Epistula ad Smyrnaeos*, 8:1; *Sources Chrétiennes* (Paris, 1942–), 10, 138, quoted in *CCC*, no. 1369.

and marriage). This is not an arbitrary arrangement: "This order, while not the only one possible, does allow one to see that the sacraments form an organic whole in which each particular sacrament has its own vital place. In this organic whole, the Eucharist occupies a unique place as the 'Sacrament of sacraments': 'all the other sacraments are ordered to it as to their end'." [10]

Sacraments of Initiation

Regarding the sacraments of initiation, it is important to see them as a unified whole, even though in the West they are usually celebrated separately. (The churches of the East celebrate all three sacraments of initiation together, including giving the infant the Precious Blood; solemn "First Communion" is a Western custom.) In the early Church, the bishop completed the rite of baptism by the imposition of hands and anointing with chrism, after which the newly baptized received the Eucharist for the first time. As communities grew and bishops were responsible for larger areas, it was not always possible for them to be present for sacramental initiation. Two solutions to this dilemma emerged: in the East, the unity of the sacraments of initiation was maintained by delegating the priest to confirm; in the West, the unity of the community around its bishop was underscored by having the priest or deacon baptize, with confirmation administered by the bishop later.

The unity of the sacraments of initiation was also affected by the decision of Pope Saint Pius X at the beginning of the twentieth century to invite young children to receive Holy Communion. This change encouraged more frequent reception of the Eucharist, but it meant that most Catholics would receive First Communion before confirmation. However, it is the holy Eucharist, not confirmation, which completes Christian initiation. Why is this important? Baptism and confirmation permanently change the recipient and can never be repeated, whereas the Eucharist is received frequently. Whenever we celebrate the Eucharist, we are in effect renewing our sacramental initiation. The liturgical reforms following the Second Vatican Council emphasize the unity of the three sacraments of initiation: adult converts receive all three sacraments in the same celebration, with the

---

[10] CCC, no. 1211 citing St. Thomas Aquinas, *Summa Theologiae*, III, 65, 3.

priest administering confirmation; when the bishop confirms candidates baptized earlier, the liturgy includes the renewal of baptismal promises and takes place within a celebration of the Eucharist.

Sacraments of Healing

After its presentation on the sacraments of initiation, the *Catechism* deals with the sacraments of healing. Certainly one of the hallmarks of Jesus' ministry was healing. He performed physical cures, but what is more striking is that he also forgave sins. Jesus continues his work as the Physician of our bodies and souls through the sacraments of the anointing of the sick and penance. As regards the former, over the centuries, it had become customary to anoint the dying, so that this sacrament came to be associated more with preparation for death than with healing. Since the Second Vatican Council, the earlier understanding of the sacrament has been recovered. Although it still is administered to the dying to prepare them for their final journey, the anointing of the sick is intended primarily to strengthen those who endure serious illness or the infirmity that accompanies old age. Another important aspect is the emphasis on the ecclesial nature of the grace of this sacrament. Illness often isolates, but anointing reminds us that the sick hold a privileged place in the Body of Christ:

> By celebrating this sacrament the Church, in the communion of saints, intercedes for the benefit of the sick person, and he, for his part, through the grace of this sacrament, contributes to the sanctification of the Church and to the good of all men for whom the Church suffers and offers herself through Christ to God the Father. (*CCC*, no. 1522)

The "last sacrament" is the Eucharist received as Viaticum (a Latin word meaning "provisions for the journey"); Christ accompanies his disciple on the last stage of his journey home. The pilgrimage of discipleship begins with the three sacraments of baptism, confirmation, and Eucharist, and it concludes with the three sacraments of penance, the final anointing of the sick, and Viaticum (Eucharist).

As to the sacrament of penance or reconciliation, we face a serious problem: relatively few Catholics celebrate this sacrament today, and fewer do so with any regularity. There are many reasons for this, some of which touch on our understanding of the sacraments in general.

For example, some people say, "I do not have to confess my sins to a priest—I can tell them directly to God." It is true that we can express our sorrow to God for our sins, but this objection ultimately nullifies the whole sacramental life. If all that matters is "me and God", then I don't need any sacraments at all. This in turn denies two central tenets of Christian faith, the Incarnation and the communal nature of salvation. Regarding the Incarnation, we believe that God forgave repentant sinners before the coming of Christ; why then did the Son of God become man? As we have seen, there were several reasons, but among them was God's desire to express his love and forgiveness to us in human terms. The words that shocked the Pharisees—"Your sins are forgiven" (Mk 2:5)—brought peace of mind to the man who heard them. The great consolation Christ offered was that the sinner could hear with his own ears the words of divine forgiveness. When we celebrate the sacrament of reconciliation, Christ speaks those words to us through the priest who acts in his name. Christ empowered his apostles to forgive sins, and he commissioned them to bring this forgiveness to the whole world (Jn 20:23; Mt 16:19; 18:18; Lk 24:47). If what was visible in our Savior has passed over into the mysteries, it would be a strange sacramental economy that excluded the forgiveness of sins.

As to the communal nature of salvation, sin does not concern only my relationship with God; it also affects my relationships with others. For a member of the Body of Christ, there is no such thing as a sin that is just "between me and God". Saint Paul taught the Corinthians: "If one member suffers, all suffer together; if one member is honored, all rejoice together" (1 Cor 12:26). Just as the whole community is strengthened by the holiness of individual members, so the whole community is wounded by the sins of each. The priest represents both Christ and the Church. To go to confession is to proclaim that love of God and love of neighbor are inextricably united: I need to be reconciled both to God and to the community.

Theological objections do not keep most of us from going to confession—we avoid it because it is humiliating to admit our failings. While it is painful to confront our sins, it is therapeutic. Sin is self-absorption, and its fruit is isolation; healing requires outside intervention. Sacramental confession is not the only way to express sorrow and receive forgiveness; the *Catechism* devotes several paragraphs to the many forms of penance in the Christian life (nos. 1434–39). But the sacrament is necessary in the case of serious sin, and regular confession is beneficial to our spiritual growth.[11] Most of us do not relish going to the doctor or the dentist, but regular check-ups help us avoid more serious problems down the road. Similarly, regular celebration of the sacrament of penance helps us deal with sinful tendencies and habits early on. But even the hardened sinner can find the grace of divine forgiveness in this sacrament. The words of absolution can lift the burden of a lifetime.

Sacraments in the Service of Communion

In addition to sacraments of healing, there are two sacraments "at the service of communion": holy orders and matrimony. The *Catechism* emphasizes that these two sacraments are directed toward the salvation of others: "If they contribute as well to personal salvation, it is through service to others that they do so" (*CCC*, no. 1534). The unity-in-diversity of the Body of Christ is manifested in the relationship between the community of the baptized and their pastors:

> While the common priesthood of the faithful is exercised by the unfolding of baptismal grace—a life of faith, hope, and charity, a life according to the Spirit—, the ministerial priesthood is at the service of the common priesthood. It is directed at the unfolding of the baptismal grace of all Christians. The ministerial priesthood is a *means* by which Christ unceasingly builds up and leads his Church. (*CCC*, no. 1547)

Ordination is for service, and those who are ordained remain members of the faithful. The word *apostle* never appears in the Gospel of John: all the followers of Jesus, even the leaders, are always "disciples".

It is natural to think of holy orders in terms of service to others in the Church, but the ecclesial importance of marriage may come as a surprise, especially in a culture that sees marriage primarily (and sometimes exclusively) in terms of a romantic relationship between the couple. While the Church defends the traditional view of marriage as beneficial for society in general, her greater concern is to counteract

---

[11] "Serious sin" is not a purely subjective judgment. There are objective criteria that can help us determine if a sin is "mortal" or "venial": see *CCC*, nos. 1854–64.

erroneous views of matrimony because they make it more difficult for believers to see the conjugal relationship properly. The Catholic understanding is that marriage involves a lifelong, faithful commitment between a man and a woman, with an openness to children. Until recently, this is what most people in the Western world assumed marriage to be; each of these elements is challenged in contemporary society. For Catholics, these characteristics have a profound religious meaning: Christ's love for his Bride, the Church, is unfailing, faithful, and life-giving, and Christian marriage is a "sacrament" of this relationship, as Saint Paul taught: " 'For this reason a man shall leave his father and mother and be joined to his wife, and the two shall become one flesh.' This is a great mystery, and I mean in reference to Christ and the Church" (Eph 5:31–32). According to the Second Vatican Council, "For as God of old made Himself present to His people through a covenant of love and fidelity, so now the Savior of men and the Spouse of the Church comes into the lives of married Christians through the sacrament of matrimony" (GS, no. 48).

Sacramentals

The seven sacraments are not the only actions that enrich our lives as Catholics. There are sacramentals, which do not confer the grace of the Holy Spirit directly, but strengthen those who receive them by virtue of the intercessory prayer of the Church; foremost among these are blessings and exorcisms. Then there are the images of Our Lord and the saints, and objects used for prayer. Holy pictures, crucifixes, statues, medals, and the like are constant reminders in our homes and on our streets of our communion with Christ and the Church. While superstition in regard to these objects must be avoided, the greater temptation in a secular culture is to discard them. When we wear a medal or hang a religious picture in our home or office, we proclaim that we want our relationship with Christ to sanctify every aspect of our lives.

The Sacramental Journey of a Catholic

I would like to conclude this chapter by recalling how the sacraments surround the Catholic throughout life. Our earthly pilgrimage of faith is framed by two journeys. At the beginning of life, family and friends carry a newborn baby to the door of the church where he is welcomed into the community of believers and takes his place in the assembly that listens to the word of God. Through prayers, exorcisms, and the invocation of the saints, the child is prepared for the sacrament of baptism. The baptism itself is more than symbolic: the infant is truly plunged into the mystery of the dying and rising of Christ; original sin is washed away; he is incorporated into the Body of Christ that is the Church. Following baptism, he is anointed with chrism, a foreshadowing of his later confirmation by the bishop. The baby is dressed in a white garment to symbolize his new life in Christ. A flame from the paschal candle is entrusted to the parents and godparents as a sign of their child's sharing in the Lord's death and Resurrection. Then he is carried to the altar, as a reminder that sacramental initiation will find its completion in the Eucharist.

The final journey begins when the dying man celebrates the sacrament of reconciliation, is anointed, and receives Holy Communion to strengthen him for his pilgrimage from this world. After death, his body is carried to the church, where the priest welcomes him for the last time. The white pall, reminiscent of the baptismal garment, is placed on his coffin, which is sprinkled with holy water. His body is carried up near the altar, where the paschal candle burns. This last Eucharist is offered for the repose of his soul, with the prayer that he may enter into the banquet of eternal life. His body is honored with incense, because it has been a temple of the Holy Spirit, and he is laid in his grave to await resurrection at the return of Christ.

Between his first and last visits to church, the Catholic swims in the great sea of the sacraments: the impressions of early childhood, when the candles, the singing, the statues, and the icons reflect something of the glory of the heavenly liturgy; the hands of the bishop laid upon his head to impart the gift of the Holy Spirit; the words of absolution lifting the burden of sin; soothing oil to strengthen him in illness; the joy, perhaps, of marriage vows, when he and his wife become a living sacrament of the love between Christ and his Bride, the Church. And most precious of all, the gift of Christ himself in the Eucharist—received in the fervor of childhood, amid the distractions of young adulthood, at funerals, weddings,

Easter, Christmas, in the quiet recollection of daily Mass. In all of these sacraments, Christ gives divine life: healing, forgiving, enlightening, nourishing body and soul. When Saint Leo taught, "What was visible in Our Savior has passed over into the mysteries", he gave the Gospel response to a question put long ago: "For what great nation is there that has a god so near to it as the LORD our God is to us, whenever we call upon him?" (Deut 4:7).

Chapter Ten

The Holy Eucharist

If the sacraments are the lifeblood of the Church, the Eucharist is her heart. Christ acts in the other sacraments, but the Eucharist *is* Christ himself. For twenty centuries, saints and theologians have tried to describe this great mystery, but the reality eludes the noblest efforts of human genius. In the last chapter, I suggested that it is impossible to do justice to a Catholic understanding of the sacraments in a few pages; it is even more impossible to do justice to the Eucharist. Fervent participation in the Mass and prayerful meditation in the presence of the Blessed Sacrament are the paths that lead us into this great mystery. However, we need to explore two fundamental Catholic beliefs about this sacrament: that the Holy Eucharist is truly the Body and Blood of Christ, and that the Eucharistic celebration is not only a meal, but also a sacrifice. We will consider the dogma of the Real Presence of Christ in the Eucharist first.

The Real Presence: What We Believe

In the Most Blessed Sacrament of the Eucharist, the Body and Blood, Soul and Divinity of Christ are truly and permanently present even though the appearances of bread and wine remain.

Some History

Saint Paul's First Letter to the Corinthians gives an early description of the Last Supper:

> For I received from the Lord what I also delivered to you, that the Lord Jesus on the night when he was betrayed took bread, and when he had given thanks, he broke it, and said, "This is my body which is

for you. Do this in remembrance of me." In the same way also the chalice, after the supper, saying, "This chalice is the new covenant in my blood. Do this, as often as you drink it, in remembrance of me." (1 Cor 11:23–25)

The apostle is reminding the Corinthians of the tradition he had handed on when he first preached the Gospel to them, within twenty years or so of the Supper itself. The three synoptic Gospel accounts of the Last Supper also describe Jesus as saying, "This is my Body" and "This is my Blood" (Mt 26:26–28; Mk 14:22–24; Lk 22:19–20). John's Gospel does not recount the institution of the Eucharist, but it does contain a lengthy discourse by Jesus on the theme of the bread of life, in the course of which he asserts, "Truly, truly, I say to you, unless you eat the flesh of the Son of man and drink his blood, you have no life in you" (Jn 6:53). Did Jesus mean these words literally? The Catholic response is that he did, although this does not exclude spiritual understandings of the Eucharist as well.

The Fathers on the Eucharist as the Body of Christ

When Jesus first proclaimed that his followers must eat his Flesh and drink his Blood, some found the idea abhorrent and left him. He let them go, and did not modify his scandalous words. Nor has the Catholic Church: she resolutely affirms that the Eucharist is truly the Body and Blood of Christ. The earliest Fathers, beginning with Saint Ignatius of Antioch, emphasized the intrinsic connection between the Incarnation, the bodily Resurrection of Christ, and his Real Presence in the Eucharist. They did so in opposition to Gnostics, who considered matter evil and sought to "spiritualize" Christian doctrines. Ignatius was adamant in the face of Gnostic repugnance. He wrote: "They abstain from the Eucharist and from prayer, because they do not admit that the Eucharist is the flesh of our Savior Jesus Christ, the flesh which suffered for our sins and which the Father, in his graciousness raised from the dead." [1] Ignatius also connected the Eucharistic presence of Christ to the unity of the Church as Christ's Body, as Saint Paul had done before him. Paul had written to the Corinthians: "The

---

[1] Ignatius of Antioch, *Letter to the Smyrneans*, no. 6, trans. Gerald Walsh in *The Apostolic Fathers: A New Translation*, ed. Francis Glimm, Joseph Marique, and Gerald Walsh (New York: Cima Publishing Co., 1947), pp. 120–21.

bread which we break, is it not a participation in the body of Christ? Because there is one bread, we who are many are one body, for we all partake of the one bread" (1 Cor 10:16–17). We find at the dawn of Christianity a constellation of doctrines that shines together through the ages: the Eucharist is truly the Body and Blood of Jesus, who was born of Mary, suffered on the Cross, and rose from the dead; those who eat his Flesh and drink his Blood are members of his Body, the Church. Belief in the presence of Christ in the Eucharist is coupled with the visible Church as the Body of Christ and to the mysteries of Christ's Incarnation and bodily Resurrection.

The Fathers affirmed that what had previously been bread and wine was now the Body and Blood of Christ, but they struggled to find language to describe this miraculous transformation. Irenaeus stated that the bread and wine *become* the very Body and Blood of Christ by the word of God; Cyril of Jerusalem said that, unlike the baptismal water and chrism for anointing, the Eucharistic elements were *changed* or *transformed*, and he compared this to the miracle at Cana, when Jesus changed one thing into another; Gregory of Nyssa held that Christ *"transelements"* the nature of visible realities in the Eucharist; Ambrose used the word *transfigured*; and John Damascene said that the bread and wine are *supernaturally transformed* into the Body and Blood of Christ, so they are not two things, but one and the same. This sampling of eminent Fathers illustrates the conviction of the Christians of the first centuries: in the Eucharistic celebration, a change takes place in the elements themselves. They are no longer bread and wine, but truly the Body and Blood of Christ. This transformation was attributed to the creative power of the Father, through the agency of the word of Christ and sanctification by the Holy Spirit.

The Fathers also spoke in figurative or symbolic terms about eating and drinking the Body and Blood of Christ. They had to counteract pagan accusations of cannibalism, and it was evident that the Eucharistic elements retained the appearances of bread and wine. But for Christians of the first millennium, it was not a choice between a real change or a symbolic one: the Eucharist provided an inexhaustible source of spiritual reflection, and teaching about the Real Presence was part of a wider catechesis. For example, the production of bread and wine from many grains of wheat and many grapes was seen as a vivid image of the many members making up the ecclesial Body of

Christ; a wealth of scriptural images and events were understood to refer to the Eucharist; and Holy Communion was seen as "figurative" in relation to the true banquet of Heaven. But it is clear that throughout the patristic era Christians considered the Eucharist to be unique because through the power of God the bread and wine became something different, the Body and Blood of Christ. The *Catechism* cites the testimony of two of the greatest Fathers of the East and West:

> Thus St. John Chrysostom declares: "It is not man that causes the things offered to become the Body and Blood of Christ, but he who was crucified for us, Christ himself. The priest, in the role of Christ, pronounces these words, but their power and grace are God's. This is my body, he says. This word transforms the things offered." And St. Ambrose says about this conversion: "Be convinced that this is not what nature has formed, but what the blessing has consecrated. The power of the blessings prevails over that of nature, because by the blessing nature itself is changed.... Could not Christ's word, which can make from nothing what did not exist, change existing things into what they were not before?" [2]

Transubstantiation

A theological controversy about the Eucharist erupted in the West in the eleventh century. The roots of the conflict go back to the writings of two monks in the ninth century, Paschasius and Ratramnus. Paschasius authored the first full-length theological treatise on the Eucharist; in it, he emphasized the identity of the Eucharistic Body and Blood with the Body born of Mary that suffered on the Cross and rose from the dead. His disciple Ratramnus took a different approach: he maintained that the Eucharist is not truly the Body and Blood of Christ, but the figure or sacrament of his Body and Blood. To some extent, the difference between these two positions was a matter of emphasis, and the debate remained a rather in-house affair at their monastery. But two centuries later, Berengarius of Tours adopted Ratramnus' position and expanded on it. He taught that the bread and wine were not changed, but a value or power was given to them so that the Body and Blood of Christ is received spiritually in Holy

[2] *CCC*, no. 1375, quoting St. John Chrysostom, *De proditione Judae*, 1:6: *PG* 49, 380, and St. Ambrose, *De mysteriis*, 9, 50, 52: *PL* 16, 405–7.

Communion. Berengarius' views are somewhat ambiguous, but it seems he thought that the Eucharist is like chrism, which after its consecration is still oil, although it is imbued with spiritual power.

Unlike the ninth-century dispute, the Berengarius affair was very public. His views gained a sympathetic hearing among the Cathars ("pure ones"), who viewed matter as evil and rejected the sacraments. The Fourth Lateran Council (1215) was convened to deal with abuses in the Church and to respond to the Cathars. At the beginning of the thirteenth century, three different understandings of the Eucharist were in circulation: (1) the bread and the wine remain what they were, but are signs or reminders of the Body and Blood of Christ; (2) the elements are both bread and wine and the Body and Blood of Christ; (3) the elements are no longer bread and wine, but the Body and Blood of Christ, although the appearances of bread and wine remained. Lateran IV recognized the third alternative as most faithful to tradition: "His body and blood are truly contained in the sacrament of the altar under the forms of bread and wine, the bread and wine having been changed in substance [*transsubstantiatis*], by God's power, into his body and blood, so that in order to achieve this mystery of unity we receive from God what he received from us."[3] This document represents the first official reference to *transubstantiation*, and since the term is so closely identified with Catholic teaching on the Eucharist, we should examine its meaning.

Like the various words used by the Fathers of the Church, the term *transubstantiation* was coined to express the conviction that a change took place in the elements of the Eucharist. The basic idea is that ordinarily the qualities our senses perceive about something point to the underlying reality of what it is. In the case of the Eucharist, however, we encounter something that is not only miraculous, but unique in human experience: the underlying reality (or "substance") of the bread and wine has been converted into the Body and Blood of Christ, even though what our senses perceive still has the appearances of bread and wine. The word *transubstantiation* does not describe *how* this change takes place. Its purpose was to exclude deficient explanations

---

[3] Fourth Lateran Council, constitution *Firmiter*, in *Decrees of the Ecumenical Councils*, vol. 1, trans. Norman Tanner (Washington, D.C.: Sheed & Ward and Georgetown University Press, 1990), p. 230.

by affirming three truths: (1) that a change takes place in the elements themselves, not simply in our understanding of them; (2) that this conversion means that the elements are no longer bread and wine, but only the Body and Blood of Christ; and (3) that the appearances of bread and wine remain, even in their physical and chemical "accidents" (attributes not essential to the nature of something), such that no physical or chemical change can be detected in the bread or wine.

The question emerged again in the sixteenth century. In response to the views of the Reformers (who professed a variety of theological positions about the nature of the Eucharist), the Council of Trent defined that the whole Christ (Body, Blood, Soul, and Divinity) to be truly, really, and substantially contained in the Eucharist, and that this change is fittingly called *transubstantiation* (*CCC*, no. 1376). The term is fitting, but it is not the only way to express the Church's faith—witness the example of the Eastern churches, which also believe in the transformation of the elements although they do not use this term.

Some theologians today question whether the term is helpful, since words like *substance* and *accidents* have a different meaning for us than they did in the Aristotelian lexicon of the Middle Ages. Various alternatives have been proposed, but each is problematic in some way. I would suggest we take the word as a helpful place-marker for one of the central mysteries of our faith: by *transubstantiation*, we mean that what looks like bread and wine is in fact not bread and wine at all, but the Body and Blood of Christ. Our senses tell us, "This is bread and wine"; Christ tells us, "This is my Body, this is my Blood"—and in faith we accept what Christ tells us. As Saint Thomas Aquinas expressed it in one of his hymns:

> Seeing, touching, tasting are in thee deceived;
> How says trusty hearing? that shall be believed;
> What God's Son has told me, take for truth I do;
> Truth himself speaks truly or there's nothing true.[4]

In the centuries since the Reformation, Catholic theology and piety have emphasized the doctrine of the Real Presence of Christ in the

---

[4] St. Thomas Aquinas [attr.], *Adoro te devote*, trans. Gerard Manley Hopkins, quoted in *CCC*, no. 1381.

Eucharist. The Second Vatican Council enshrined this teaching in the broader context of the many ways Christ is present in the liturgy:

> He is present in the sacrifice of the Mass, not only in the person of His minister ... but especially under the Eucharistic species. By His power He is present in the sacraments, so that when a man baptizes it is really Christ Himself who baptizes. He is present in His word, since it is He Himself who speaks when the holy scriptures are read in the Church. He is present, lastly, when the Church prays and sings, for He promised: "Where two or three are gathered together in my name, there am I in the midst of them." (*SC*, no. 7)

However varied and powerful as these manifestations of Christ in our midst are, his presence in the Blessed Sacrament is unique, as Pope Paul VI emphasized: "This presence is called 'real'—by which is not intended to exclude the other types of presence as if they could not be 'real' too, but because it is presence in the fullest sense: that is to say, it is a *substantial* presence by which Christ, God and man, makes himself wholly and entirely present." [5]

Implications

How is the Eucharist related to the risen Christ in Heaven? The Church affirms two truths in this regard: (1) Christ is present in his bodily form properly speaking only "at the right hand of the Father" in Heaven; (2) in the Eucharist, the same risen body of Christ is present in a different way. The Church has never defined how these truths are interrelated; she only professes *that* Christ is truly, really, and substantially present in the Blessed Sacrament, not *how*. Some have suggested that since Christ is God, and God is everywhere, then this is why Christ is present in the Eucharist. But this explanation contradicts the dogma of the Incarnation. In his divine nature, the Son is everywhere (so that he did not leave the Father in coming to earth), but it is an attribute of a human body to be present in only one place. The *incarnate* Son of God was in the womb of Mary, or teaching by the lake, or hanging on the Cross. Christ's human nature was transformed by his Resurrection, but it did not lose its "localized" quality: he ascended to the Father, and from there he will return. The risen body of Christ

5 Paul VI, *Mysterium Fidei* (1965), no. 39, quoted in *CCC*, no. 1374.

locally present at the right hand of the Father is sacramentally present in the Eucharist.

Since the elements are no longer bread and wine, but solely the Body and Blood of Christ, in Holy Communion we receive the Flesh of the risen Christ. He gives his Body and Blood not only to nourish us, but to transform us. Every other food we eat becomes part of us; when we eat the Eucharist we are raised up into the life of Christ glorified. In the words of Saint Irenaeus, "our bodies, which partake of the Eucharist, are no longer corruptible, but possess the hope of resurrection".[6]

The Lord who is locally present in Heaven and sacramentally present in the Eucharist has one Body. This Body is wholly present in each consecrated Host, and in each part of the Host, and in every drop of the Precious Blood. There is not more of the Body of Christ in many Hosts, nor do we receive less if we receive only a fragment. When the Host is divided, only the sacramental sign is affected; Christ remains one and entire in each part. The significance of this truth becomes apparent when we recall one of the names for the Eucharist in the New Testament: "the Breaking of Bread". After Saint Paul reminded the Corinthians that "the bread which we break is a communion in the body of Christ", he added, "Because there is one bread, we who are many are one body, for we all partake of the one bread" (1 Cor 10:17). The one body of the risen Christ, received by many individual believers, unites us into his Mystical Body. The Eucharist makes the Church. The apostle warns the Corinthians, "For any one who eats and drinks without discerning the body eats and drinks judgment upon himself" (1 Cor 11:29); this "discerning" refers to recognizing that the Eucharist is the sacramental Body of Christ and that those who partake of it are members of the ecclesial Body of Christ.

Sharing in the Eucharist should make us generous in sharing other things as well. The *Epistle of Barnabas* (early second century) gives this advice: "Share with your neighbor whatever you have, and do not say of anything, this is mine. If you both share an imperishable treasure, how much more must you share what is perishable."[7] Saint John Chrysostom called his congregation to task for not recognizing Christ in the poor: "You have tasted the Blood of the Lord, yet you

---

[6] St. Irenaeus, *Adversus haereses*, 4, 18, 4–5: PG 7/1, 1028–29, quoted in *CCC*, no. 1000.
[7] *Epistle of Barnabas*, chap. 19 (Office of Readings, Wednesday in Eighteenth Week in Ordinary Time).

do not recognize your brother.... You dishonor this table when you do not judge worthy of sharing your food someone judged worthy to take part in this meal." [8]

Because we recognize in faith that the Eucharist is truly the Body of Christ, we adore him present in the Blessed Sacrament. In the words of Saint Augustine: "No one eats that Flesh unless he has first adored it ... and we sin by not adoring." [9] Although we use the term *Real Presence* in connection with the Eucharist, we should not imagine this presence to be a static reality. Because it is the living, risen Lord who abides with us, his presence is dynamic and active. At the heart of that activity is the *sacrifice* of Christ, and it is to that reality we now turn.

Mass as Sacrifice: What We Believe

In the celebration of the Eucharist, Christ's sacrifice on the Cross is re-presented and memorialized, and its saving power is applied for the forgiveness of sins. The Eucharist is Christ's sacrifice: he is the Priest who offers, and it is his sacrifice on the Cross that is offered, but in an unbloody manner. The Church as the Body of Christ participates in the offering made by Christ her Head.

Some History

Jesus celebrated a final meal with his apostles on the night before he died, and told them: "Do this in memory of me." The Christian Eucharist is the fulfillment of that command. But this was no ordinary gathering: it was a Passover meal, the solemn feast when the Jews celebrate their deliverance from slavery. [10] In this meal, the participants relive the dramatic events of the Exodus—the unleavened bread suggests the haste surrounding the Israelites' departure; the roast lamb recalls the blood of

[8] St. John Chrysostom, *Homiliae in primam ad Corinthios*, 27, 4: PG 61, 229–30; cf. Mt 25:40, quoted in *CCC*, no. 1397.

[9] Augustine, *Enarrationes in Psalmos*, 98, 9; quoted in James T. O'Connor, *The Hidden Manna: A Theology of the Eucharist* (San Francisco: Ignatius Press, 1988), p. 59. Much of the material presented in this chapter is based on this fine book.

[10] The synoptic Gospels describe the Last Supper as a Passover meal. In the Fourth Gospel, the meal takes place before the Passover; nor does John describe the institution of the Eucharist. He links Jesus to the Passover by having him crucified while the lambs are sacrificed in the Temple for the feast, and he explains that the soldiers did not break the legs of Jesus because the bones of the paschal lamb were not to be broken (Jn 19:36).

the lamb that delivered God's people from the avenging angel. It was in this atmosphere, already suffused with sacred associations, that Jesus broke the bread and said, "This is my Body, given for you"; and at the end of the meal, he gave them the cup, telling them it was the cup of the New Covenant of his Blood, shed for the forgiveness of sins.

To appreciate the significance of the Last Supper, it is important to emphasize that the Passover meal does not simply commemorate an event in the distant past: "This is how Israel understands its liberation from Egypt: every time Passover is celebrated, the Exodus events are made present to the memory of believers so that they may conform their lives to them" (CCC, no. 1363). But at the Last Supper, it was not just a past event that became present—an event from the future was made present, too. Jesus united what he did at table that evening with what he was to do the next day: lay down his life on the Cross. Where formerly the blood of many lambs delivered one nation from slavery, now the Blood of the Lamb of God was being poured out to deliver the whole human race from the slavery of death, and to begin an Exodus into the Promised Land of eternal life. The meal and the sacrifice were inextricably linked. Saint Paul was aware of this, and he told the Corinthians: "For Christ, our Paschal Lamb, has been sacrificed. Let us, therefore, celebrate the festival ... with the unleavened bread of sincerity and truth" (1 Cor 5:7–8). Further on, after recalling the words of Jesus, "This cup is the new covenant in my blood. Do this, as often as you drink it, in remembrance of me." Paul added, "For as often as you eat this bread and drink the chalice, you proclaim the Lord's death until he comes" (1 Cor 11:26).

The earliest Christians saw the Eucharist as a sacrificial meal. The *Didache*, which may have been written as early as the end of the first century, and second-century Fathers like Justin Martyr and Irenaeus described the Christian Eucharist as the fulfillment of a prophecy found in the Book of Malachi: "For from the rising of the sun to its setting my name is great among the nations, and in every place incense is offered to my name, and a pure offering" (Mal 1:11). In the Old Testament, sacrifices could be offered in only one place, the Temple in Jerusalem. These offerings prefigured the one perfect sacrifice of Christ on the Cross; this is one of the principal themes in the Letter to Hebrews (e.g., Heb 10:1–18). Since Christ's glorification, his one perfect sacrifice is offered up all over the world in the Eucharistic celebration.

The doctrine that the Eucharist is sacrificial runs through the patristic writings of both East and West. The integral relationship between the Last Supper, the Cross, and the Eucharist was not called into question until the Protestant Reformation in the sixteenth century. The fundamental objection of the Reformers to the sacrifice of the Mass came from their opposition to "works righteousness". To their minds, the practice of offering the sacrifice of the Mass was the lynchpin of a whole ecclesiastical system whereby Christians tried to earn salvation. Furthermore, it seemed to call into question the adequacy of Christ's self-offering on the Cross. Since, as the Letter to the Hebrews clearly taught, "when Christ had offered for all time a single sacrifice for sins, he sat down at the right hand of God" (Heb 10:12), the Reformers considered it blasphemous to suggest that any other sacrifices were either necessary or beneficial.

Unlike the doctrine of the Real Presence, which had been denied centuries before, the Protestant challenge to the sacrificial nature of the Eucharist was something new. The connection between the upper room, Calvary, and the altar had never been questioned. The Fathers at Trent rejected the Protestant contention that the Mass was an "additional" sacrifice to that offered by Christ on the Cross. Rather, the Eucharistic sacrifice was given by Christ to the Church so that his one perfect sacrifice could be "re-presented, its memory perpetuated until the end of the world, and its salutary power be applied to the forgiveness of the sins we daily commit".[11] The Cross and the Eucharist constitute one single sacrifice: Christ is the Priest who offers and the Victim offered; his great act of redemption on Calvary is offered sacramentally in an unbloody manner. Trent did not define how the Mass is a sacrifice, nor has the Church subsequently done so.

Implications

Two ideas are fundamental to the Eucharist as sacrifice: the permanence of Christ's priesthood and our participation in it as members of his Body.

---

[11] Council of Trent (1562): DS 1740, quoted in *CCC*, no. 1366. Cf. 1 Cor 11:23; Heb 7:24, 27.

Jesus Christ, a Priest Forever

The principal scriptural source for our theology of Christ the Priest is the Letter to the Hebrews. Much of this book contrasts the priesthood of the Old Covenant with that of Christ. The offering of sacrifice is part of most religions. It is a concrete way to show our dependence on God: sacrifices are made to express praise and thanks, to atone for sins, and to seek divine help. Even a cursory review of the Old Testament reveals how central sacrifice was to the Jewish people. When Abraham was commanded to spare his son Isaac, he sacrificed a ram in his place. This is a dramatic instance of "substitution": the blood of an animal is offered in place of a human sacrifice. Blood was held to be the principle of life, and as such it belonged to God. While there were many kinds of sacrifice offered in the Old Testament, blood sacrifices were the most solemn. The Temple, its priesthood, and its sacrifices were at the heart of Israel's religion; as the Letter to Hebrews observes, "Indeed, under the law almost everything is purified with blood, and without the shedding of blood there is no forgiveness of sins" (Heb 9:22).

The understanding of Christ as the Lamb of God who takes away the sins of the world led naturally to the idea of his priesthood. Jesus was not an unwilling victim. He had come to give his life as a ransom for the many, and he did so with sovereign freedom: "No one takes it [my life] from me, but I lay it down of my own accord" (Jn 10:18). Christ was Priest as well as Victim on Calvary. The Letter to the Hebrews describes several ways in which Christ's priesthood differs from the priesthood of the Temple. Israel's priests were only human, and sinners; Christ is the Son of God, higher than the angels, who out of love for us became our Brother in all things except sin. The priests of the Old Covenant offered as a sacrifice something other than themselves; Christ offered himself. And, because he is both the Son of God and our Brother, Christ's sacrifice represents both the greatest act of God's condescension to us and the supreme offering by man to God. The old sacrifices were provisional and had to be repeated frequently; Christ's sacrifice is definitive. In fact, the priesthood of Christ is qualitatively different: whereas the Temple priests are descendants of Aaron, he is a Priest after the order of Melchizedek.

Melchizedek is a mysterious figure who appears briefly in the Book of Genesis: he offers bread and wine, blesses Abraham, and receives a tithe from him (Gen 14:18–20). The author of Hebrews describes him as having neither beginning nor end of days, and no genealogy (unlike the Temple priests, for whom genealogy was essential to their office). The distinguishing characteristic of the priesthood of Melchizedek in Hebrews is that it lasts forever. Christ offered a single sacrifice for sins: "He has appeared once for all at the end of the age to put away sin by the sacrifice of himself" (Heb 9:26), but that priestly offering is permanent: "Consequently he is able for all time to save those who draw near to God through him, since he always lives to make intercession for them" (Heb 7:25).

Christ is risen and cannot die again, yet he bears in his glorified body the wounds of his Passion. His self-offering on the Cross summed up his whole life: by that one act Christ expressed to the full his loving obedience to the Father and his merciful compassion for us. Priest and Victim are not roles that Christ assumed when he mounted the Cross; they are constitutive of who he is: not just a Priest for three hours, but a Priest forever. The Letter to the Hebrews depicts Jesus entering Heaven, the true Holy of Holies, with his own Blood, "thus securing an eternal redemption" (Heb 9:12). In Heaven, he remains Victim as well as Priest; the Book of Revelation describes "a Lamb standing, as though it had been slain" (Rev 5:6). Christ's priestly offering does not pass away, and it is accessible to us in the Eucharist. Toward the end of the Letter to the Hebrews, we are told, "We have an altar from which those who serve the tent [where the sacrifices of the Old Covenant are offered] have no right to eat" (Heb 13:10). That altar is the holy table where the Christian Passover, both meal and sacrifice, is celebrated.

Our Participation in Christ's Sacrifice

We proclaim the death of the Lord until he comes again because Christ has transformed what had been the end of all human hopes into the gateway of eternal life. His sacrifice is the center of human history, and the fact that he lets us take part in it is an example of his merciful condescension. Christ invites us to offer ourselves with him; he lets his sacrifice become our sacrifice. The Church is the Body of Christ, and the offering of the Eucharist is the offering of the whole Christ, Head and members.

Does this imply, as the Reformers feared, that the death of Christ was not sufficient to redeem us? No, the Catholic Church has always taught that redemption comes only from Christ and his Cross. Yet even Saint Paul, who was himself so adamant on this point, wrote to the Colossians, "Now I rejoice in my sufferings for your sake, and in my flesh I complete what is lacking in Christ's afflictions for the sake of his body, that is, the Church" (Col 1:24). Christ makes us participants in his work of redemption. And this should not surprise us, if we recall that salvation draws us into the communion of trinitarian life. God invites us to give as well as to receive. Here we encounter a paradox: salvation is a pure gift, but it demands our active involvement; Christ's sacrifice is all-sufficient, and yet he allows us to unite our sacrifices with his. When the Church offers her sacrifice together with that of Christ her Head, it is not because otherwise his sacrifice would be inadequate; it is because Christ asks us to imitate, in our limited way, his generous love. Again, we turn to the Letter to the Hebrews: "So Jesus also suffered outside the gate in order to sanctify the people through his own blood. Therefore let us go forth to him outside the camp, bearing abuse for him" (Heb 13:12–13). For twenty centuries, Christians have made their own the plea of Saint Ignatius of Antioch: "Let me imitate the sufferings of my God." [12]

Of course, whatever we have to offer is first of all God's gift to us. As we take part in the Eucharistic sacrifice, we are like a child who spends her allowance on a present for her mother. The girl was given the money by her mother, so in a sense she is simply returning something she received, and yet, what parent would not treasure the gift more than the money? What makes the gift precious is not its monetary value, but the love it expresses. Similarly, when we unite our sacrifices to the perfect self-offering of Christ, the only thing we are "adding" is our love, but this makes it truly our sacrifice as well as his.

We can unite our sacrifice to Christ's because we are members of his Body. Our offering is never for our individual needs alone; it is part of the oblation of the whole Church. This means, first of all, the

---

[12] Ignatius of Antioch, *Letter to the Romans*, no.6 (Office of Readings, Tuesday of the Tenth Week in Ordinary Time).

community of believers throughout the world, given a human face in the Eucharistic Prayer with the mention by name of our own bishop and the pope, the shepherd of the whole earthly flock. The Catholic Church is a communion of communities gathered at altars all over the world, offering the many sacrifices that are one sacrifice. We offer the Eucharistic sacrifice also for those who have died. In the fourth century, Saint Cyril instructed his people in Jerusalem: "Then, we pray [in the anaphora] for the holy fathers and bishops who have fallen asleep, and in general for all who have fallen asleep before us, in the belief that it is a great benefit to the souls on whose behalf the supplication is offered, while the holy and tremendous Victim is present." [13] We offer the Eucharist for the needs of the entire world, and, in the frank language of the Roman Canon, we offer it for ourselves and for those who are dear to us.

In this same Eucharistic Prayer, the priest begs God to look favorably upon our offering, as once he did the sacrifices of Abel, Abraham, and Melchizedek. This prayer proclaims that the offerings in the Old Covenant prefigured the sacrifice of Christ and were acceptable because in some way they were related to it. More broadly, these three figures can be taken to represent all mankind (Abel), the chosen people (Abraham), and the Gentiles (Melchizedek). Thus, not only the sacrifices offered in the Old Testament, but every human expression of devotion to God is caught up into Christ's sacrifice.

We should not presume that our sacrifice will be accepted simply because it is united to Christ's: our offering needs to be ratified in our lives. As members of "a chosen race, a royal priesthood, a holy nation" (1 Pet 2:9), we all share in the priesthood of Christ, albeit in different ways as lay people and ordained priests. But any priesthood modeled on Christ's demands self-sacrifice. Jesus did not offer his sacrifice in the Temple sanctuary. He was driven out of the holy city, and we must follow him there and share in his Passion. For this reason, Saint Paul appealed to the Romans "by the mercies of God, to present your bodies as a living sacrifice, holy and acceptable to God, which is your spiritual worship" (Rom 12:1). Jesus' command "Do this in memory of me" means several things: gather for this

[13] St. Cyril of Jerusalem, *Catecheses mystagogicae*, 5, 9, 10: PG 33, 1116–17, quoted in CCC, no. 1371.

meal, offer this sacrifice ... and lay down your lives for one another as I have for you.

In a sermon on the martyrs, Saint Augustine applied a piece of practical advice from the Old Testament to the Eucharist. He cites the Book of Proverbs as teaching this: "You have sat down at a great table. Diligently consider what is set before you because it is necessary for you to prepare the same things" (see Prov 23:1).[14] At the great table of the Eucharist, Augustine taught, Christ feeds us with his very self; the martyrs recognized this and willingly shed their blood. Most of us are not asked literally to lay down our lives, but all of us are called to make sacrifices. Some will be small and some great, but all of them have meaning when we unite them to Christ's self-oblation.

Conclusion

The two dogmas we have considered in this chapter make it clear why Saint Thomas called the Eucharist the greatest of Christ's miracles. There are many reasons to go to Mass, but certainly the most imperative are these: first, we are privileged to offer our gifts, our sacrifices, and our lives to our heavenly Father in union with Christ's infinitely perfect self-offering; no greater expression of thanksgiving is possible. Second, we receive the very Body and Blood of Christ himself in Holy Communion. These two truths have a common foundation: Christ's ardent love for us. Saint Louis de Montfort observed:

> Eternal Wisdom, on the one hand, wished to prove His love for man by dying in his place in order to save him, but on the other hand, he could not bear the thought of leaving him. So he devised a marvelous way of dying and living at the same time, and of abiding with man until the end of time. In order to satisfy his love, he instituted the sacrament of the Holy Eucharist and went to the extent of changing and overturning nature itself.[15]

---

[14] Taken from the Office of Readings for September 26.
[15] St. Louis de Montfort, *Love of Eternal Wisdom*, no. 71, in *God Alone: The Collected Writings of Saint Louis Marie de Montfort* (Bay Shore, N.Y.: Montfort Publications, 1987), p. 68.

The Eucharist is so amazing that many find these truths hard to accept. When Jesus first announced this mystery, some disciples left him. He asked the Twelve, "Do you also wish to go away?" May we respond to Christ the Bread of Life now as Saint Peter did then: "Lord, to whom shall we go? You have the words of eternal life; and we have believed, and have come to know, that you are the Holy One of God" (Jn 6:68–69).

Chapter Eleven

The Communion of Saints

We call the Eucharist "Holy Communion": it is our communion with Christ and also with the other members of his Body. The closer we draw to him, the closer we come to one another. Awareness of this bond points to another article of the Creed: the communion of saints. The Latin term *communio sanctorum* has two meanings: *sanctorum* can be translated as either neuter, "a sharing in holy things", or masculine, "a community of holy people". The meanings are mutually related; the community is holy because it shares in the holy gifts of God.

What We Believe

Our union with Christ binds us to the other members of his Body, both those on earth and those who have died. By our prayers and works of charity, we build up the Body of Christ. Just as we can help one another on earth, so we are aided by the prayers of the saints, and we can assist the dead who are preparing to enter into the glory of Heaven.

Some History

The hallmark of the early Christians was mutual love: "Now the company of those who believed were of one heart and soul, and no one said that any of the things which he possessed was his own, but they had everything in common" (Acts 4:32). What did they share? On the most basic level, faith in the God who had raised Jesus from the dead; this faith was the very reason for the community's existence. Where formerly God's people had been bound together by the ties of blood, the new Israel was made up of all those, Jew and Gentile alike, who proclaimed Jesus as Lord. They also shared a common hope: to welcome

Christ when he returned in glory and enter into eternal life. And they shared a common love—the divine life they had received from the indwelling of the Holy Spirit.

We Can Pray and Do Penance for One Another

This communion in charity can be shown in many ways, great and small. As the *Catechism* notes, even the least of our actions done with love benefits everyone (*CCC*, no. 953). One important expression of mutual support is intercessory prayer. The great leaders of the Old Testament, such as Abraham and Moses, interceded before God on behalf of the people. The Letter to the Hebrews tells us that the risen Christ lives forever to make intercession for us (Heb 7:25), and Saint Paul teaches that the Holy Spirit "intercedes for us with sighs too deep for words" (Rom 8:26). The idea of intercession occurs often in the Letters of Saint Paul, who prays frequently for others and asks for their prayers for him. Nor does he limit intercession to the needs of believers: "First of all, then, I urge that supplications, prayers, intercessions, and thanksgivings be made for all men, for kings and for all who are in high positions" (1 Tim 2:1–2). When we recall that the "kings and those in high positions" were hunting down Christians and putting them to death, it is clear that the disciples took seriously Jesus' command to pray for their persecutors.

Love is expressed in deeds, too. Christ showed his love for us by laying down his life on the Cross, and the early Christians recognized that martyrdom sanctified not only the one who endured it, but others as well. Saint Paul described his death as a libation poured upon the sacrificial offering of his disciples' faith (Phil 2:17), and as Ignatius of Antioch journeyed to Rome for execution, he assured the Ephesians that he was offering his life for them as well as for himself. The disciple's suffering is united to the Master's; when Jesus likened his death to the grain of wheat that yields a rich harvest, he added: "If anyone serves me, he must follow me; and where I am, there shall my servant be also" (Jn 12:26). The intimate bond between Christ and his followers helps us understand the audacious words of Saint Paul: "Now I rejoice in my sufferings for your sake, and in my flesh I complete what is lacking in Christ's afflictions for the sake of his body, that is, the Church" (Col 1:24).

From the very beginning, then, Christians have recognized that the reward God gives to one person (merit) can be shared with others, and that the suffering of one member can make up for what is lacking in another (satisfaction). We have already discussed the Catholic understanding of merit in chapter nine above: it is the reward God gives to those who love him and who, with the help of his grace, perform good works. Satisfaction for sin is the penance we undertake or the suffering we accept to show our love for God and to undo the effects of sin. Here is how the *Catechism* describes it:

> Many sins wrong our neighbor. One must do what is possible in order to repair the harm.... Simple justice requires as much. But sin also injures and weakens the sinner himself, as well as his relationships with God and neighbor. Absolution takes away sin, but it does not remedy all the disorders sin has caused. Raised up from sin, the sinner must still recover his full spiritual health by doing something more to make amends for the sin: he must "make satisfaction for" or "expiate" his sins.[1]

We do not do penance to *earn* God's forgiveness; God freely and generously forgives us as soon as we turn to him in repentance. Nor should we imagine that we can make satisfaction apart from Christ. The Council of Trent taught:

> The satisfaction that we make for our sins, however, is not so much ours as though it were not done through Jesus Christ. We who can do nothing ourselves, as if just by ourselves, can do all things with the cooperation of "him who strengthens" us. Thus man has nothing of which to boast, but all our boasting is in Christ ... in whom we make satisfaction by bringing forth "fruits that befit repentance." These fruits have their efficacy from him, by him they are offered to the Father, and through him they are accepted by the Father.[2]

Why do we need to make satisfaction? Since our age is marked by a lively concern for ecology, it might help to think of sin as a kind of spiritual pollution: works of charity restore the spiritual environment that has been damaged by selfishness. Prayer, fasting, and works of mercy are traditional forms of penance and have always been central

---

[1] *CCC*, no. 1459; cf. Council of Trent (1551): DS 1712.
[2] Council of Trent (1551): DS 1691, quoted in *CCC*, no. 1460. Cf. Phil 4:13; 1 Cor 1:31; 2 Cor 10:17; Gal 6:14; Lk 3:8.

to Christian discipleship. We can do penance not only for our own sins but also on behalf of others.

This mutual cooperation undergirds the doctrine of indulgences. The granting of an indulgence has nothing to do with the forgiveness of sin; it is an act by which the Church mitigates a penance on the basis of shared membership in the Body of Christ. In the communion of saints, "the holiness of one profits others, well beyond the harm that the sin of one could cause others. Thus recourse to the communion of saints lets the contrite sinner be more promptly and efficaciously purified of the punishments for sin" (*CCC*, no. 1475). In the early centuries, a Christian who had denied the faith during persecution was required to perform a rigorous penance. Another Christian enduring imprisonment or awaiting execution could offer his sufferings on behalf of the weaker member, whose penance would be lightened or lifted altogether. Over time this mutual support found expression in the practice of the Church granting an indulgence, whereby a person could obtain for himself, or a soul in Purgatory, a lessening of the penance required to make satisfaction for sins. It is true that the practice of granting indulgences led at times to abuses, but the doctrine itself is both sound and biblical. It is simply a concrete expression of the commandment of Saint Paul: "Bear one another's burdens, and so fulfil the law of Christ" (Gal 6:2; see 1 Cor 12:26). This generous assistance ought to elicit generosity in turn: "Thus the Church does not want simply to come to the aid of these Christians, but also to spur them to works of devotion, penance, and charity." [3]

So, as members of the Body of Christ we can intercede for one another, share the reward for good works, and do penance for one another. But this sharing in spiritual goods is not limited by the horizons of this world. Even during his earthly ministry, Jesus taught that the God of Abraham, Isaac, and Jacob "is not God of the dead, but of the living; for all live to him" (Lk 20:38). It is all the more true after his Resurrection that those who have gone before us in death are alive in Christ, and we are united with them in him. The communion of saints includes those already in Heaven and those undergoing their final purification after death.

---

[3] *CCC*, no. 1478; cf. Paul VI, apostolic constitution, *Indulgentiarum doctrina*, 5.

The Saints Pray for Us

The word *saints* was used in the New Testament to describe the community of believers, those who had been sanctified by their immersion into the death and Resurrection of Christ and the reception of the Holy Spirit. In time, the term was applied in a more restricted sense to the righteous dead, especially the martyrs, who were held in veneration by the community.

The earliest description we possess of a martyr's death (aside from the biblical account in Acts of the first martyr, Saint Stephen) is that of Saint Polycarp, ca. 155. Irenaeus, who knew Polycarp, said that he had been instructed by the apostles themselves; he is one of the earliest figures after the New Testament era. The account of his execution bears witness to devotion to the saints very early in the life of the Church. The *Martyrdom of Polycarp* distinguishes this veneration from adoration, which is given to God alone: "We worship Christ as God's Son; we love the martyrs as the Lord's disciples and imitators, and rightly so because of their matchless devotion towards their king and master." [4] The account also refers to the day of Polycarp's martyrdom as his "birthday" and mentions that the community commemorated the anniversary of his death by celebrating the Eucharist, a practice recorded by early writers such as Tertullian and Cyprian as well. Finally, the *Martyrdom* describes the honor accorded to Polycarp's relics by the community:

> And so, afterwards, we took up his bones, more valuable than precious stones and finer than gold, and put them in a proper place. There, as far as we are able, the Lord will permit us to meet together ... to celebrate the birthday of his martyrdom, both in memory of those who fought the fight and for the training and preparation of those who will fight. [5]

The early Christians did not only honor the saints; they sought their prayers. (Properly speaking, we do not pray *to* the saints, but ask the saints to pray for us.) Inscriptions on Christian graves and

---

[4] *Martyrium Polycarpi*, 17: *Apostolic Fathers* II/3, 396, quoted in *CCC*, no. 957.

[5] *The Martyrdom of Polycarp*, chap. 18, trans. Francis Glimm, in *The Apostolic Fathers: A New Translation*, ed. Francis Glimm, Joseph Marique, and Gerald Walsh (New York: Cima Publishing Co., 1947), p. 160.

writings of the Fathers testify to the antiquity of the practice of invoking the intercession of the saints. Following the era of persecution, impressive shrines were raised over the tombs of martyrs, which became the goal of pilgrimages. Devotion to the saints continued to grow throughout the Middle Ages, nourished by vivid stories of their lives and by miracles granted by God through their intercession. Along with official liturgical commemoration, expressions of love for the saints were shaped by popular piety, and Church leaders sought—not always with success—to root out superstitious practices in connection with the saints and their relics. The Council of Trent defended the legitimacy of the veneration of the saints in response to Protestant condemnations of the practice, while exhorting pastors to oppose any superstition connected with the invocation of the saints and the veneration of their relics and images. The Second Vatican Council has reiterated the importance of the intercession of the saints:

> For by reason of the fact that those in heaven are more closely united with Christ, they establish the whole Church more firmly in holiness, lend nobility to the worship which the Church offers to God here on earth and in many ways contribute to its greater edification. For after they have been received into their heavenly home and are present to the Lord, through Him and with Him and in Him they do not cease to intercede with the Father for us, showing forth the merits which they won on earth through the one Mediator between God and man.... Thus by their brotherly interest our weakness is greatly strengthened. (*LG*, no. 49)

We Pray for Those Who Have Died

Heroic sanctity was no more common in the first centuries of the Church than it is today, so the early Christians also prayed *for* their deceased friends and relatives. Prayer for the dead is mentioned in the Old Testament: the Second Book of Maccabees relates that Judas Maccabeus offered sacrifice to atone for the sins of his slain soldiers (2 Macc 12:39–45). As we saw in chapter seven above, it is unclear what canonical status this book held in the first century, but at the very least it suggests that the practice of praying for the dead was known in Jewish circles at the time of Jesus. The Christian understanding is that our eternal destiny is determined at the end of earthly life—"It is appointed for men to die once, and after that comes judgment" (Heb 9:27)—but there are hints in the New Testament of the possibility for some kind of repentance after death. For example, there is Paul's enigmatic reference to baptism on behalf of the dead (1 Cor 15:29), an allusion to Christ preaching among the souls of the ancestors in prison (1 Pet 3:19), and his teaching that blasphemy against the Holy Spirit will not be forgiven "either in this age or in the age to come" (Mt 12:32), which implies that some sins *will* be forgiven in the age to come.

The writings of Fathers, inscriptions in catacombs, and ancient liturgical texts testify that the early Christians prayed for the dead. Tertullian held that, although there was no explicit scriptural directive, the custom went back to the apostles. It is not clear how our ancestors thought their prayers benefited the faithful departed, but the practice assumes some kind of interim state or condition after death for those who have been saved but who must still undergo some kind of purification. Eastern Christianity has always encouraged prayers for the dead, but has tended to avoid extensive speculation regarding the nature of this interim state.

Purgatory

The West manifested greater curiosity about this matter, and by the end of the Middle Ages, the doctrine of Purgatory played an important role in Catholic life. In the wake of Saint Augustine's conflict with Pelagianism, Western Christianity emphasized the healing power of grace and the need to undo the effects of sin. This preoccupation with sin and repentance extended to the next world: if someone died with his sins forgiven, but with the effects of sin not yet removed by penance, how was the healing completed? A favored biblical image was that of purifying fire. Along with scriptural references to metals cleansed by fire, a specific reference in Saint Paul was also appealed to: "Now if any one builds on the foundation with gold, silver, precious stones, wood, hay, straw—each man's work will become manifest; for the Day will disclose it, because it will be revealed with fire.... If any man's work is burned up, he will suffer loss, though he himself will be saved, but only as through fire" (1 Cor 3:12–15). The great Latin

Doctors—Ambrose, Augustine, Jerome, and Gregory—all applied this text to the purification of the just after death.[6]

Over time, the desire to assist the faithful departed grew. The feast of All Souls was established in the tenth century, an annual commemoration for the dead. In addition, prayers and Masses were offered to ease the sufferings of the souls in Purgatory. The nature of those sufferings was the subject of much speculation, from crude images of torture to the sublime insights of Dante's *Divine Comedy*. The situation of these souls was viewed with ambivalence: on the one hand, it was commonly thought that the least suffering in Purgatory was greater than any earthly pain; on the other hand, the "holy souls" were joyful because their salvation was assured, and they welcomed the purification that prepared them to enter the all-holy presence of God.

The Protestant Reformers initially objected to superstitious practices and greed connected with the doctrine of Purgatory, and eventually rejected the doctrine itself. They opposed the practice of praying for the dead: those in Heaven had no need for our prayers, and those in Hell could not be helped by them. Given the vehemence of the Reformers' condemnation of Purgatory, and its prominence in the popular piety of the time, the teaching of the Council of Trent on this doctrine is notable for its sobriety. The council simply stated "that purgatory exists, and that the souls detained there are helped by the prayers of the faithful and most of all by the acceptable sacrifice of the altar."[7] The decree then cautions pastors to avoid difficult and subtle questions and needless speculation regarding the doctrine. Trent's treatment of Purgatory illustrates how important it is to distinguish the defined teaching of the Church from popular expressions of that teaching. However individual Catholics choose to picture the condition of

---

[6] In the third century, Origen had used the image of purifying fire in connection with a doctrine that every creature, including Satan, would ultimately be saved after a purification by fire—in effect, that there is a Purgatory, but no Hell. This idea was condemned by the Second Council of Constantinople (553). When the Greeks and Latins discussed Purgatory at the reunion Councils of Lyons and Florence, the Greeks feared that the condemned doctrine was lurking beneath the language of "purifying fire". In deference to their concerns, the idea of purifying fire has never been defined as essential to the doctrine of Purgatory.

[7] Council of Trent, "Decree on Purgatory", trans. Norman Tanner, *Decrees of the Ecumenical Councils*, vol. 2 (Washington, D.C.: Sheed & Ward and Georgetown University Press, 1990), p. 774.

the faithful departed, all that we are required to believe is that there is some kind of purification after death, and that our prayers and especially the offering of the Eucharist can assist those experiencing it. This is what Christians believed in the second century, and it is what Orthodox and Catholic Christians have professed ever since.

Implications

The communion of the saints proclaims that love is stronger than death and that our union with Christ connects us to all the members of his Body. Our awareness of this bond with the saints and the faithful departed is not as strong today as it was formerly. Some Catholics have the wrong impression that the Second Vatican Council "got rid of" Purgatory.[8] In fact, the council taught the doctrine explicitly (see LG, nos. 49–51); more fundamentally, prayer for the dead remains an integral part of Catholic life. We assist the dying with prayers, and we intercede for them in our funeral liturgy; we pray for our departed loved ones and offer the sacrifice of the Mass for them, especially on the anniversary of their deaths; in every Mass, we pray for all the faithful departed.

Our Need of Final Purification

We do not give much thought to Purgatory because, truth to tell, we do not think much about Heaven or Hell, either; the attractions and cares of this world crowd out awareness of the world to come. It is also true that many people today have an attenuated sense of the

---

[8] A word might be said here about Limbo. On the basis of Christ's teaching that one must be born again of water and the Holy Spirit to enter into the Kingdom of God (Jn 3:5), Saint Augustine and others concluded that an unbaptized child was damned. Great though his prestige was, some theologians found Augustine's teaching too harsh. They proposed that infants who died without baptism, while not being admitted to Heaven, enjoy a state of natural happiness forever. This condition was known as Limbo, derived from the Latin word for *threshold*. This doctrine has never been defined as Church teaching. The *Catechism* does not refer to Limbo, but simply states: "The Church does not know of any means other than Baptism that assures entry into eternal beatitude; this is why she takes care not to neglect the mission she has received from the Lord to see that all who can be baptized are 'reborn of water and the Spirit.' *God has bound salvation to the sacrament of Baptism, but he himself is not by bound by his sacraments*" (*CCC*, no. 1257); and, "As regards *children who have died without Baptism*, the Church can only entrust them to the mercy of God, as she does in her funeral rites for them" (*CCC*, no. 1261; italics in original).

corrosive effect sin has on us. There are two images for each of us: the person God created us to be, and the person we have made ourselves. We will be truly happy only when these two images are the same, and this demands that we root out the reserves of self-centeredness and petty pride that our sinful choices have left in our character. It is not a question of being forgiven—God bestows his mercy freely—but it is about becoming the free, generous, and holy persons God created us to be. It takes effort to keep in shape physically; similarly, spiritual health demands the regimen of penance. Any virtue or talent can be developed only with practice, discipline, and effort. If this is true for earthly well-being, why should it not be the case with spiritual health? The purification of penance must happen here or hereafter.

Some people reject the dogma of Purgatory because they are uncomfortable with the idea of a "punishing" God. And yet Catholic tradition holds that the souls in Purgatory *welcome* their purification because they know they need it. This was one of the principal themes of Dante's *Divine Comedy*. He depicted the inhabitants of Hell as unrepentant, resentful people who continually justify their selfish behavior; those in Purgatory, in contrast, rejoice to do penance because they know this is the way to spiritual wholeness. We know nothing about the condition of souls in the next life and, consequently, nothing of the nature of what "suffering" means for them. But it is commonly held that the greatest affliction of the souls in Purgatory is their temporary separation from God. Saint Catherine of Genoa (d. 1510) began her description of the souls in Purgatory this way:

> These souls cannot think, "I am here, and justly so because of my sins," or "I wish I had never committed such sins for now I would be in paradise," or "That person there is leaving before me," or "I will leave before that other one." They cannot remember the good and evil in their past nor that of others. Such is their joy in God's will, in His pleasure, that they have no concern for themselves but dwell only on their joy in God's ordinance, in having Him do what He will. They see only the goodness of God, His mercy toward men.[9]

In the Letter to the Hebrews, the apostle exhorted the first Christians: "Let us also lay aside every weight, and sin which clings so closely,

---

[9] Catherine of Genoa, *Purgation and Purgatory; The Spiritual Dialogue*, trans. Serge Hughes (New York: Paulist Press, 1979), p. 71.

and let us run with perseverance the race that is set before us" (Heb 12:1). That is a good description of discipleship: to strip away anything and everything that separates us from God. Some heroic souls manage to do this in the course of their earthly life; most of us go to our grave with some of that race still to be run. It is comforting to know that, just as we can help one another during our earthly contest, so we also can assist the dead on the final lap of their race.

The idea that suffering can purify us must be embraced with prudence. It is both a false and a harmful docility to meet every affliction with the advice to "offer it up": there *are* wrongs that can be righted, and Christians have a duty to oppose injustice. But even with our best efforts, this world will always be an imperfect place, and some misfortunes are both unfair and unavoidable. These sufferings, meaningless and even evil in themselves, can be transformed into expressions of love when we, like Saint Paul, bear them for the sake of Christ's Body, the Church. At the heart of Christianity stands the Passion and death of the most innocent man in human history, willingly embraced by him out of love. We are not innocent, but by offering our sufferings for others, we follow, in our own limited and imperfect way, the example of Christ.

The Saints Help Us, and We Honor Them

As we can assist the faithful departed with our prayers, so we can also be helped by the prayers of those who have finished their race. The Letter to the Hebrews describes the saints as a cloud of witnesses surrounding us, filling the stands and cheering us on (Heb 12:1). To ask their prayers is no slight to God, because it is their intimacy with him that makes their intercession so powerful. Can we not pray to God directly? Of course we can, and we do—almost all of the prayers in the Catholic liturgy are addressed to the Father through Christ our Lord. Christ is the one Mediator between the Father and us, but often he exercises that mediation through the members of his Body. The glorified Christ met Paul on the road to Damascus, and, had he wished to, he could have shown himself in the same way to others. Instead, he entrusted the preaching of the Gospel to his disciples. Paul himself was very conscious of his role as a mediator of Christ: "So we are ambassadors for Christ, God making his appeal through us" (2 Cor 5:20).

The saints are effective mediators because they are close to God and to us. They are like the four men who were so anxious to bring their paralyzed friend to Jesus that they lowered him down through the roof on his bed. We are told, "And when Jesus saw their faith, he said to the paralytic, 'Child, your sins are forgiven' " (Mk 2:5). It was in response to *their* faith that Jesus forgave the man's sins and healed him. When we ask other people to pray for us, it is not because we think God prefers them to us. But we believe the prayers of others help, and the more so the closer they are to God. How could those who are with him now in Heaven *not* help us by their prayers?

Many Protestants find one aspect of the Catholic and Orthodox devotion to the saints particularly disturbing: the veneration of their images and relics. We all treasure pictures or keepsakes of loved ones from whom we are separated, and this holds true for the saints. Is such reverence idolatry? No: we know very well that the saints are only human, so we do not worship them; and the honor we show to their icons and statues is directed to the person, not the image itself. Their images in our churches and homes remind us that Christ has broken the reign of death, and that the saints are alive in him. The Second Council of Nicaea taught:

> We rightly define with full certainty and correctness that, like the figure of the precious and life-giving cross, venerable and holy images of our Lord and God and Savior, Jesus Christ, our inviolate Lady, the holy Mother of God, and the venerated angels, all the saints and the just . . . are to be exhibited in the holy churches of God, on sacred vessels and vestments, walls and panels, in houses and on streets.[10]

Can such practices give rise to superstition? Certainly, but it is not easy to distinguish faith from superstition, especially when judging the behavior of others. A sick woman believed that if she merely touched the hem of Jesus' garment, she would be healed (Mt 9:20-21). People carried their sick into the street to be healed by Peter's shadow, and handkerchiefs that had touched Paul's body were laid on the sick (Acts 5:15; 19:12). Superstition, or confidence in the power of God? It is very easy to misjudge the motivations of others. We would do

---

[10] Council of Nicaea II (787): DS 600, quoted in *CCC*, no. 1161.

well to heed the advice of Saint Ignatius Loyola that we ought to be more ready to put a good interpretation on another's position rather than to condemn it as false (*Spiritual Exercises*, no. 22).

The saints do not only help us with their prayers—they challenge us by their example. Saint Francis de Sales suggested that the lives of the saints are to the Gospel what the concert is to the sheet music: we learn what the teaching of Christ means in practice from observing the friends of God. When we are tempted to be content with mediocrity, to settle for the lowest common denominator, the saints raise our sights and spur us on to greater generosity. Holy friends help us become holy. There are saints to suit every taste, and the varied forms that holiness has taken over the past two thousand years is like a prism refracting the white light of God's love into a rainbow of colors. That divine light is too bright in itself for our mortal eyes, but we can look upon it filtered through the lives of heroic disciples.

Angels

We include angels in the communion of saints because, although their nature is different from ours, they are part of the same spiritual creation and have been created, like us, to enjoy the vision of God. Angels are pure spirits possessing an intellect to know God and a will to love him. Much of our knowledge about them is speculative; we can only imagine what life would be like if our intellect and will were unhampered by the limitations of a material body. Angels appear all through Scripture, and they perform various functions: worshipping God, acting as his messengers, battling evil spirits, and manifesting God's love and protection toward men. Their mission continues today as we unite with them in worship, seek their assistance in our struggle against evil, and rejoice in their protection. Although angels are superior to us by nature, we are their companions because Christ is the Lord of all creation, seen and unseen:

> He is the image of the invisible God, the first-born of all creation; for in him all things were created, in heaven and on earth, visible and invisible, whether thrones or dominions or principalities or authorities—all things were created through him and for him. He is before all things, and in him all things hold together. (Col 1:15–17)

"In him all things hold together": just as God has entrusted the care of the earth to us, so he has entrusted us to the stewardship of the angels. The idea of angelic protection is attested to in both the Old Testament and the New, and belief in "guardian angels" is ancient. Commenting on the words of Jesus, "See that you do not despise one of these little ones; for I tell you that in heaven their angels always behold the face of my Father who is in heaven" (Mt 18:10), Saint Jerome wrote: "So great is the dignity of souls that each of them has an angel assigned to it from the moment of its birth to protect it." [11]

While on the subject of angels, I should say a word about devils. Our modern culture is of two minds on this topic: on the one hand, a sophisticated, secular worldview dismisses the idea of devils as nonsense; on the other hand, there is a tremendous fascination with the power of evil. (The film *The Exorcist* is often rated the scariest movie of all time.) The Catholic understanding of Satan and the other fallen angels is as follows: (1) they were created good but became evil by their own choice; (2) their rejection of God was radical and irrevocable; they cannot repent; and (3) because they are creatures, their power, unlike God's, is limited (*CCC*, nos. 391–95). Opposition to Satan is at the heart of Jesus' mission: "The reason the Son of God appeared was to destroy the works of the devil" (1 Jn 3:8). One of the great contributions of C. S. Lewis in the field of Christian apologetics was his ability to communicate the malice and cleverness of the fallen angels, who are far superior to us in intellect.

We have considered various parts of the communion of saints: the earthly community of believers on pilgrimage, the departed souls completing their purification, the saints and angels in Heaven. God's saving work sanctifies the whole of creation and unites everything seen and unseen into a communion of love. We hope to share one day in the glory of the vision of God, but we are already one with the saints and angels in charity. Since we are creatures of time and space, Heaven seems to be "the world to come", but in Christ that glorious future is already present to us in some way. As Saint Paul exhorted the Philippians, "If then you have been raised with Christ, seek the things that are above, where Christ is, seated at the right hand of God. Set

---

[11] St. Jerome, *Com. in Matt.*, 18, 2: *PL* 26, 130. See *CCC*, no. 336 for a similar teaching by St. Basil the Great.

your minds on things that are above, not on things that are on earth. For you have died, and your life is hidden with Christ in God" (Col 3:1–3).

The Future Church Is Already Present

Thinking about the Church in glory reveals something unique about the spiritual dynamism that energizes the Body of Christ. We can view the mystery of the Church from the perspective of history: the call of Abraham, the saga of the patriarchs, the drama of Exodus and Exile, the coming of the Son of God in the fullness of time, the commissioning of the disciples to carry the Good News to all creation. Seen from this angle, God's love flows to us from the past; history is the conduit of divine life. But when we seek "the things that are above", we become aware that there is also an energy attracting us from the future. The pilgrim Church on earth and the souls in Purgatory are being drawn into the communion of saints that even now rejoices around the heavenly throne. Within history, the apostles scattered to preach the Gospel to the ends of the earth; beyond history, the apostles are reunited around their Master. Jesus promised them at the Last Supper: "You are those who have continued with me in my trials; as my Father appointed a kingdom for me, so do I appoint for you that you may eat and drink at my table in my kingdom, and sit on thrones judging the twelve tribes of Israel" (Lk 22:28–30). The communion of saints celebrates the reality that the Church is both *in* history and *beyond* history, still on pilgrimage and already home.

Christ described the apostles gathered around him as being in the Kingdom while he sat with them at the Last Supper. The Eucharistic celebration provides our most intense experience of the communion of saints on this side of the grave. Each congregation gathered around its altar is united sacramentally with all the other communities of their local church and with the Church all over the world. But the catholicity of communion is temporal as well as geographical. The Eucharist reaches back through history because it is the Lord's Supper made present in our midst. That meal has been bound forever by Jesus to his one perfect sacrifice, which fulfilled every offering back through time to Abel. The saving blood and water have flowed from the pierced side of Christ down through the centuries, nourishing the martyrs and saints, and that stream of Christ's love flows into our Eucharistic celebration. But the Mass lifts our gaze beyond history as well. The Eucharistic liturgy is the first course of a banquet that will never end. In the words of the Second Vatican Council:

> In the earthly liturgy we take part in a foretaste of that heavenly liturgy which is celebrated in the holy city of Jerusalem toward which we journey as pilgrims, where Christ is sitting at the right hand of God, a minister of the sanctuary and of the true tabernacle; we sing a hymn to the Lord's glory with all the warriors of the heavenly army; venerating the memory of the saints, we hope for some part and fellowship with them; we eagerly await the Saviour, Our Lord Jesus Christ, until He, our life, shall appear and we too will appear with Him in glory. (SC, no. 8)

The story of salvation history began with the creation of Adam and Eve, and it concludes with the marriage of the Lamb and his Bride, the Church. The words of the angel announcing those nuptials are proclaimed by the priest just before we come forward to receive Holy Communion: "Blessed are those who are invited to the marriage supper of the Lamb" (Rev 19:9).

The "holy communion" that makes us one *with* Christ makes us one *in* Christ: like the spokes of a wheel, the closer we come to the center, the closer we come to one another. For this reason, the greatest impetus to Christian unity comes from holy lives. Theological agreements are important, common charitable activities are beneficial, but various Christian denominations will draw closer together the more their members draw close to Christ. The saints and the faithful departed are near to us because they are so close to him. Paradoxically, it is the saint closest to Christ, and therefore nearest to us, whose place in the communion of saints is most problematic for many Protestants: Mary, the Mother of Jesus. What do we Catholics believe about her?

Chapter Twelve

Mary, Virgin and Mother

Devotion to Mary is a characteristic element of Catholic life, but it is a stumbling block for many Protestants. She has inspired more great art than any other woman in history, but the very splendor of these works is disquieting to those who fear idolatry. Nor is this concern limited to Protestants. Love for the Mother of Jesus arises spontaneously among the faithful, and at times Church leaders have had to defend doctrinal truths while reining in exuberant expressions of popular piety. Even bishops disagree: one of the most heated debates at the Second Vatican Council concerned the question of whether to issue a separate document about Mary, or to include what the fathers wanted to say about her in the Dogmatic Constitution on the Church.

Given the strong emotions Mary provokes, it is important for us to distinguish between doctrine and piety. Although Marian devotions are a part of Catholic spirituality, the Church allows her children great liberty in their regard. For example, since Marian apparitions are instances of private revelation, no Catholic is bound to accept them. On the doctrinal level, the Catholic Church affirms four dogmas about Mary: she remained a virgin her whole life; she is the Mother of God; she was preserved from original sin; at the end of her life, she was taken up body and soul to Heaven. These are not simply biographical details; because these are *dogmatic* truths, they pertain to the Gospel, the saving truth entrusted to the Church. In order to understand their significance, we must bear in mind that what the Church teaches about Mary is to be understood in terms of her relationship to her Son and to the Church. These teachings developed at different times over the past two thousand years, so we will examine them in turn in this chapter and the next, beginning with Mary's virginity.

Mary's Virginity: What We Believe

Mary conceived and gave birth to Jesus as a virgin, and she remained so after his birth. This dogma is known as the "perpetual virginity of Mary".

Some History

At the outset, it might be helpful to distinguish three terms that often get confused: *virginal conception* means that Mary conceived Jesus miraculously while remaining a virgin; *virgin birth* means that Mary remained a virgin in giving birth to Jesus; and *Immaculate Conception* (that is, the conception of Mary within *her* mother) means that, although she was conceived in the normal way, Mary was preserved from original sin.

The Gospels of Matthew and Luke both testify to the virginal conception of Jesus. At the beginning of his Gospel, Matthew provides a genealogy for Jesus, "the son of David, the son of Abraham". He lists three sets of fourteen generations, from father to son, but at the end, when the reader would logically expect Matthew to conclude, "and Joseph the father of Jesus", he does not; rather, he writes, ". . . and Jacob the father of Joseph the husband of Mary, of whom Jesus was born, who is called Christ" (Mt 1:16). He then says that before Joseph and Mary had come together she was found to be with child. In a dream, an angel revealed to Joseph that "that which is conceived in her is of the Holy Spirit" (Mt 1:20). Matthew then adds, "All this took place to fulfil what the Lord had spoken by the prophet: 'Behold, a virgin shall conceive and bear a son, and his name shall be called Emmanuel' (which means, God with us)" (Mt 1:22–23). For Matthew, Joseph is Jesus' father in a legal sense, which is why Jesus can be described as "Son of David". But he is not the father of Jesus in a biological sense: Mary has conceived her child by the Holy Spirit, so that he is "Son of God", a title used of Jesus ten times in this Gospel. Matthew sees the virginal conception of Mary's child as the fulfillment of a prophecy in Isaiah.[1]

---

[1] As far back as the second century, the objection was raised that, in the Hebrew, Isaiah 7:14 reads *a young girl* will conceive, which the Septuagint translated by the Greek word for *virgin*. In its original context, the "sign" spoken of by Isaiah did not refer to the manner of the child's conception, but to the fact that a child was about to be born who would manifest in some way God's providential care for his people. Matthew's citation of Isaiah

Luke's infancy narrative describes Jesus' conception from Mary's point of view. Twice he refers to her as "virgin", and, when she asks how it is possible for her to conceive since she has not had relations with any man, the angel answers, "The Holy Spirit will come upon you, and the power of the Most High will overshadow you; therefore the child to be born will be called holy, the Son of God" (Lk 1:35). This is a unique event in salvation history: Scripture relates several instances of conceptions that were wondrous because the woman was past child-bearing years (from Sarah to Mary's relative Elizabeth), but never a woman who conceived as a virgin. Thus the Gospels present two independent traditions about the origins of Jesus that agree on several points: Jesus did not have a human father; Mary conceived through the power of the Holy Spirit; and for this reason, Jesus can be called the Son of God.

The early Christians faced opposition to the idea of Jesus' virginal conception on three fronts: those who believed that Jesus was only human, the natural son of Joseph and Mary; those who rejected the idea of any kind of conception, because they believed that Jesus was a purely divine being; and those who thought that such a claim turned Jesus into a demigod, like the offspring of gods and mortals in Greek mythology. Ignatius of Antioch emphasized that Jesus was truly born, he truly died, and he truly rose again. But while defending the true humanity of Jesus, Ignatius several times referred to his being born of a virgin, and he wrote that this was a profound spiritual reality: "Mary's virginity and giving birth, and even the Lord's death escaped the notice of the prince of this world: these three mysteries worthy of proclamation were accomplished in God's silence."[2] The early Christians held the pagan myths to be both ridiculous and repugnant, and they pointed out that there is no suggestion in the Gospels of the Holy

---

suggests a very early Christian interpretation of the verse. Matthew did not believe in the virginal conception of Jesus on the basis of the prophecy of Isaiah; a conviction of this truth existed in Christian circles before he wrote his Gospel. Matthew finds the citation apt because it bears witness to a fundamental theme in his infancy narrative: Jesus is both Son of David and Son of God. The virginal conception was not an assertion invented to fulfill a prophecy; it was an event that revealed that this Old Testament passage was prophetic.

[2] St. Ignatius of Antioch, *Ad Eph.* 19, 1: *The Apostolic Fathers*, ed. J.B. Lightfoot (New York: Macmillan, 1889–1890), II/2, 76–80; *Sources Chrétiennes* (Paris, 1942–), 10, 88, quoted in *CCC*, no. 498. Cf. 1 Cor 2:8.

Spirit assuming a human form and impregnating Mary.[3] As we saw in chapter three, it took centuries for the Church to craft a vocabulary expressive of her faith that Christ is truly God and truly man; the next section of this chapter will examine Mary's place in that development. But the biblical accounts of the virginal conception contributed to the understanding that Jesus was both human and divine.

A more developed theological reflection on Mary's role in the work of redemption emerged in the second century, especially in the writings of Justin and Irenaeus, who spoke of Mary as the "New Eve". Saint Paul had described Christ as the New Adam; just as Adam's Fall had been prepared for by Eve's disobedience, so Mary prepared the way for Christ. In the words of Saint Irenaeus: "The knot of Eve's disobedience was untied by Mary's obedience: what the virgin Eve bound through her disbelief, Mary loosened by her faith."[4] God has brought about a new creation in Christ, and this new creation was reflected in an intuition that Jesus' birth was also remarkable in some way. Finally, since Mary's virginity manifested her utter dedication to God's will, it was also held that she remained a virgin after the birth of her Son. These ideas appear in the second-century *Protoevangelium of James*, one of the earliest New Testament apocrypha. The Church does not base her doctrinal teachings on the apocryphal Gospels, but what the *Protoevangelium* demonstrates is that ideas about the virgin birth and Mary's lifelong virginity were circulating in Christian communities immediately after the New Testament era. The early Fathers were divided on the idea of the virgin birth. Some feared that to speak of Mary giving birth as a virgin threatened the doctrine that Jesus was truly born as man; however, others argued that "the sign" spoken of by Isaiah was that a virgin would conceive and a virgin would give birth—why, if the first had happened, could not the second have?

Mary's virginity after the birth of Jesus was seen as an expression of her discipleship. In the third century, Origen proposed Jesus and Mary as models for male and female virgins, respectively. As the ascetical and monastic movements grew more widespread in the Church, interest in the virginal examples of Jesus and Mary increased. Some opposed

---

[3] We do not ascribe gender to God, but it is noteworthy vis-à-vis pagan myths that the conception of Jesus is not attributed to God the Father, but to the Spirit, a word that is feminine in Hebrew and neuter in Greek.

[4] St. Irenaeus, *Adversus haereses*, 3, 22, 4: PG 7/1, 959A, quoted in *CCC*, no. 494.

the idea of Mary's perpetual virginity, but great Fathers of East and West—Athanasius, Epiphanius, Basil, Ambrose, Augustine, Jerome, and others—all vigorously defended the doctrine. As Saint Augustine preached in one of his sermons, Mary "remained a virgin in conceiving her Son, a virgin in giving birth to him ... always a virgin".[5] These Fathers asserted Mary's lifelong virginity even as they defended the goodness of marriage against Gnostic claims that the material world was evil. By the sixth century, the doctrine of Mary's perpetual virginity was universally accepted, and in creeds and prayers of both East and West, she was frequently described as "ever virgin". The perpetual virginity of Mary has never been explicitly defined, but it is accepted as dogmatic teaching by the Orthodox and Catholic churches. The principal Protestant Reformers—Luther, Zwingli, and Calvin—believed in Mary's perpetual virginity, but subsequently Protestantism has by and large denied the doctrine.[6]

Implications

The subject of virginity prompts mixed emotions. The mystery of the Incarnation stands at the heart of Christianity, and Catholicism is a very sacramental, bodily religion. At the same time, since its beginning, Christianity has been haunted by the specter of dualism, a philosophical outlook that disparages material reality. Even while opposing dualism, the Church has been influenced by it, and for some people, the doctrine of Mary's virginity is simply an example of the Catholic Church's uneasiness about the sexual realities of life. Add to this the idea of ritual purity found in some religions, the double standard in

---

[5] St. Augustine, *Sermones*, 186, 1: *PL* 38, 999, quoted in *CCC*, no. 510.

[6] There are some notable exceptions. For example, John Wesley, the founder of Methodism, professed belief in Mary's perpetual virginity. The general abandonment of this doctrine in Protestantism can be explained in part by the rejection of religious life in the wake of the Reformation, but the principal scriptural objection is the references to the brothers and sisters of Jesus in the Gospels. The alternative explanations to the obvious meaning of these words are that they refer to relatives of Jesus, but not siblings (there being no other word for *cousin* in Greek, the word for *brother* was used for this relation as well), or to Joseph's children from a previous marriage. Whether these explanations are persuasive will depend on one's presuppositions, but certainly Origen, Jerome, Athanasius, Ambrose, Augustine, and many other great Fathers (and Luther and Calvin!) were aware of the passages referring to the brothers and sisters of Jesus, yet did not find that they created an obstacle to professing Mary's perpetual virginity.

many cultures that demands chastity from women, but not from men, and the Augustinian notion (not espoused by the Church, but influential for many centuries nonetheless) that original sin is connected with sexual pleasure, and it is understandable that many prefer to ignore this particular dogma. Virginity is not prized in a culture that exalts sexual "liberation". Contemporary society almost treats virginity as a childhood disease, with the presumption that its loss is essential to maturity. In the past, virginity was admired, although that admiration was often accompanied by a dose of hypocrisy; today it is often ridiculed.

Our cultural context makes it difficult for us to approach the dogma of Mary's virginity dispassionately. With that caveat in mind, I return to the basic principle stated at the outset of this chapter: the dogmatic teachings about Mary must be understood in terms of their theological meaning. What does it say about Christ and about us when the Church teaches that Mary conceived her Son as a virgin, gave birth to him as a virgin, and remained a virgin after his birth?

Mary's Virginal Conception of Jesus

The fundamental import of Jesus' virginal conception is that Mary's Son is truly a man like us, and he is also the Son of God incarnate. This idea will be explored in the next section, on the dogma of Mary as the Mother of God. The conviction that Jesus' conception proclaims his unique identity has been professed since the New Testament. A more recent, post-Enlightenment question has arisen: Do the infancy narratives describe historic events, or are they legends invented to express a belief about who Jesus is? The infancy narratives are a genre distinct from the rest of the Gospels, more charged with symbolism than the accounts of Jesus' ministry and death. But they also are unlike the apocryphal Gospels, which are replete with fantastic details. To claim that these narratives are simply historical reports ignores the fact that, while grounded in history, the Gospels are proclamations of Christian faith. On the other hand, to dismiss them as fiction because "miracles cannot happen" is to allow an a priori prejudice to skew our reading of the biblical text. Matthew and Luke clearly believed the virginal conception really took place. However, their primary interest was in the theological truth it proclaimed: Jesus is truly man, born of a woman, and he is also truly the Son of God.

What does Mary's virginal conception mean for us? In one sense, the event is utterly unique: of the billions of women who have ever lived, only Mary was privileged to give birth to the incarnate Son of God. And yet, we see Mary as a model of discipleship; it is possible for us to share in her prerogative in some way. Christ himself suggested how when a woman praised his Mother, "Blessed is the womb that bore you, and the breasts that you sucked!" he responded, "Blessed rather are those who hear the word of God and keep it!" (Lk 11:27–28). Jesus was not rejecting praise for his Mother, but indicating that Mary's faith is even more praiseworthy than her maternity. In fact, it was because she heard the word with such faith that the Word became flesh. The Fathers of the Church were fond of saying that Mary conceived in her heart before she conceived in her womb; Augustine went so far as to say, "Mary is more blessed because she embraces faith in Christ than because she conceives the flesh of Christ."[7] As the one who conceived Christ in the flesh, Mary stands alone; as one who embodies faith in Christ, she is an example worthy not only of honor, but also of imitation.

The Virgin Birth

In regard to the virginal birth of Jesus, the Church simply affirms *that* Mary retained her virginity when she gave birth, without determining how this is to be understood physiologically. The Second Vatican Council demonstrated an admirable reserve in its articulation of this dogma: Christ's birth "did not diminish His mother's virginal integrity but sanctified it" (*LG*, no. 57).[8] For the Fathers of the Church, Jesus' wondrous birth was connected to other mysteries of his life. Some related it to the Resurrection, when Christ was able to pass through the sealed tomb and locked doors; for others, the virginal birth of the Son in time was a created reflection of his ineffable birth from the Father in eternity. As the New Adam, Christ proclaimed the new creation by his birth; as the

---

[7] St. Augustine, *De sancta virginitate*, 3: *PL* 40, 398, quoted in *CCC*, no. 506.

[8] The council references the Lateran Council (649), the *Tome* of Leo the Great, the Council of Chalcedon, and the writings of Saint Ambrose. The words used in *Lumen Gentium* are taken from a seventh-century liturgical text, the Prayer over the Gifts for the feast of the Nativity of Mary, which is still used: "he, who at his birth from the Blessed Virgin did not diminish but consecrated her integrity".

New Eve, Mary was exempt from the pains of childbearing that resulted from the disobedience of our first parents.

If the Fathers saw the virgin birth as an earthly reflection of the Son's eternal generation from the Father, it was also an image of Christ's wondrous birth in the believer by faith and baptism. Only once in human history did the Son of God literally assume a human nature as his own, a nature drawn from the flesh of Mary. But in a spiritual sense, Christ "takes on" the humanity of each believer and comes to birth in each of us. Saint Paul compared his apostolic efforts to a woman in labor: "My little children, with whom I am again in travail until Christ be formed in you!" (Gal 4:19). The same Holy Spirit who made Mary a mother while she remained a virgin descended upon the disciples at Pentecost to make the Church fruitful with new "christs". For this reason, the Second Vatican Council presents Mary as an image of the Church as Virgin Mother, barren and useless in the estimation of worldly wisdom, but life-bearing by virtue of God's grace: "By receiving the word of God in faith [the Church] becomes herself a mother. By her preaching she brings forth to a new and immortal life the sons who are born to her in baptism, conceived of the Holy Spirit and born of God. She herself is a virgin, who keeps the faith given to her by her Spouse whole and entire" (*LG*, no. 64). The virgin birth of Jesus happened only once in history, but it takes place mystically in every baptism.

Virginity and Discipleship

All Christian denominations with a tradition of monasticism affirm that Mary remained a virgin after the birth of her Son, whereas Protestants generally reject it. So, did Mary's example give rise to a virginal way of life in the early Church, or did a virginal way of life give rise to the idea of Mary's lifelong virginity? Rather than attempting to answer this question with the limited data available from the early centuries of the Church, I would like to begin with the life and teaching of Jesus. This must be primary, because what Mary has to teach us only has value in connection with the Gospel.

Marriage has been central to the culture and religion of the Jewish people throughout its history; one is born into the chosen people. In biblical times, children were seen as a blessing from God, and barrenness was a source of shame. As in many traditional cultures, virginity before marriage was valued; also, temporary abstention from conjugal relations was practiced as a means of purification by priests serving in the Temple and by soldiers going into battle. However, lifelong virginity was not an ideal for the Jews. Jesus upheld the importance of marriage in his preaching—in fact, his prohibition of divorce went beyond the commonly held rabbinical views, indeed, beyond the Law of Moses itself.

Yet we find another thread running through the Gospels. Jesus was an itinerant preacher, and he invited some of his disciples (both men and women) to travel about with him. These disciples left behind their work, their homes, and their families to accompany Jesus. Christ taught that the claims of the Kingdom trumped the ties of family. He was impatient with those who appealed to family obligations as an excuse to decline the invitation to follow him; he proclaimed that he had come to divide families; and he went so far as to say: "If any one comes to me and does not hate his own father and mother and wife and children and brothers and sisters, yes, and even his own life, he cannot be my disciple" (Lk 14:26). In response to Jesus' firm opposition to divorce, some of his disciples said that in that case it would be better not to marry. Jesus responded, "Not all men can receive this precept, but only those to whom it is given. For there are eunuchs who have been so from birth, and there are eunuchs who have been made eunuchs by men, and there are eunuchs who have made themselves eunuchs for the sake of the kingdom of heaven. He who is able to receive this, let him receive it" (Mt 19:11–12).

Jesus did not teach that only those who set aside family ties could be his disciples. He did *not* ask everyone to leave home and family to follow him—in fact, only a small number of his followers. His basic message was that the Kingdom must have first priority, whatever a person's state in life. Most disciples were to live out their calling in the context of family, but others, as virgins, would be free to "follow the Lamb wherever he goes" (Rev 14:4) and to witness to the Kingdom, where, "in the resurrection they neither marry nor are given in marriage, but are like angels in heaven" (Mt 22:30). By word and example, Jesus upheld the ideal of virginity.[9]

---

[9] Recently, some have suggested that Jesus was married. The impression is given that ancient writings, suppressed for centuries by the Church, testify to this. This impression

The idea of lifelong virginity for the sake of the Kingdom was advocated by Saint Paul. In his First Letter to the Corinthians he writes:

> The unmarried man is anxious about the affairs of the Lord, how to please the Lord; but the married man is anxious about worldly affairs, how to please his wife, and his interests are divided. And the unmarried woman or virgin is anxious about the affairs of the Lord, how to be holy in body and spirit; but the married woman is anxious about worldly affairs, how to please her husband. I say this for your own benefit, not to lay any restraint upon you, but to promote good order and to secure your undivided devotion to the Lord. (1 Cor 7:32–35)

Of course, Paul also saw marriage as an expression of discipleship. In the Letter to the Ephesians, he describes the union of husband and wife as a profound mystery, a sacramental expression of Christ's love for the Church. This is the Epistle in which he instructs wives to be submissive to their husbands. This teaching grates on modern sensibilities, but we should not miss what is revolutionary in Paul's teaching: "Be subject to one another out of reverence for Christ" (Eph 5:21). The apostle teaches that the subjection between spouses should be *mutual*, and it is rooted in the recognition of, and service to, Christ in one's partner. Both husband and wife are called upon to imitate the sacrificial love of Christ in their relations with one another.

Two forms of discipleship emerge from the New Testament: those who express their love for Christ within the bonds of marriage and family, and those who remain unmarried (or do not marry again) in order to attend completely to the Lord. As the Church grew in the

---

has no foundation in fact: even the Gnostic Gospels do not describe Jesus as married. Some maintain that, given the cultural world of first-century Palestine, Jesus *must* have been married, and that this was so normal that it was not mentioned in the Gospels. An argument from silence proves nothing either way; indeed, the fact that it has always been assumed that Jesus was unmarried suggests that the burden of proof lies with those who make the novel claim that he was. I believe that the ancient conviction that Jesus did not marry emerged from the convergence of several factors: (1) his example—Jesus' itinerant ministry implies that he did not have family responsibilities; (2) his teaching—while honoring and defending marriage, Jesus repeatedly emphasized that the claims of the Kingdom were greater; and (3) his followers—with the exception of a few ascetical communities, lifelong virginity was not prized in the ancient world, and yet from the time of the New Testament on it appears as an approved form of Christian discipleship. This last point takes on added significance when we recall that encouraging virginity could be construed as giving ammunition to their Gnostic adversaries, and yet the early Christians still endorsed it.

early centuries, both these ways were encouraged, and they were under-
stood to be complementary, as Saint John Chrysostom makes clear:
"Whoever denigrates marriage also diminishes the glory of virginity.
Whoever praises it makes virginity more admirable and resplendent." [10]

With these two patterns of Christian life in mind, let us return to
the figure of Mary. If the heart of discipleship is union with Christ,
then it makes sense that the early Christians understood Mary to be
the disciple par excellence. She was involved at each key moment in
the mission of Christ: at his birth and throughout his childhood, obviously, but also at the beginning of his public ministry, his crucifixion,
and the birth of the Church at Pentecost. It was natural to assume that
he would be her only child since Mary's entire life was centered on
Christ.

Mary would not have loved Jesus less if he had had brothers and
sisters; good mothers love each of their children entirely, and uniquely.
Rather, her choice to have no other children is the other side of her
virginal motherhood: her maternal virginity. We must keep in mind
that Christian virginity is not tied to ritual purity or a feeling that sex
is "dirty"—virginity is valued "for the sake of the Kingdom", that is,
as an expression of a total gift of oneself to the Lord. As Jesus taught,
some are eunuchs by birth or human intervention; others make themselves such spiritually for the sake of the Kingdom. Even Saint Augustine, whom some blame for what they consider to be the Catholic
Church's preoccupation with sexual purity, taught that virginity as such
is not what matters. In his commentary on the parable of the foolish
virgins who ran out of oil for their lamps, Augustine interpreted the
oil as a symbol of charity: what the bridesmaids lacked was not virginal chastity, but charity.

If we understand virginity to be a gift of self to God, then the
virginal conception of Jesus is a remarkable manifestation of Mary's
discipleship. Her faith was so profound, her reliance on God so absolute, that the impossible happened: she conceived a child while remaining a virgin. After the birth of her Son, Mary remained a virgin because
she was the Mother of Christ. The distinctive mark of Christian charity is to see and love Christ in others. Our love for him holds the first

---

[10] St. John Chrysostom, *De virginitate*, 10, 1: *PG* 48, 540, quoted in *CCC*, no. 1620;
cf. John Paul II, *Familiaris consortio*, no. 16.

place in our lives and shapes all of our other relationships. Mary's case was unique: her Son really, literally, *was* Christ. She loved him as his Mother, but more importantly, she loved him as his disciple. Her maternal love was virginal, because it was a love dedicated totally to Christ. The doctrinal meaning of Mary's perpetual virginity is tied to the identity of her Son, and it is to that dogma that we now turn.

Mother of God: What We Believe

Because the child born of Mary is from all eternity the Son of God, she is rightly called "Mother of God" (*Theotokos*).

Some History

The dogma that Mary is the Mother of God was solemnly defined at the Council of Ephesus in the year 431. The issue at that council was not Mary, but Jesus—specifically, what it means to profess that he is both God and man. In the chapter on the Incarnation, we looked at the Church's struggle to find an adequate way (or better, the least inadequate way) to answer Jesus' question, "Who do you say that I am?" The doctrine of Mary's divine maternity emerged from that struggle.

It all started with a sermon. Sometime around the year 428, a priest named Proclus preached in the cathedral of Constantinople in the presence of the patriarch Nestorius. Several times Proclus referred to Mary as *Theotokos*, a title that had been used of her for at least a century. The Greek word is usually rendered as "Mother of God" in English, but it is a rather elusive term: literally, it means "she who gave birth to the one who is God".[11] After the sermon, Nestorius angrily criticized the title for several reasons: it seemed to equate Mary with the goddesses of pagan religion; it implied that the eternal Son of God was a creature; it suggested that Jesus was not truly man. Proclus appealed to

---

[11] The word was difficult to put into Latin as well. The most literal translation is *Deipara* ("Birth-giver of God"); another variation is *Dei Genetrix* ("God-bearer"). Although anti-Catholic polemicists sometimes claim that our devotion to Mary is the revival of pagan worship of a mother goddess, the Fathers were anxious to avoid such confusion, and for this reason, they initially did not translate *Theotokos* as *Mater Dei* ("Mother of God"). This term became common only when the orthodox understanding of Mary's divine maternity was firmly established.

the Patriarch of Alexandria, Cyril, and quickly the familiar mix of religion and politics muddied the waters. Theologically, the Antiochene school to which Nestorius belonged emphasized the true humanity of Jesus, while the Alexandrian approach of Proclus and Cyril stressed the unity of the divine and human natures in the Person of the Son of God; politically, there was a rivalry between Alexandria and Constantinople, since the new imperial capital was claiming a position ahead of Alexandria.

Cyril of Alexandria denounced Nestorius to Pope Celestine, who summoned a synod in Rome that examined the issue and condemned the position of Nestorius. Meanwhile, the emperors called for an ecumenical council to meet at Pentecost, 431, at Ephesus to decide the matter. At that gathering, Cyril's position was judged to be correct: since Christ possessed both a divine nature and human nature but was one Person, the Son of God, it was proper to call Mary *Theotokos*. The title "Mother of God" was paradoxical, but it was orthodox: paradoxical, because Mary as a creature could not be the Mother of God *as God*; orthodox, because to assert that Jesus was truly born of Mary *and* was the eternal Son of God effectively proclaimed that he was fully human and fully divine.

The Council of Ephesus was concerned to express the truth about the identity of Jesus, but Mary's pivotal role in the expression of that truth encouraged greater popular devotion to her. All over the Christian world, churches were erected in her honor; notable among these is the basilica of Saint Mary Major in Rome, built immediately after the council. Although Mary already had a place in the liturgical celebrations of Christmas and Epiphany, after Ephesus, feasts in her honor were added to the calendar. The Mother of Jesus was celebrated in sermons, praised in hymns, and depicted in art.

Implications

Mother and Son

The dogma of the *Theotokos* was theologically effective because it captured in one word the Christian belief that Christ is true God and true man. Terms like *nature*, *Incarnation*, and *hypostasis* are abstract; to say that Mary is the Mother of God gave concrete expression to the Church's faith. Once the doctrinal issue was settled, people began to reflect more on the intimate bond between Mary and Jesus. She did not simply give him his human nature—she was his *Mother*. The bond between mother and child is among the closest of human ties, and Mary was privileged to share this relationship with the Son of God himself.

And yet even this, the most intimate of human ties, is eclipsed by something greater: Christ is the Redeemer and Mary is redeemed; he is the Lord and she is the handmaid of the Lord. At the beginning of Canto XXIII of the *Divine Comedy*, Dante addresses Mary with paradoxical yet beautiful language: she is "*Vergine Madre, figlia del tuo Figlio*", "Virgin Mother, daughter of your Son". It was her faith that allowed Mary to conceive miraculously; her motherhood is rooted in her discipleship. Mary's faith was tested most radically on Calvary. Many years before, the angel had promised her: "He will be great, and will be called the Son of the Most High; and the Lord God will give to him the throne of his father David, and he will reign over the house of Jacob for ever; and of his kingdom there will be no end" (Lk 1:32–33). Mary had believed then that nothing was impossible with God, and she continued to believe this as she watched her child die. The events that distanced her as a mother from her Son—his remaining behind in the Temple at the age of twelve, the leave-taking as he set out on his ministry, the final separation of death—bound her to him more closely by virtue of her faith.

Mary, Our Mother in Faith

What does Mary's divine maternity mean for us? First of all, since Christ took his human nature from Mary, it is through her that the Son of God is united to the human race. That alone would be reason enough for all generations to call her blessed (Lk 1:48). But the Scriptures suggest another connection: Mary's faith not only unites her to Christ; it also unites her to his disciples. In Luke's Gospel, it is Mary who first brings Christ to others: to Elizabeth, even before his birth; to the shepherds at Bethlehem; to Simeon and Anna in the Temple. At the beginning of the Acts of the Apostles, Luke describes the community of believers at prayer, and Mary is among them.

John's Gospel draws us more deeply into the mystery of Mary's relationship to the other disciples. He has no account of the infancy of

Jesus, but he presents Mary at two key moments: the beginning of
Jesus' ministry and his death. At the wedding feast of Cana, "the mother
of Jesus" (John does not give her name) tells her Son that the wine
has run out. Jesus answers: "O woman, what have you to do with me?
My hour has not yet come" (Jn 2:4). In answer to this reproof, Mary
instructs the waiters to do whatever Jesus tells them to, and he then
turns the water into wine. John points out that through this, the first
of Jesus' signs, his glory was manifested, causing his disciples to believe
in him (Jn 2:11). Mary had appealed to her Son as his Mother; Jesus
refused her request. The situation seemed hopeless, but Mary showed
the confidence of a disciple: in response to this faith, Jesus performed
his first sign, and his disciples believed in him. Mary's faith encouraged faith in the disciples.

The dynamic of Cana comes into clearer relief when we turn to
Mary's second appearance in John's Gospel, at the crucifixion. The
same protagonists are present again, but in a different configuration—
at the wedding feast, the story opened with two distinct entities: "Jesus
and his disciples" and "the mother of Jesus"; now, Jesus hangs on the
Cross alone, and Mary and the beloved disciple stand together beneath
it. They are not there as mere bystanders: she endures the anguish of
a Mother at the horrendous death of her Son, and John, the desola-
tion of a disciple witnessing the brutal humiliation of his Master. On
a level even deeper than these emotions, they stand near the Cross in
faith: now "the hour" has come, and *this* is how Jesus manifests his
glory! They believe that nothing is impossible with God, that divine
love is stronger than human cruelty. And they unite themselves to
Christ's self-offering. The conviction that had filled Mary's heart as a
young woman sustains her now: "Behold, I am the handmaid of the
Lord; let it be to me according to your word" (Lk 1:38). Toward the
end of Jesus' agony, moments before his death, Saint John tells us:
"When Jesus saw his mother, and the disciple whom he loved standing near, he said to his mother, 'Woman, behold, your son!' Then he
said to the disciple, 'Behold, your mother!' And from that hour the
disciple took her to his own home" (Jn 19:26–27).

Those last words have been interpreted as evidence that Mary had
no other children; in a final act of filial piety, Jesus arranged that his
Mother would not be bereft. But there is a deeper significance to
what Saint John relates. Immediately after uttering these words, the

Evangelist says that Jesus knew that all was now finished—finished, not simply because he was dying, but finished because he had completed his work. By his obedience unto death, Christ brought about a new creation: Mary and the beloved disciple were the nucleus of a new family, bound together, not by ties of blood, but by faith. Christ is the New Adam, transforming the tree of death into the tree of life; the Church is the New Eve, born from his pierced side; and Mary is the image and embodiment of that New Eve, "the mother of all the living" (Gen 3:20). The beloved disciple did not take Mary to his own home simply because she had no other children to care for her; he did so because all the disciples of Jesus have become his sisters and brothers, and she has become their Mother in faith.

Some people find Catholic devotion to "our Blessed Mother" too sentimental. But the Catholic conviction that Mary is our Mother goes deeper than May crownings and smiling Madonnas, as the Second Vatican Council teaches:

> She conceived, brought forth and nourished Christ. She presented Him to the Father in the temple, and was united with Him by compassion as He died on the Cross. In this singular way she cooperated by her obedience, faith, hope and burning charity in the work of the Saviour in giving back supernatural life to souls. Wherefore she is our mother in the order of grace. (*LG*, no. 61)

We can see how Mary is our Mother in faith when we consider what Saint Paul says about Abraham in his Letter to the Romans. He calls Abraham "the father of us all" by virtue of his faith. Abraham showed his tremendous faith especially in two ways: he believed that God would give him a son even in old age, and he was willing to sacrifice that son at God's command. Abraham believed in a God "who gives life to the dead and calls into existence the things that do not exist" because he trusted "that God was able to do what he had promised" (Rom 4:17, 21). By faith, Abraham and Sarah were able to conceive when beyond childbearing age. Mary for her part conceived while remaining a virgin because she "believed that there would be a fulfilment of what was spoken to her from the Lord" (Lk 1:45). Abraham was willing to offer up Isaac because "he considered that God was able to raise men even from the dead; hence he did receive him back and this was a symbol" (Heb 11:19). The angel of God halted his sacrifice at the last moment, and Isaac was raised from the dead as a symbol (the Greek literally says "as a parable"). Mary offered her Son, but no angel intervened. Her Son died, and still she believed in a God who gives life to the dead.

The figure of Mary beneath the Cross has captured the imagination of artists and poets over the centuries—the sorrowful mother witnessing the death agony of her child. But the Church perceives something more profound, as the Second Vatican Council taught:

> After this manner the Blessed Virgin advanced in her pilgrimage of faith, and faithfully persevered in her union with her Son unto the cross, where she stood, in keeping with the divine plan, grieving exceedingly with her only begotten Son, uniting herself with a maternal heart with His sacrifice, and lovingly consenting to the immolation of this Victim which she herself had brought forth. Finally, she was given by the same Christ Jesus dying on the cross as a mother to His disciple with these words: "Woman, behold thy son." (*LG*, no. 58)

The disciple took her to his home; Mary took him to her heart. And so it has gone on ever since: the disciples of Jesus turn instinctively to Mary, not simply because she is our sister in sorrow, but more especially because she is our Mother in faith.

Chapter Thirteen

Mary's Origin and Destiny

The second two Marian dogmas, her Immaculate Conception and Assumption, constitute a serious ecumenical challenge. To many Orthodox and Protestant Christians, they represent much that they find most objectionable about Catholicism: unilateral definitions of dogmatic truths by the pope, doctrines not found explicitly in Scripture or taught by the great Fathers of the early Church, the apotheosis of Mary. From the Catholic perspective, they are examples of how the Holy Spirit guides the Church to an ever-deeper understanding of the faith she has received from Christ and the apostles. We will consider first the dogma of the Immaculate Conception.

Immaculate Conception: What We Believe

By a singular grace and privilege, and in virtue of the merits of Christ's redemptive death, Mary was preserved from original sin from the first moment of her existence.

Some History

Pondering the Redemption of Mary

In the last chapter, we saw how the understanding of the significance of Mary's virginity and motherhood grew during the first several centuries of the Christian era. At the heart of the matter was an intuition, already attested to in the New Testament, that Mary was a preeminent example of faith and discipleship. She heard the word of God and acted on it, and did so with such complete dedication that the Word-made-flesh was born from her. Union with God's will is the source of holiness, and as Christians meditated on Mary's role as the Mother of

God, they grew to appreciate her remarkable sanctity. Mary possessed a unique dignity: she, a mere creature, had given birth to the divine Savior. Surely God must have lavished tremendous graces upon her for this sublime vocation.

A few of the early Fathers imputed personal failings to Mary, but as reflection on her absolute openness to God's will deepened, so did the conviction that she never sinned. Freedom from sin did not make Mary "superhuman"; rather, she was *fully* human. As was pointed out in the chapter on the Incarnation, to sin is to act in a way contrary to our nature as God intended it: we are less truly ourselves when we act selfishly. Christ never sinned because he could not—his human will, though free, was always guided by his personal identity as the Son of God. Unlike Jesus, Mary was only human, but she did not sin; she always chose to do God's will. Awareness of her sublime holiness grew, and in the wake of the Council of Ephesus, adjectives like "all-holy", "pure", "sinless", and "immaculate" were applied to her more and more frequently throughout the Christian world.

At the same time that the title *Theotokos* was being debated in the East, the Church in the West was struggling with Pelagianism. Saint Augustine, following his great teacher Ambrose, taught that Mary had never sinned. Pelagius sought to use this to his advantage, arguing that this meant that it was possible for someone always to do God's will. Yes, Augustine replied—but only with the assistance of grace. God's grace did not rob Mary of her free will; she always cooperated with that grace. Mary's reliance on God, her discipleship, is what enabled her to avoid sin. As the debate wore on, Augustine increasingly emphasized the pervasiveness and power of original sin, and he claimed that although Mary had not committed any personal sins, she was not free of original sin. The discussions in the West about Mary's holiness would be conducted for fourteen centuries beneath the shadow of that judgment by Augustine.

In the wake of the Council of Ephesus, many feasts in Mary's honor were added to the liturgical calendar, especially in the East. One of these was the feast of the Conception of Mary by Saint Anne, instituted in Constantinople in the eighth century. It celebrated the beginning of Mary's life as the prelude to the symphony of the new creation brought about by Christ. Byzantine preachers and theologians praised Mary's sanctity, but the feast was more devotional than doctrinal.

The feast of Mary's Conception found its way to England, where, transplanted into Western soil with its Augustinian emphasis on original sin, it sparked theological controversy. No less an ardent devotee of Mary than Saint Bernard opposed the feast because it seemed to challenge the universality of Christ's redemptive work. A fundamental conviction going back to Saint Paul was that Christ had died for all people (2 Cor 5:15). Bernard held that if Mary had never sinned, and she had been conceived without original sin, then she did not need to be saved. This issue was vigorously debated for hundreds of years: How could we affirm Mary's complete holiness without denying that Christ saved the whole human race without exception? Scripture said that Jeremiah and John the Baptist had been sanctified in the womb, and theologians were willing to recognize the same privilege in Mary. By the end of the twelfth century, the commonly held position in the West was that original sin was the universal inheritance of the descendants of Adam, including Mary; that by his death, Christ had redeemed the whole human race; and, in virtue of her unique vocation as Mother of the Savior, that Mary was sanctified at some point before her birth. Most of the great Scholastic teachers of the thirteenth century, including Saint Thomas, espoused this view.

It was a great Franciscan theologian, John Duns Scotus, who resolved the dilemma of Mary's holiness and Christ's universal redemption. As to Mary's being conceived without original sin, Scotus reasoned that what God does ordinarily at baptism he could certainly do at the very beginning of Mary's life. Given her future role as the Mother of God, it was fitting that she should be as holy as humanly possible. Did this exempt Mary from the need of redemption? On the contrary, Scotus argued: she was in fact *more completely* redeemed than any other man because she was dependent on God's saving grace at every moment of her existence. In this unique instance, Christ the Redeemer demonstrated his mastery over evil, not by healing the wound of original sin, but by preserving innocence. Mary's initial sanctification did not negate Christ's role as universal Redeemer; it manifested it more completely.

Scotus proposed this solution at the beginning of the fourteenth century, but it took five hundred years of intense and often rancorous debate to settle the matter. Scotus' own Franciscan order rallied to his position, while the Dominicans by and large opposed it. Battles were fought over terminology, such as the distinction between "the Conception of the Immaculate Virgin" or "the Immaculate Conception of the Virgin". While theologians argued, the feast of Mary's Conception continued to spread at the popular level. Its meaning was subject to various interpretations; those who opposed the Immaculate Conception considered it to be a commemoration of the sanctification of Mary in the womb of her mother.

The Holy See adopted a stance of prudent reserve on the question and sought to maintain peace between contending parties. In 1477, Pope Sixtus IV authorized the celebration of the feast of the Conception of Mary in Rome, but he also forbade either side to denounce the other as heretical. The question of the Immaculate Conception was raised during the Council of Trent, but the fathers sidestepped the matter by declaring that it was not their intention to include Mary in their teaching on original sin. In 1661, Pope Alexander VII indicated that Rome was favorable to the doctrine, but that it remained an open question. By the beginning of the nineteenth century, many bishops and religious orders were petitioning the pope to define the Immaculate Conception. One example of how the tide had turned was that in 1834 the Holy See announced that dioceses and religious orders could ask permission to add the word *Immaculate* to *Conception* in the Preface for the feast, and by 1847, nearly three hundred requests were received— including one from the Master General of the Dominicans!

Soon after his election, Pope Pius IX sent a letter to all the bishops of the world canvassing them on the matter. They were to give the views of their clergy and people as well as their own. Of the 603 bishops contacted, 546 favored the definition. Over the next few years, a commission of theologians hammered out a series of schemas addressing various aspects of the doctrine. Finally, on December 8, 1854, the pope defined as dogmatic faith of the Church that "the most Blessed Virgin Mary was, from the first moment of her conception, by a singular grace and privilege of almighty God and by virtue of the merits of Jesus Christ, Savior of the human race, preserved immune from all stain of original sin." [1] The decree states concisely that Mary's sanctification from the beginning of her existence is the fruit of Christ's redemptive death.

[1] Piux IX, *Ineffabilis Deus* (1854): DS 2803, quoted in *CCC*, no. 491.

The "Sense of the Faith" in the Church

When treating the teaching office of the Church in chapter six above, we saw that the Holy Spirit protects the whole body of the faithful from error in matters of belief: "They manifest this special property by means of the whole people's supernatural discernment [*sensus fidei*] in matters of faith when 'from the Bishops down to the last of the lay faithful' they show universal agreement in matters of faith and morals" (*LG*, no. 12). The history of the dogma of the Immaculate Conception illustrates how this *sensus fidei* is a living reality. It took centuries for theologians to clarify the proper meaning of the doctrine. The Magisterium of the Church did not act precipitously, but allowed the debates to go on; Rome resisted the efforts of contending parties to force a decision one way or the other. Meanwhile, among the People of God, two fundamental intuitions continued to deepen: that Christ is the Redeemer of the whole human race, and that Mary must have received unequaled gifts of grace to fulfill her vocation as the Mother of God. Rather than imposing a new doctrine on believers, Pope Pius IX was responding to repeated requests from all parts of the Catholic world to recognize the Immaculate Conception as part of the dogmatic patrimony of the Church. In the words of Cardinal Newman:

> To that large class of minds, who believe in Christianity, after our manner,—in the particular temper, spirit, and light, (whatever word is used,) in which Catholics believe it,—there is no burden at all in holding that the Blessed Virgin was conceived without original sin; indeed, it is a simple fact to say, that Catholics have not come to believe it because it is defined, but that it was defined because they believed it.[2]

Implications

"The Almighty Has Done Great Things for Me"

Mary's freedom from sin must be understood in light of her relationship to Christ. As the Mother of the one who is "holy, blameless, unstained, separated from sinners, exalted above the heavens" (Heb 7:26), it was fitting that she should be as holy as humanly possible.

---

[2] John Henry Newman, *Apologia pro vita sua* (London: Oxford University Press, 1913), p. 346. Newman wrote his *Apologia* ten years after the definition of this dogma.

This holiness was the fruit of her Son's saving death, so that the Church sees Mary as redeemed in a more sublime manner. We might gain some insight into the nature of this redemption from an image used by Saint Thérèse. She described a clever physician who heals the limb of his child who has tripped over a stone. Suppose instead that the doctor ran ahead and moved the stone out of the child's way: When the child became aware of this, would she not love her father even more? Thérèse adds: "Well, I am this child, the object of the *foreseeing love of a Father* who has not sent His Word to save the *just*, but *sinners*. He wants me *to love* Him because He *has forgiven* me not much but ALL."[3] The saint used the somewhat paradoxical language that the Lord had forgiven her in advance by preventing her from falling; this is what God did in a singular way for Mary.

Christ's saving mission is inseparable from that of the Holy Spirit, so we should also see Mary's holiness as the work of the Spirit. This relationship has been emphasized in the East, and it provides a balance to our Western preoccupation with sin and redemption. We speak of the "stain" of original sin, but really this condition is the privation of something—communion with God. Grace is not a commodity, but the life of union with God, and this comes from the presence and activity of the Holy Spirit. The *Catechism* draws our attention to this teaching of the Second Vatican Council: "The Fathers of the Eastern tradition call the Mother of God 'the All-Holy' (*Panagia*) and celebrate her as 'free from any stain of sin, as though fashioned by the Holy Spirit and formed as a new creature'."[4] At the beginning of Luke's Gospel, the angel Gabriel told Zechariah that his son John would be filled with the Holy Spirit even from his mother's womb (Lk 1:15). This promise was fulfilled when Mary came to Elizabeth, carrying the unborn Jesus, whom she had conceived by the Holy Spirit. John the Baptist leaped for joy in his mother's womb, and Elizabeth was filled with the Holy Spirit. Christ and the Spirit sanctified John before his birth; it is certainly fitting that they sanctified Mary at the very beginning of her life.

The Son and the Spirit were sent from the Father for our salvation and sanctification. What Saint Paul wrote to the Ephesians can be

---

[3] St. Thérèse of Lisieux, *The Story of a Soul: The Autobiography of Saint Thérèse of Lisieux*, ed. John Clarke (Washington, D.C.: ICS Publications, 1996), p. 84.

[4] *CCC*, no. 493, citing *LG*, no. 56. In a footnote, *Lumen Gentium* cites writings of Germanus of Constantinople, Anastasius of Antioch, St. Andrew of Crete, and St. Sophronius.

applied in a particular way to Mary: "Blessed be the God and Father of our Lord Jesus Christ, who has blessed us in Christ with every spiritual blessing in the heavenly places, even as he chose us in him before the foundation of the world, that we should be holy and blameless before him" (Eph 1:3–4). This blessing bestowed "before the foundation of the world" is completely gratuitous and unmerited. Mary's Immaculate Conception is an eminent example of that divine generosity: that she is graced from the very beginning of her existence precludes any suggestion of "merit". One of the watchwords of the Protestant Reformation was *sola gratia* (grace alone)—meaning that salvation is a free gift, and not something we earn. Whatever ecumenical difficulties the doctrine of the Immaculate Conception presents, it certainly can be seen as an instance of free, unmerited grace.

Mary Immaculate and the Church

Of course, the Letter to the Ephesians is not speaking specifically about Mary: all who are in Christ have been chosen to be holy and blameless. Paul describes how this is accomplished toward the end of the Letter: "Christ loved the Church and gave himself up for her, that he might sanctify her, having cleansed her by the washing of water with the word, that he might present the Church to himself in splendor, without spot or wrinkle or any such thing, that she might be holy and without blemish" (Eph 5:25–27).[5] Mary is a member of this Church, a preeminent member because she gave birth to the Savior, but only one member nonetheless. Yet she also embodies personally what is realized collectively in the Mystical Body of Christ. The whole Church is the Bride of Christ, whom the Savior sanctified by giving himself up to death for her; each member is cleansed by water and the word to be holy and without blemish; that purification is most fully realized in Mary, all-holy and immaculate.

This relationship between Mary and the Church is reflected in the last book of the Bible. The twelfth chapter of the Book of Revelation describes two great portents: a woman about to give birth and a fierce dragon seeking to devour her child. This dramatic vision hearkens back to the scene in Eden, when God cursed the serpent after the Fall

---

[5] The Greek word "*amomos*" translated as "without blemish" here is the same word translated as "blameless" in Eph 1:4. Its Latin equivalent is "*immaculati*".

of Adam and Eve: "I will put enmity between you and the woman, and between your seed and her seed; he shall bruise your head, and you shall bruise his heel" (Gen 3:15).[6] Who is "the woman" in Revelation? Primarily, the Church—understood as the community stretching back through the Old Testament and continuing on earth after the Ascension of Christ. This community is Israel (the sun, moon, and twelve stars allude to the patriarch Joseph in Genesis 37), and it is from this people that the Messiah is born: "She brought forth a male child, one who is to rule all the nations" (Rev 12:5). The child eludes the dragon and is snatched up to God and his throne, but "the woman" remains on earth and brings forth other offspring who bear testimony to Jesus, against whom the dragon makes war. A feminine personification of the People of God is a common biblical image: the prophets spoke of Israel as the bride of God, as does the Song of Songs; the remnant of Israel left after the Exile was called "the Daughter of Zion"; and in the New Testament, both Paul and the Book of Revelation describe the Church as the Bride of Christ.

If the People of God encompasses Israel, the disciples of Jesus, and the Church after his Ascension, Mary is the central female figure uniting all three communities: she was there before the coming of Jesus, throughout his entire life, and after his return to the Father. Mary can be seen as the flowering of Israel's long centuries of expectation for the Messiah. In the words of the *Catechism*:

> Throughout the Old Covenant the mission of many holy women *prepared* for that of Mary. At the very beginning there was Eve; despite her disobedience, she receives the promise of a posterity that will be victorious over the evil one, as well as the promise that she will be the mother of all the living. By virtue of this promise, Sarah conceives a

---

[6] *The New Jerusalem Bible* has a helpful footnote on the history of the translation of this verse: "The Hebrew text, by proclaiming that the offspring of the snake is henceforth at enmity with the woman's descendants, opposes the human race to the devil and his 'seed', his posterity, and hints at ultimate victory; it is the first glimmer of salvation, the *proto-evangelium*. The Greek version has a masculine pronoun ('he', not 'it' will bruise . . .), thus ascribing the victory not to the woman's descendants in general but to one of her sons in particular, and thus providing the basis for the messianic interpretation given by many of the Fathers. The Latin version has a feminine pronoun ('she' will bruise . . .) and since, in the messianic interpretation of our text, the Messiah and his mother appear together, the pronoun has been taken to refer to Mary." *The New Jerusalem Bible* (New York: Doubleday, 1985), p. 21.

son in spite of her old age. Against all human expectation God chooses those who were considered powerless and weak to show forth his faithfulness to his promises: Hannah, the mother of Samuel; Deborah; Ruth; Judith and Esther; and many other women.[7]

Mary represents the people that gave birth to the Messiah, and she herself did so literally. She remained in the midst of the community of believers after the Ascension, and her virginal motherhood in faith is an image of the Church, which gives birth to other children who witness to Jesus. These offspring will struggle against the dragon until the Lord's return in glory, but in Mary they see the first fruits of Christ's definitive victory over the serpent: a bride holy and unblemished, utterly sanctified by his sacrificial death. Saint Paul tells us: "For those whom he [God] foreknew he also predestined to be conformed to the image of his Son, in order that he might be the first-born among many brethren. And those whom he predestined he also called; and those whom he called he also justified; and those whom he justified he also glorified" (Rom 8:29–30). As Christians reflected on Mary's origins, it was only natural that they should also give thought to her destiny. Just as they became convinced that she had been predestined and justified in an eminent degree, so they came to believe that she already shares in the glory of her Son's Resurrection. This is the doctrine of the Assumption.

The Assumption: What We Believe

Mary already shares fully, body and soul, in the risen life of Heaven.

Some History

We might picture the dogma of the Immaculate Conception as a stream arising in the consciousness of the Christian people, which had to wend its way around various obstacles and finally reached its full expression in the nineteenth century. The dogma of the Assumption enjoyed a more placid history: here, too, the doctrine emerged from the People of God, but the belief that Mary shares in the glory of Heaven met with little resistance. The proclamation of the dogma in 1950 did not

[7] CCC, no. 489, cf. Gen 3:15, 20; 18:10–14; 21:1–2; 1 Cor 1:17; 1 Sam 1.

settle a controversy; it recognized the dogmatic status of a long-cherished belief.[8]

The first explicit reference to Mary's destiny appears in a letter of Saint Epiphanius written in the year 377. It is an expression of frank agnosticism: Epiphanius has never heard anything of her death, or of her tomb, and he judges that Scripture was silent about the matter so as not to overwhelm us with what must have been a prodigious event. Epiphanius imitated this silence; later Fathers were not so taciturn.

Following the Council of Ephesus, a feast of the *Theotokos* was instituted in Jerusalem on August 15. Since saints' days ordinarily commemorated the anniversary of their death, by the sixth century this feast was associated with Mary's passing from this world. People naturally wondered: How did this happen? Pious legends described the event; the earliest extant accounts date to the fifth century, although these texts record stories that had been in circulation for some time. Church Fathers sought to sift theological gold from the sand of popular imagination: whatever the reliability of these stories, it certainly seemed appropriate that there was something special about the end of Mary's life. The feast came to be known by different names: Mary's Assumption, or Passing, or Dormition ("falling asleep"). A feast commemorating the end of Mary's life was instituted also beyond the Byzantine Empire in the Coptic, Abyssinian, and Armenian churches. Around the year 600, the Byzantine emperor extended the feast of Mary's Dormition to his entire kingdom, and it became the principal Marian celebration.[9]

From the sixth century on, eminent Greek Fathers, among them Theoteknos, Germanus of Constantinople, Andrew of Crete, and John Damascene, preached about Mary's "falling asleep". They avoided the fanciful legends surrounding the event; their theological reasoning was

---

[8] Although it is commonly said that Pius IX defined that Mary was conceived without original sin, or that Pius XII defined that Mary was assumed into Heaven, this is not strictly speaking accurate. What these popes defined was that these beliefs were *dogmas*, that is, doctrines recognized by the Church to be truths revealed by God for our salvation and as such an essential part of her faith.

[9] There was another Marian feast in Constantinople dating back to at least the middle of the sixth century, in honor of a relic of Mary: a veil. Marian shrines have been favored destinations of pilgrimage over the centuries and have been associated with articles of clothing, images, or places where Mary appeared. No church has ever claimed to possess Mary's body. Of course, this does not prove Mary's bodily Assumption, but given the great interest in relics (real or spurious) since the second century, it does suggest that in the popular mind such corporeal relics of the Mother of God were not thought to be available.

that she who had given birth to God should not suffer corruption, and they affirmed that Mary was now with her Son. The Scriptures record how Enoch and Elijah had been snatched from this world at the end of their lives, and that, at the death of Jesus, bodies of saints were raised from the dead and appeared to many people (Gen 5:24; 2 Kg 2:11; Mt 27:52–53). Thus, there were biblical precedents for bodily glorification after death, and who was more deserving of such a reward than the Mother of the Word incarnate? The Fathers taught that it was only fitting that she who had given flesh to the Savior should experience in her flesh the glory of her Son's Resurrection. The feast of the Dormition became one of the greatest feasts in the Orthodox calendar.

The feast of August 15 came to be celebrated in Rome toward the middle of the seventh century, and it became very popular in the West as well. One obstacle arose in the ninth century: a letter mistakenly attributed to Saint Jerome dismissed the bodily Assumption of Mary as fanciful. But in the tenth century, translations of the Greek patristic homilies on the Assumption became available in the West, and in the late eleventh century, another document (this time wrongly attributed to Augustine) presented solid theological reasons for Mary's bodily Assumption. While noting the silence of Scripture on the matter, "Augustine" argued that it was reasonable to believe that Mary was with her Son, body and soul, for the same reasons given by the Greek Fathers. The doctrine of the Assumption came to be universally accepted in the Catholic Church in the twelfth century.

Pius IX received requests to define it as dogmatic, but he judged that the time was not ripe. The requests continued to arrive, and in the first half of the twentieth century, they became a floodtide: bishops, religious communities, theological faculties, and millions of ordinary Catholics from all over the world wrote, asking for the proclamation of the Assumption. Finally, on November 1, 1950, Pope Pius XII solemnly declared as dogmatic faith of the Catholic Church "that the Immaculate Mother of God, the ever Virgin Mary, having completed the course of her earthly life, was assumed body and soul into heavenly glory".[10]

---

[10] Pope Pius XII, *Munificentissimus Deus*, no. 44. René Laurentin makes two interesting observations about the wording of the Holy Father's statement. First, although the definition is concise, it is dogmatically dense: in defining the Assumption, Pius XII recalls

Implications

The source of Mary's glory is her union with her Son in his redemptive work. She was not simply an instrument used by God for the Word to become flesh—she shared heart and soul in Christ's whole mission, from the Annunciation to Calvary. Because Mary was so closely united with her Son in his life and death, it is appropriate for her to be united with him in his Resurrection. On the eve of his death, Jesus told his disciples that he was departing to prepare a place for them, and then he promised: "And when I go and prepare a place for you, I will come again and will take you to myself, that where I am you may be also" (Jn 14:3). Christ will return to raise us up in glorified bodies into the Kingdom of Heaven, as Saint Paul teaches: "For as in Adam all die, so also in Christ shall all be made alive. But each in his own order: Christ the first fruits, then at his coming those who belong to Christ" (1 Cor 15:22–23). Yet Heaven begins here on earth: in baptism, we are plunged into the paschal mystery of Jesus' death and Resurrection, and we are already united with him in Heaven: "But God, who is rich in mercy, . . . raised us up with him, and made us sit with him in the heavenly places in Christ Jesus" (Eph 2:4, 6). Mary, the New Eve, is the first fruits of those brought into the heavenly places by the New Adam. Redeemed from the first moment of her life by her Son's death, she already shares fully in his victory.

Mary and the Church in Glory

In one sense, Mary's bodily Assumption is a singular privilege: she who gave flesh to the Son of God is the first disciple to experience in her flesh the glory of the Resurrection. But she does so as one of us. When Pius XII proclaimed the dogma of the Assumption, he expressed the hope that it would strengthen belief in our own future resurrection.

---

other dogmatic teachings of the Church—Mary's Immaculate Conception, perpetual virginity, and role as the Mother of God. All of these doctrines are interconnected and should be understood in relation to the whole of revelation. Secondly, although we commonly picture Mary as being taken "up" to Heaven, the definition avoids such spatial imagery: "*Assumere*" in Latin means "to take to oneself"; God took Mary, body and soul, to himself. While we cannot avoid thinking of Heaven as a place, it is better understood as a relationship with God. René Laurentin, *A Short Treatise on the Virgin Mary* (Washington, N.J.: AMI Press, 1991), pp. 249–50.

This it can do if we keep in mind Mary's relationship with us. Mary's heavenly glory is a sign that we, too, are destined to share body and soul in Christ's victory over death. Christ is truly our Brother, but he is also the Son of God. Can we, mere creatures, hope to share in his glorious Resurrection? The Assumption of Mary, a creature who is, like us, only human, proclaims that we can. And her *bodily* Assumption reminds us that Christ did not come to save "souls"—he saves us completely, body and soul. Long ago, Tertullian succinctly expressed a truth at the heart of Christianity: *caro cardo salutis* (the flesh is the hinge of salvation).[11] The dogma of the Assumption proclaims that, through the power of Christ's Resurrection, the hope expressed in the Old Testament is fulfilled: "From my flesh I shall see God" (Job 19:26).

Because she is one of us, one of the faithful redeemed by Christ, Mary in Heaven is the image of the whole Church in glory. The Bible ends with an invitation: "The Spirit and the Bride say, 'Come'" (Rev 22:17). That Bride is the Church in her homeland at the end of her journey, and Mary is her living icon. As the Second Vatican Council teaches: "In the interim, just as the Mother of Jesus, glorified in body and soul in heaven, is the image and beginning of the Church as it is to be perfected is the world to come, so too does she shine forth on earth, until the day of the Lord shall come, as a sign of sure hope and solace to the people of God during its sojourn on earth" (*LG*, no. 68).

When we speak of Mary as an "image" of the Church, we need to avoid reducing her to an abstraction. She was a real person, a Jewish woman of the first century. That is who she still is, though transfigured by Resurrection glory. In the mystery of the Incarnation, the Son of God did not just become "man"; he became Jesus of Nazareth. The Resurrection did not erase Jesus' identity; although his human nature was transformed, he is the same man who had preached in the villages of Galilee and died on Calvary. Similarly, after her Assumption, Mary is still the woman who gave birth to Jesus, the woman who stood beneath the Cross, the woman who was at prayer with the other disciples at Pentecost. In picturing the world to come, we are speaking of realities beyond our earthly experience, and such knowledge as we have, we see "in a mirror dimly" (1 Cor 13:12). Still,

---

[11] Tertullian, *De resurrectione carnis*, 8, 2: PL 2, 852, quoted in *CCC*, no. 1015.

contemplating Mary in heavenly glory helps us appreciate how her relationship to her Son and to us has been transformed.

Mary Our Mother

In the First Letter of John, we are told that "we know that when he appears we shall be like him, for we shall see him as he is" (1 Jn 3:2). On earth, Mary walked by faith and not by sight: like the other disciples, her approach to Christ's divine identity was through his humanity. And her union with her Son was partial, marked by the limitations of this world as well as by her separation from him during his ministry and after his death and Resurrection. In Heaven, Mary sees Jesus "as he is", and beholds his humanity—the humanity she gave him—now in the full splendor of his divinity. Her union with him is perfect and without a shadow of separation. She also sees *us* in her Son, and this is why she can exercise her maternal role in a more eminent way than she could when she was on earth. Jesus gave Mary as a mother to "the disciple" beneath the Cross, and for the remainder of her earthly life, she must have enjoyed a privileged place in the affections of his followers. She could assist them by her prayer, but the extent of both their need and her influence was limited by the horizons of this world and the obscurity of faith. But now she sees each and every one of us in Christ, individually and perfectly, as do all the saints. But she knows us with a mother's love; and for a mother, to know that one's child is in need is to act.

Because all of us are "in Christ", Mary's intercession is universal; because she is a mother, it is particular and personal. A mother's love for her children is tailored to the unique needs of each. This is why different cultures, even different towns, can honor "their" Madonna. In a poem entitled "The Black Virgin", Chesterton evoked Mary's many images—rooted deep in Chartres, the White Lady of Walsingham, a little shepherdess, a mysterious figure darker than violet vestment—and observed:

> One in thy thousand statues we acclaim thee
> On all thy thousand thrones acclaim and claim
> Who walk in forest of thy forms and faces
> Walk in a forest calling on one name
> And, most of all, how this thing may be so
> Who know thee not are mystified to know

That one cries "Here she stands" and one cries "Yonder"
And thou wert home in heaven long ago.[12]

When we think of Mary's motherly intercession, we should not
imagine that by her mercy she tempers the justice of her Son. In God,
justice and mercy are one, and her maternal prayer is but the echo of
her Son's merciful love for us. The secret of Mary's discipleship was
her wholehearted cooperation with the will of God; this is the basis
of her prayer now. (We might do well to picture her intercession, not
in terms of her telling her Son, "They have no wine", but of her
saying to us, "Do whatever he tells you.") In this regard, it is noteworthy that the Second Vatican Council taught: "For all the salvific
influence of the Blessed Virgin on men originates, not from some
inner necessity, but from the divine pleasure. It flows forth from the
superabundance of the merits of Christ, rests on His mediation, depends
entirely on it and draws all its power from it" (*LG*, no. 60). The
council speaks of her influence on *us*; she is not a manipulative mother
wheedling treats for her children from a miserly father; rather, she is
the model disciple who by her love and prayer helps us to embrace
fully God's will.

Conclusion

Mary can help us do the will of God because during her earthly life
she, too, had to walk by faith. As we conclude our reflection on the
Immaculate Conception and the Assumption, it is good to recall that
these are privileges in manner, not in substance: they are blessings God
also gives to us in a different way. Mary was preserved from original
sin; we are cleansed of it in baptism. She shares fully now in the risen
life; we will do so when Christ returns. These dogmas became explicit
over many centuries, but they are rooted in the saving events recorded
in the New Testament. The primitive Christian image of Mary as the
New Eve emerged from her biblical portrait as a disciple totally devoted
to hearing the word of God and obeying it. These dogmas express
fundamental biblical truths: God's grace always has the primacy; Christ's

---

[12] G. K. Chesterton, "The Black Virgin", *The Collected Works of G. K. Chesterton*, vol. X:
Poetry, Part I (San Francisco: Ignatius Press, 1994), p. 122.

victory over sin and death is complete; each human person possesses infinite value and is destined for an eternal weight of glory.

The doctrines of the Immaculate Conception and Assumption were the fruit of long and loving meditation by the People of God on Mary's place in God's plan, but their importance as "saving truth" became clear only in recent times. The nineteenth century was characterized by unbridled optimism regarding human achievement; the anthem for the age was penned by the poet Swinburne: "Glory to Man in the highest! for Man is the master of things!" In answer to this vaunting of human accomplishment, Pope Pius IX proclaimed in the dogma of the Immaculate Conception the priority of God's grace, our need for redemption by Christ, and the beauty of a life lived in total dependence on God's will. Overweening confidence in human progress collapsed in the horrific events of the twentieth century; the smokestacks of Auschwitz and the mushroom cloud of Hiroshima revealed what terrors befall vast numbers of ordinary people when "Man is the master of things". Millions of people died in wars; millions more were degraded by totalitarian regimes. All over the world, individuals and races were sacrificed on the altar of "the State". In the face of this brutality, Pope Pius XII invited the world to contemplate the intrinsic dignity and glorious destiny of each human person, manifested in the heavenly splendor of a Jewish woman who had lived long ago in an obscure corner of the mighty Roman Empire.

The dogma of the Assumption has meaning for us because the glory of Heaven is the last chapter God intends for every human biography, and by her earthly pilgrimage, Mary shows us how to reach it. Those who are puzzled by Catholic devotion to Mary sometimes point out that we know very little about her. She lived in obscurity and passed most of her life carrying out the ordinary round of human duties. But hers was a life of utter dependence on God, total dedication to Christ, unstinting and discreet charity to those in need. If all generations call her blessed, she herself tells us why: "He who is mighty has done great things for me, and holy is his name" (Lk 1:49). God will do great things for us, too, if we let him; and unlike earthly fame, heavenly splendor is not diminished but increased when it is shared. A figure clothed with the sun, adorned with stars, the moon beneath her feet: this is Mary, but it can also be each one of us.

Chapter Fourteen

Life Everlasting

The thought of Mary and the saints in glory directs our attention to God's greatest gift to us: eternal life. Saint Peter, with his customary bluntness, once pointed out to Jesus that the apostles had left everything to follow him, and then asked: "What then shall we have?" Jesus answered,

> Truly, I say to you, in the new world, when the Son of man shall sit on his glorious throne, you who have followed me will also sit on twelve thrones, judging the twelve tribes of Israel. And every one who has left houses or brothers or sisters or father or mother or children or lands, for my name's sake, will receive a hundredfold, and inherit eternal life. (Mt 19:28–29)

Heaven is the ultimate "Good News". But is it true?

What We Believe

At a moment known only to God, Christ will return in glory to judge the living and the dead. This world will give way to the Kingdom of God in its fullness. The universe will be transformed, death and suffering will be banished, and charity will unite the saints and angels in the communion of the Holy Trinity. At Christ's return, every man will receive a spiritual body. This general judgment is preceded by a particular judgment for each individual at the moment of death. The blessed enter Heaven, either immediately or after purification, and the damned enter Hell.

Some History

Our final topic brings us back to our first: the Resurrection of Christ. Christians believe in life everlasting because Jesus Christ rose from the dead. The disciples understood from their encounters with the risen Jesus "that Christ being raised from the dead will never die again;

death no longer has dominion over him" (Rom 6:9). Christ shares his victory with us. Saint Paul believed that to deny our resurrection from the dead was to deny Christ's own Resurrection: "If there is no resurrection of the dead, then Christ has not been raised" (1 Cor 15:13).

Several points emerge from the biblical accounts of the Resurrection appearances. First, the disciples do not testify simply to the continued existence of Jesus' soul or spirit after his death—his dead body was restored to life. Second, this body was not a reanimated corpse, like that of Lazarus or the young girl Jesus had raised from the dead; Christ's human nature was transformed by the Resurrection. For this reason, Saint Paul taught that at our resurrection we will receive a celestial body, whose properties exceed anything we can now imagine. Third, by his Ascension, Jesus showed that the risen life, although begun on earth, finds its full expression in the Kingdom of Heaven. That is where we will experience eternal life: "But our commonwealth is in heaven, and from it we await a Savior, the Lord Jesus Christ, who will change our lowly body to be like his glorious body, by the power which enables him even to subject all things to himself" (Phil 3:20–21).

Christ's Resurrection radically changed the meaning of death. Human pride had ushered in death, but the reign of death was broken by the humble obedience that brought Christ to the Cross. Christ abolished death (2 Tim 1:10) and made it the gateway to true life. His death becomes the pattern for disciples to imitate (Phil 3:10); we proclaim the death of the Lord in the Eucharist (1 Cor 11:26); believers are baptized into his death (Rom 6:3–5). Christians still experience physical death, but this holds no terrors because even in death we belong to Christ: "Whether we live or whether we die, we are the Lord's. For to this end Christ died and lived again, that he might be Lord both of the dead and of the living" (Rom 14:8–9). Saint Paul confidently asserted: "For me to live is Christ, and to die is gain" (Phil 1:21). The apostles and many other disciples bore witness to this conviction not only by their preaching, but by their martyrdom.

Christ Our Judge

Eternal life is God's gift, but we have our part to play as well. Christ is not only our Savior; he is also our Judge. The doctrine of eternal damnation creates an insuperable obstacle for many people; how can such a terrifying idea be associated with a loving God? Christians believe in Hell for the same reason that we believe in Heaven: from the teaching of Jesus himself. Various religions and philosophies offer conjectures about life after death; even much of Christian theology on the nature of that life is speculative. But the fact of eternal reward or punishment comes to us from a uniquely qualified source: the only Person who has actually been where we are going. We read the following in John's Gospel, when the Baptist bore witness to Jesus: "He who comes from above is above all; he who is of the earth belongs to the earth, and of the earth he speaks; he who comes from heaven is above all. He bears witness to what he has seen and heard, yet no one receives his testimony. . . . He who believes in the Son has eternal life; he who does not obey the Son shall not see life, but the wrath of God rests upon him" (Jn 3:31–32, 36). It is impossible to take the Gospels seriously and deny that Jesus proclaimed a message of eternal reward or punishment.

It is a sobering exercise to read through the Gospels and note how often Jesus speaks of judgment or the eternal consequences of our actions and attitudes: the idea appears over thirty times in the Gospel of Matthew, and judgment is one of the main themes of John's Gospel. Salt that turns insipid is trampled underfoot, wheat is collected into barns while the chaff is burned, fish caught in the net are kept, but the refuse is thrown away. When it comes to entering the Kingdom, no sacrifice is too great (one's family, an eye or a limb, life itself), nor is any act of kindness too small (a cup of cold water). Like many prophetic figures before him, Jesus warned the greedy, the cruel, and the complacent of divine retribution. What disturbed many of his listeners was that Christ claimed that *he* would be the Judge, although judgment is a divine prerogative; and further, he told them that their eternal destiny depended on their relationship to him. For example, Jesus warned the towns of Bethsaida, Capernaum, and Chorazin that they would be brought down to Hades because they had not been moved to repent by the signs he had worked (Mt 11:20–24). In Jerusalem, Jesus claimed, "I told you that you would die in your sins, for you will die in your sins unless you believe that I am he" (Jn 8:24). And, after his Resurrection, Christ commissioned his followers to preach the Gospel to the whole creation: "He who believes and is baptized will be saved; but he who does not believe will be condemned" (Mk 16:16).

These are hard sayings. It is not surprising that many people choose to ignore them, especially in a culture where it is considered bad form to be "judgmental". However, the theme of judgment is not marginal to Jesus' mission; there is an urgency to his preaching that can be explained only if it is true that what we believe and how we act have eternal consequences. And it is evident that his disciples took this teaching seriously: the earliest New Testament writings speak about Jesus returning as Judge.

What are Heaven and Hell like? Jesus tells us very little. His favorite image for the Kingdom of Heaven is a wedding feast, an occasion that must have been one of the most joyful celebrations in the villages of his day. When referring to Hell, Jesus sometimes used the word *Gehenna*. This was a refuse dump on land cursed by the Jews because in earlier times people had sacrificed their children to the god Moloch there. Others before Jesus had used this desolate pit of continually smoldering rubbish to portray the fate of evildoers. We should not make too much of the biblical imagery for Heaven and Hell; suffice it to say that Heaven is far more wonderful than anything we can imagine, and Hell is far worse than any picture can convey.

The return of Christ in glory will mark the end of the world of time and space as we know it, and the inauguration of the Kingdom of God in its fullness. The time of probation will be over. Jesus concludes the parable of the sheep and the goats with two final verdicts: "And they will go away into eternal punishment, but the righteous into eternal life" (Mt 25:46). Christ's judgment includes those who have already died: "Do not marvel at this; for the hour is coming when all who are in the tombs will hear his [the Son's] voice and come forth, those who have done good, to the resurrection of life, and those who have done evil, to the resurrection of judgment" (Jn 5:28–29).

The Particular Judgment

What about those who die before the return of Christ? Several biblical passages suggest that some kind of judgment takes place at the end of life and that each person's reward or punishment begins at the moment of death. Such a state of affairs is presumed in Jesus' parable of the rich man and Lazarus, but is more explicit in the words he spoke to one of the criminals crucified with him: "Truly, I say to you, today you will be with me in Paradise" (Lk 23:43). We read in the Letter to the Hebrews: "It is appointed for men to die once, and after that comes judgment" (Heb 9:27). We have one lifetime in which to shape our character; who we are at the end of life determines our destiny forever.

The General Judgment

We might see the individual human life as a microcosm for the whole of creation. "In the beginning", God brought the universe into being, and it has its own life story. This biography will reach its fulfillment when Christ returns; creation will have attained its final purpose. That fulfillment is as shrouded in mystery as the origins of the universe. We do not know when this will take place, and we will grasp the meaning of creation only when we get to the last chapter. As the Second Vatican Council teaches: "At that time the human race as well as the entire world, which is intimately related to man and attains to its end through him, will be perfectly reestablished in Christ" (*LG*, no. 48). This claim seems audacious to the secular mind, and yet Christians have always seen Christ as the key to the purpose of the universe: "For he [God the Father] has made known to us in all wisdom and insight the mystery of his will, according to his purpose which he set forth in Christ as a plan for the fulness of time, to unite all things in him, things in heaven and things on earth" (Eph 1:9–10).

The basic dogmas about what are known as the "Four Last Things" (death, judgment, Heaven, and Hell) appear throughout the New Testament: death as the way to eternal life; a bodily resurrection; individual judgment at death; a general judgment at the end of time; and finally, everlasting blessedness or misery. In nearly two thousand years, there has been little doctrinal development regarding these matters.

There has been much *imaginative* attention paid to them, because people are naturally very curious about the afterlife. Theological speculation has emerged at what we might call the "frontier" between human history and the Second Coming of Christ. In every age, some have claimed that they discerned signs of the imminent return of Christ (a final trial, a great apostasy, the appearance of the Antichrist). The Catholic view is that while we should live in eager expectation of Christ's return, predictions about the specific date of the Second Coming should be avoided. For some Christians, another sign preceding the end of the world will be a thousand-year reign of Christ on earth. "Millenarianism" has taken many forms throughout history: several early Fathers espoused it, and strains of apocalyptic thought have been part of the Church's experience for two thousand years. However, the idea of an earthly reign of the glorified Christ is not Catholic doctrine (CCC, no. 676).

As to the frontier between physical death of individuals and the return of Christ, the principal dogmatic development is the doctrine of Purgatory, the belief in a final purification before entering into communion with the all-holy God. The souls in Heaven already see God face-to-face; once we pass from this world, we live, no longer by faith, but by sight.[1]

Implications

Many Christians today give little thought to the life to come. The great Lutheran philosopher Søren Kierkegaard lamented this state of affairs already in the nineteenth century: "The hereafter has become a joke, an exigency so uncertain that not only does no one any longer respect it but no one even envisages it, so that people are actually amused at the thought that there used to be a time when this idea transformed everyone's existence."[2] The traditional depictions of Heaven and Hell strike people as childish, and when modern tourists visit the historic churches of Europe, they sometimes leave with the impression that past generations were haunted by the terrors of Hell. It is true that a depiction of the Last Judgment was a prominent element in the iconography of most churches, but our fascination with these paintings might testify more to the perennial attraction of the macabre than to the medieval

---

[1] The only dogmatic teaching in this area apart from Purgatory, and one of the very few dogmas defined by a pope, is that the souls in Heaven "see the divine essence with an intuitive vision, and even face to face, without the mediation of any creature" (Pope Benedict XII, *Benedictus Deus* [1336]; CCC, no. 1023). Benedict's immediate predecessor, Pope John XXII, had presented as a private opinion the theory that, prior to the Second Coming, the souls in Heaven behold only the risen humanity of Christ, and not God himself. Benedict's fundamental point is that while here on earth we know God through the mediation of our senses and in the obscurity of faith; in Heaven we will behold God directly.

[2] S. Kierkegaard, *Concluding Postscript*, 4, quoted in Raniero Cantalamessa, *Jesus the Holy One of God*, trans. Alan Neame (Collegeville, Minn.: Liturgical Press, 1991), p. 80.

fear of damnation. The torments of the damned occupied a small part in the decoration of churches, most of which was given over to depicting the life of Christ and the glory of the saints.

What the great monuments of Christian art demonstrate is that our ancestors had a vivid sense of the correlation between our world and the spiritual realm. Christians in the past viewed the natural world, including human mortality, from a religious perspective. Today the sophisticated dismiss such a perspective as primitive. One wonders how earlier generations would appraise our culture, which does everything possible to deny the fact of death and seems content to remain indifferent to what awaits us on the other side of it. Certainly, the traditional belief that at death we each face divine judgment is more faithful to the teaching of Christ than the modern assumption that everything will just work out somehow in the next life. The only "immortality" our post-Christian society can offer is an extension of earthly existence lived out in relative comfort. What Christ offers is true life, compared to which our earthly existence is hardly life at all: "I came that they may have life, and have it abundantly" (Jn 10:10).

Death, the Gateway to Life Everlasting

Faith alone offers a glimpse of the abundant life of Heaven, but there is an analogy in our human experience that might help us appreciate the connection between this world and the next. Each of us spent nine months, more or less, in the womb. What "life" meant then was to dwell in a dark and confined space. During that time, we were developing the organs that would enable us to apprehend this world— eyes and ears, tongues and noses, hands and feet. Those organs were useless to us in the womb; they were being shaped for our future life. Once born into this world, we appreciate through our senses how utterly beautiful creation is: the sound of birdsong, the majestic sweep of the ocean, the look of love in the eyes of another. Those nine months were preparing us to experience the wide world outside the womb. The revelation of the glorified humanity of the risen Christ taught his disciples that our earthly existence is but a time of gestation in which we are being equipped for an existence whose beauty is beyond our comprehension now: *that* will be true life. There is continuity as we move from this world to the next, as there was when we came out of the womb. In the next life, we will be who we are now, but freed from the confines of this earthly creation.

Death is our portal from this limited existence to true life. Why then do we fear it? There is the instinct for self-preservation that we share with animals, but there is also the anticipation of the separation of soul and body that death entails. Disembodied souls or soulless bodies are unnatural to us; that is why we are unsettled by ghosts and corpses. And, because the risen life is lived on an entirely new plane, to leave this world seems like the end of everything. If by some miracle, we could talk to an unborn baby and describe something of the beauty of our world, the child would not understand us, and he would resist being born: life outside the womb is so utterly different that it would seem to that baby to be death, not life. So, it is not surprising that we fear death; Jesus himself trembled at the prospect of it.

Death marks the end of earthly growth. Jesus said, "We must work the works of him who sent me, while it is day; night comes, when no one can work" (Jn 9:4). Once I leave this world my "self" has reached its maturity. That spiritual ripeness cannot be gauged by earthbound measures. At the beginning of life, the average time of gestation is nine months, but some of us are born early and others are born late; mothers know well that nature's clock is not calibrated to our calendars. If death is our birth to new life, then the "average" life span is similarly imprecise. This is a consoling realization when we face one of the greatest heartaches, the death of a child. It is natural to regret all that the little one will miss here on earth, and to feel that he (and we) has been cheated. But if the purpose of this life is to form us for the life to come, then even as we mourn we can take comfort that the child was called from this world because he was ready for a better one. We find a presentiment of this in the Old Testament Book of Wisdom: "Being perfected in a short time, he fulfilled long years; for his soul was pleasing to the Lord, therefore he took him quickly from the midst of wickedness" (4:13–14). But it is above all our faith in Christ, who died and rose from the dead, that enables us to bear the sorrow of separation from those we love, and to know that they enjoy a life infinitely more wondrous than that which they knew here on earth. Our prayer should be that the moment of death finds us prepared to go to God. That is why in the Litany of Saints we pray, "From a sudden and unforeseen death, deliver us, O Lord." In the Hail Mary, we ask the Mother of God to pray for us at the only two moments that really matter: now, and at the hour of our death.

Saint Francis of Assisi welcomed "Sister Death" because, even though he ardently sang the canticle of created beauty, he had lived in this world with his heart set on the world to come. In our Catholic liturgy, there is room for mourning; Jesus himself wept at the grave of Lazarus. But at the heart of our rites surrounding the dying and the dead there is the assurance that "if we have been united with him in a death like his, we shall certainly be united with him in a resurrection like his" (Rom 6:5). The ancient prayer of Commendation for the Dying sounds a note of triumph as the Christian sets out on the last leg of his pilgrimage:

> Proficiscere, anima Christiana, de hoc mundo!
> Go forth upon thy journey, Christian soul!
> Go from this world! Go, in the Name of God
> The Omnipotent Father, who created thee!
> Go, in the Name of Jesus Christ, our Lord
> Son of the living God, who bled for thee!
> Go, in the Name of the Holy Spirit, who
> Hath been pour'd out on thee! Go, in the name
> Of Angels and Archangels; in the name
> Of Thrones and Dominations; in the name
> Of Princedoms and of Powers; and in the name
> Of Cherubim and Seraphim, go forth!
> Go, in the name of Patriarchs and Prophets;
> And of Apostles and Evangelists,
> Of Martyrs and Confessors; in the name
> Of holy Monks and Hermits; in the name
> Of Holy Virgins; and all Saints of God,
> Both men and women, go! Go on thy course;
> And may thy place to-day be found in peace,
> And may thy dwelling be the Holy Mount
> Of Sion:—through the Same, through Christ, our Lord.[3]

---

[3] This is Cardinal Newman's translation, found in *The Dream of Gerontius*, in John Henry Newman, *Prayers, Verses and Devotions* (San Francisco: Ignatius Press, 1989), pp. 696–97.

This prayer gives voice to the Catholic conviction that Christ has turned death from a moment of separation into a moment of meeting. The departed soul enters into the communion of life that is the Triune God and into the heavenly assembly of angels and saints.

God's Judgment Ratifies Our Choices

Heaven is homecoming—but will we be at home there? That is the essence of judgment. We should not equate God's judgment with condemnation. Saint Paul told the Corinthians: "It is the Lord who judges me. Therefore do not pronounce judgment before the time, before the Lord comes, who will bring to light the things now hidden in darkness and will disclose the purposes of the heart. Then every man will receive his commendation from God" (1 Cor 4:4–5). What does God commend? He commends charity: "Then the King will say to those at his right hand, 'Come, O blessed of my Father, inherit the kingdom prepared for you from the foundation of the world; for I was hungry and you gave me food, I was thirsty and you gave me drink' " (Mt 25:34–35). He commends mercy: "If you forgive men their trespasses, your heavenly Father also will forgive you" (Mt 6:14). He commends perseverance: "He who endures to the end will be saved" (Mk 13:13). He commends faith: "This is the will of my Father, that every one who sees the Son and believes in him should have eternal life; and I will raise him up at the last day" (Jn 6:40).

What, then, does God not commend? He does not commend selfishness: "Then he will say to those at his left hand, 'Depart from me, you cursed, into the eternal fire prepared for the devil and his angels; for I was hungry and you gave me no food, I was thirsty and you gave me no drink' " (Mt 25:41–42). He does not commend resentment: "If you do not forgive men their trespasses, neither will your Father forgive your trespasses" (Mt 6:15). He does not commend vacillation: "No one who puts his hand to the plow and looks back is fit for the kingdom of God" (Lk 9:62). He does not commend hypocrisy: "Not every one who says to me, 'Lord, Lord,' shall enter the kingdom of heaven, but he who does the will of my Father who is in heaven" (Mt 7:21). God cannot commend selfishness, resentment, equivocation, and duplicity because God is love. God banishes no one from his presence, but those who are self-absorbed turn away from him: "And this is the judgment, that the light has come into the world, and men loved darkness rather than light, because their deeds were evil. For every one who does evil hates the light, and does not come to the light, lest his deeds should be exposed" (Jn 3:19–20).

Although we hear language that suggests God sends people to Hell, in fact damnation is a self-inflicted punishment; that is one of its most awful aspects. As C. S. Lewis observed, the doors of Hell are locked from the inside. The unrepentant sinner does not want to be with God, he wants to be in God's place—that is the essence of sin. The selfish man wants everything and everyone to serve him, and he reduces subjects to objects, objects to be exploited. In the parable of the rich man and Lazarus, even in torment, the rich man cannot see Lazarus as a person; he is merely a tool: "Send Lazarus to dip the end of his finger in water and cool my tongue; ... send him [Lazarus] to my father's house, for I have five brothers, so that he may warn them" (Lk 16:24, 27). For such a person, it is Hell to be in Heaven. The fire that burns him is God's love, which is refused. Almost the final words of the Old Testament describe a blaze that is both punishment and reward: "For behold, the day comes, burning like an oven, when all the arrogant and all evildoers will be stubble; the day that comes shall burn them up, says the Lord of hosts, so that it will leave them neither root nor branch. But for you who fear my name the sun of righteousness shall rise, with healing in its wings" (Mal 4:1–2). That Sun of Righteousness rises at the beginning of the New Testament: Jesus Christ is the day who dawns upon us from on high "to give light to those who sit in darkness and in the shadow of death, to guide our feet into the way of peace" (Lk 1:79). But the divine love that provides warmth and life to help the good branches produce the fruit of charity is also the fire that burns up the dead branches of selfish egotism.

The Letter of Jude provides apt images for these lost souls: "waterless clouds, carried along by winds; fruitless trees in late autumn, twice dead, uprooted; wild waves of the sea, casting up the foam of their own shame; wandering stars for whom the deepest darkness has been reserved for ever" (Jude 12–13). Clouds without water are useless, uprooted trees are lifeless; the turbulent passions of the wicked foam out their own confusion; released from the gravitational pull of love, the lost travel aimlessly forever through empty space. One moment's repentance would empty Hell, but the damned *will not* repent. For his part, God will not overrule their choice, he will not violate their freedom to reject his love.

Although we understand that free will implies the possibility of eternal misery, we wonder: Could people really choose this state? Our sensibilities are shaken by Hell, and we instinctively turn away from the idea. The notion of "an eternal Hell eternally empty" is appealing, but we must bear two things in mind. The first is the urgency of Christ's preaching: he often warned that our earthly choices bring us to either eternal joy or eternal misery. Jesus would be a contemptible teacher if he sought to control us with imaginary terrors, like parents who keep their child from wandering at night with stories of monsters under the bed. Christ would not have warned us of eternal punishment if such a possibility did not exist. The second thing to recall is human obstinacy. We have all known people (or *been* people!) who found themselves in a situation where they *refused* to enjoy themselves and tried to hold others hostage to their foul mood. Perhaps one way to think of the difference between Heaven and Hell is that everyone is at the same celebration, but those in Hell are determined not to have a good time, and the fact that others around them are enjoying themselves only increases their resentment.

The Heart of the Gospel: The Mercy of God

Jesus warned us of the dire consequences of sin, but the fundamental theme of his preaching was the mercy of God. By his manner, his message, and his actions, Christ proclaimed the Father's love. Far from being on the watch to catch us out, God "desires all men to be saved and to come to the knowledge of the truth" (1 Tim 2:4). It is true that the awareness of God's love should not make us complacent. Saint Paul warned the Romans: "Or do you presume upon the riches of his kindness and forbearance and patience? Do you not know that God's kindness is meant to lead you to repentance?" (Rom 2:4). But the words of Jesus to the criminal crucified near him, "Truly, I say to you, today you will be with me in Paradise" (Lk 23:43), assure us that God will welcome us even at the last moment if we desire to be with him. "God so loved the world that he gave his only-begotten Son" (Jn 3:16); the Father not only gave his Son by sending him into the world; he gave him up to death on the Cross. When we contemplate Christ crucified, we see the lengths to which God has gone to invite us back into a communion of love with him.

This communion of love is what we mean by Heaven. In attempting to describe it, we are like the unborn child in relation to this world: it is a reality in which we already live, but we can apprehend practically nothing of what it is like. Even Saint Paul, who saw the Risen Christ and had a mystical experience of "the third heaven" or "Paradise" (2 Cor 12:2–3), admitted that he had heard things he was unable to repeat. When speaking of heavenly glory, he began by quoting a scriptural passage about "what no eye has seen, nor ear heard, nor the heart of man conceived, what God has prepared for those who love him", but then added, "God has revealed to us through the Spirit" (1 Cor 2:9–10). The testimony of our senses and the reasoning of our intellect can offer no certain knowledge of Heaven. Only the truth revealed by God affords us a glimpse of what God has prepared. We must return one last time to the two great dogmas of our faith, the Incarnation and the Trinity, to see what light they shed on the mystery of eternal life.

The risen humanity of God incarnate teaches us that there is a connection between this world and Heaven. Scripture speaks of "new heavens and a new earth" (2 Pet 3:13; Rev 21:1), but they blossom from the present creation. Here we recall Saint Paul's teaching on the relationship between the earthly body and the spiritual body: "What is sown is perishable, what is raised is imperishable" (1 Cor 15:42). This continuity might provide an affirmative answer to the question: "Will my dog or cat go to Heaven?" Because all that God has created is good, is it not possible that everything he has made (apart from those personal beings who definitively reject God) will be part of the new heavens and the new earth? The Book of Revelation describes how all creation takes part in the heavenly liturgy: "And I heard every creature in heaven and on earth and under the earth and in the sea, and all therein, saying 'To him who sits upon the throne and to the Lamb be blessing and honor and glory and might for ever and ever!'" (Rev 5:13).

Whatever the fate of other creatures, for us men the connection between this world and the new creation means that what we do now prepares the way for what is to come. Attention to the Kingdom of Heaven, far from distracting us from the needs of this world, in fact increases our efforts to do good here, as the lives of the saints bear witness. There is a startling passage at the end of the Second Letter of Peter: after an apocalyptic description of the end of the world, the author continues: "Since all these things are thus to be dissolved, what sort of persons ought you to be in lives of holiness and godliness, waiting for and hastening the coming of the day of God ... !" (2 Pet 3:11–12). Why would we want to hasten such a catastrophic event? Because it is only catastrophic from our earthly point of view—just as leaving the womb might seem cataclysmic to the baby. We hasten the coming of the Kingdom by holiness and godliness because these are the elements that endure to eternal life. The "dissolution" Scripture speaks of is the burning away of all that is evil, sad, or mortal.

The Risen Christ Is the Source of Eternal Life

The original perishable seed sown was the humanity of Jesus; every imperishable body must take its origin from him. As his death drew near, Jesus said,

> The hour has come for the Son of man to be glorified. Truly, truly, I say to you, unless a grain of wheat falls into the earth and dies, it remains alone; but if it dies, it bears much fruit.... If any one serves me, he must follow me; and where I am, there shall my servant be also; if any one serves me, the Father will honor him. (Jn 12:23–24, 26)

The risen Jesus is the true vine imparting divine life to the branches that abide in him. The necessity of our union with the risen Lord cannot be emphasized too much. Although the title "Christ" is used infrequently of Jesus in the Gospels, it occurs well over four hundred times in the rest of the New Testament, and in the majority of cases, it refers to *our* being "in Christ". The fact that eternal life comes to us from the risen Christ helps explain his categorical claims: "Truly, truly, I say to you, unless one is born of water and the Spirit, he cannot enter the kingdom of God" (Jn 3:5); "Truly, truly, I say to you, unless you eat the flesh of the Son of man and drink his blood, you have no life in you" (Jn 6:53); "I am the way, and the truth, and the life; no one comes to the Father, but by me" (Jn 14:6). Advocates of religious pluralism reject such words as arrogant, but Jesus' teachings simply state a fact: resurrection life can come to us only through the resurrected Christ.

Does this mean that only Christians can be saved? From the very first sermon on Pentecost morning, the Church has proclaimed that we are saved by being united to Christ through faith and baptism (Acts 2:38). But is it possible that those who have never heard the Gospel—or rejected it because of the failures of Christians—and yet have been Christlike in their charity, are "in Christ" and so can receive eternal life? The Catholic answer is affirmative. The Second Vatican Council teaches: "For, since Christ died for all men, and since the ultimate vocation of man is in fact one, and divine, we ought to believe that the Holy Spirit in a manner known only to God offers to every man the possibility of being associated with this paschal mystery" (*GS*, no. 22).

By our union with the incarnate Son of God, we experience the life of the Trinity from within, so far as we can as mere creatures. This is already true here on earth, although we see it obscurely by faith. God has sent the Spirit of his Son into our hearts, so that even now we have "the mind of Christ" and can know something of the thoughts of God through his Spirit (1 Cor 2:16; 2:10–11). By virtue of the indwelling of the Holy Spirit, "through God you are no longer a slave but a son, and if a son then an heir" (Gal 4:7). The inheritance God gives us is unique, because unlike other legacies, *we* have to die to receive it. The First Letter of John describes how our heavenly inheritance will enrich us: "Beloved, we are God's children now; it does not yet appear what we shall be, but we know that when he appears we shall be like him, for we shall see him as he is" (1 Jn 3:2). Saint Paul contrasts earth and Heaven in this way: "For now we see in a mirror dimly, but then face to face. Now I know in part; then I shall understand fully, even as I have been fully understood" (1 Cor 13:12).

Heaven: The Communion of Saints in the Communion of the Trinity

Our Catholic tradition calls this "face-to-face" experience of God the Beatific Vision. It is different from any knowledge we can have on earth. Here below, our knowledge is mediated through our senses, it is the result of reasoning, and it is always somewhat obscure. The knowledge of God we will enjoy in Heaven is immediate, intuitive, and clear, although as creatures we can never fully comprehend the mystery of God. Unless you are of a philosophical bent, discussion of the Beatific Vision can seem rather abstract. It might help to recall experiences that thrilled you to the core of your being—a spectacular vista, the power of great music, the loving gaze or embrace of another. We feel a momentary rush at such times. These emotions are transitory; our memory can retain some image of the moment, but the intensity of the original experience eludes us. In Heaven, the ecstasy is endless, so we need not fear that the moment will pass. We will know (in a way beyond anything we can now imagine) the love of the Holy Spirit who unites us to Christ. We will experience the mutual love between the Father and the Son in a way infinitely greater than we have known any loves here on earth. When we say "Our Father" in Heaven, we will do so with the ardor of the Son himself; and when we hear the Father say to us, "You are my beloved in whom I am well pleased", we will be caught up in an unending torrent of joy.

Freed from the limits of this world, we will contemplate the humanity of Christ in all its glory. The beauty of his Mother and the saints will fill us with happiness; and since our family members and friends will, we pray, be among them, we will have the joy of seeing our loved ones completely happy. The words of Saint Paul, "Now I know in part; then I shall understand fully, even as I have been fully understood", apply to our relationships with one another as well as our relationship with God. We will see and be seen through and through because we will know one another in God. Heaven is a communion of love: our unique identity, shaped by our ties with God and others here on earth, will flower there. Far from losing ourselves in some divine "essence", we will become our truest selves in communion; the trinitarian dynamic of total self-giving and unlimited reception of the other will be our life.

Unbelievers ridicule Heaven as "pie in the sky when you die". C. S. Lewis answered such derision by pointing out that either there is pie in the sky or there is not: if there is no Heaven, then Christ was wrong and Christianity is meaningless; if it exists, the prospect of gaining it or losing it must influence everything we do. We believe Jesus was speaking the truth, that God has prepared a home for us beyond anything we can imagine. But we also believe that we taste the pie already: our eternal life began when we were plunged into the death of Christ and rose again with him in baptism. We are already receiving divine life, we are already united to the communion of saints, and in the Eucharist, we already enjoy a foretaste of the heavenly Wedding Feast of the Lamb.

This infusion of divine life implants and nourishes in us the theological virtues of faith, hope, and charity. Saint Ignatius of Antioch described the trajectory of the Christian journey this way: "These are the beginning and the end of life: faith the beginning, love the end. When these two are found together, there is God, and everything else concerning right living follows from them." [4] Faith and hope accompany us on our pilgrimage, but in Heaven, they will disappear and only love will remain. Indeed, Heaven is nothing other than the bonds of love we have forged here on earth finding their full expression at last. The *Catechism* speaks of our destiny this way: "This perfect life with the Most Holy Trinity—this communion of life and love with the Trinity, with the Virgin Mary, the angels and all the blessed—is called 'heaven'. Heaven is the ultimate end and fulfillment of the deepest human longings, the state of supreme, definitive happiness" (*CCC*, no. 1024).

Jesus is the great shepherd of the sheep whom the God of peace has raised from the dead (Heb 13:20), and it is he who leads us to the green pastures of eternity: "My sheep hear my voice, and I know them, and they follow me; and I give them eternal life, and they shall never perish, and no one shall snatch them out of my hand" (Jn 10:27–28). Long ago, Saint Gregory the Great exhorted his flock to hear the voice of the Good Shepherd and follow him:

> Beloved brothers, let us set out for these pastures where we shall keep joyful festival with so many of our fellow citizens. May the thought of their happiness urge us on! Let us stir up our hearts, rekindle our faith, and long eagerly for what heaven has in store for us. To love thus is to be already on our way. No matter what obstacles we encounter, we must not allow them to turn us aside from the joy of that heavenly feast. Anyone who is determined to reach his destination is not deterred by the roughness of the road that leads to it. Nor must we allow the charm of success to seduce us, or we shall be like a foolish traveler who

---

[4] Ignatius of Antioch, *Letter to the Ephesians*, 14:1 (Office of Readings, Monday of the Second Week in Ordinary Time).

is so distracted by the pleasant meadows through which he is passing that he forgets where he is going.[5]

May each of us, too, hear the voice of the Good Shepherd who calls us by name and leads us home.

[5] Gregory the Great, *Homily 14*, nos. 3–6 (Office of Readings, Fourth Sunday of Easter).

Conclusion

The Tree in the Middle of the Garden

A simple antiphon in the Catholic liturgy professes a profound truth: "See how the Cross of the Lord stands revealed as the tree of life." [1] This conviction finds artistic expression in a mosaic that adorns the apse of Rome's cathedral church. At the center of the mosaic stands a glorious Cross, above which hovers a dove symbolizing the Holy Spirit. Four streams of water flow from the base of this Cross; majestic stags drink from these rivers, and sheep slake their thirst in green pastures. The scene evokes an event at the beginning of the Bible when God planted the Tree of Life in Eden, and from the middle of the Garden flowed four rivers (Gen 2:9–10). I would like to conclude this book with a meditation on this mosaic and its setting.

Today we associate the pope with Saint Peter's and the Vatican, but for a thousand years, Christians thought of "the Lateran" in this way. The emperor Constantine donated the palace of the Laterani family to the Bishop of Rome, and it served as the papal residence until the end of the fourteenth century. Dedicated in the first quarter of the fourth century, the Archbasilica of the Most Holy Savior is one of the world's oldest churches. The building has suffered much throughout its long history—sacked by the Vandals, ruined by earthquake, severely damaged by fire twice. The entire edifice was redone in a rather baroque style by Borromini in the seventeenth century, so many visitors to Saint John Lateran (as it is popularly known) may not be aware of its antiquity.

The mosaic in the apse has a long history, too. What we see today is a late nineteenth-century reproduction of a mosaic executed at the end of the thirteenth century by Jacopo Torriti and Jacopo da Camerino. These artists in turn had copied a mosaic that may go back to the fifth

[1] Antiphon for Psalm 1 (Office of Readings, Sunday Week I).

century, or even earlier. The pedigree of the image is more ancient still: in his commentary on the Book of Daniel, written around the year 200 B.C., Saint Hippolytus of Rome says this: "This stream of the four waters flowing from Christ we see in the Church. He is the stream of living waters, and he is preached by the four evangelists. Flowing over the whole earth, he sanctifies all who believe in him."[2]

The basilica and its mosaic stand as monuments to a community that has preached the Catholic Gospel since the days of the apostles. "The Cross of the Lord stands revealed as the tree of life!" This is the message of salvation, and the Church as the "living Gospel" has proclaimed this message for two thousand years. The Gospel is living; so, too, is the Church's tradition. Here is how the Second Vatican Council described this vital process:

> This tradition which comes from the Apostles develops in the Church with the help of the Holy Spirit. For there is a growth in the understanding of the realities and the words which have been handed down. This happens through the contemplation and study made by believers, who treasure these things in their hearts (see Luke, 2:19, 51), through a penetrating understanding of the spiritual realities which they experience, and through the preaching of those who have received through Episcopal succession the sure gift of truth. For as the centuries succeed one another, the Church constantly moves forward toward the fullness of divine truth until the words of God reach their complete fulfillment in her. (*DV*, no. 8)

Reviewing the dogmatic teachings presented in this book, we might take the vertical arm of the Cross as representing the continuity of the Gospel of salvation through time, and the horizontal arm as representing the breadth and depth that this message has attained over the centuries. There is both continuity and growth, as befits a living tree.

The Continuity of the Church throughout History

The continuity of the community of the People of God is particularly significant at three stages: from the Old Testament to the New Testament; in the lives of the disciples before and after the Resurrection;

---

[2] Quoted in Timothy T. O'Donnell, *Heart of the Redeemer* (San Francisco: Ignatius Press, 1989), p. 81. Irenaeus was the first Father to liken the Gospels to the four rivers of Paradise. There is a tradition that Hippolytus was a disciple of Irenaeus; while most scholars doubt this, it is very likely that he was at least familiar with Irenaeus' writings.

and in the community of believers from the time of Jesus to the present day. Regarding the first, we are acutely aware today of how important it is to see Jesus in the context of first-century Judaism. For this reason, the *Catechism* devotes many paragraphs to the topic "Jesus and Israel" (*CCC*, nos. 574–98). As the Gospel spread to the Gentiles, it moved out of its Jewish matrix: Mark had to explain the meaning of certain Jewish customs to his readers, and by the time the Gospel of John was written, "the Jews" were considered an alien—and hostile—community. At their best, Christians understood with Saint Paul that the Church was made up of Jew *and* Gentile. On the back wall of Santa Sabina church, not far from Rome's cathedral, there is a fifth-century mosaic that portrays two women, one identified as *Ecclesia ex circumcisione* (the Church from among the circumcised), the other as *Ecclesia ex gentibus* (the Church from among the nations). Unfortunately, the inclusion of the Gentiles came to be understood by many Christians as a rejection of the Jews. In some of the great gothic cathedrals, Christ is depicted in majesty over the main door, and again we find two women. One, her face radiant, is turned toward the Lord—the Church. The other, head bent and shrouded in a veil, has turned her back on the Lord—the Synagogue. Thankfully, relations between Jews and Christians are improving, although it is inexpressibly sad that it took the horrific events of the twentieth century to start this process. As the Christian understanding of Jesus deepens by our seeing him and his disciples in their Jewish milieu, this will create new challenges as well as new opportunities in relations between Christians and Jews. Still, it is certainly remarkable to have a pope at the beginning of the twenty-first century write a book about Jesus in which he enters into dialogue with a Jewish scholar.[3]

The second important stage of continuity is in the community of disciples during and after the public ministry of Jesus. There can be no doubt that Jesus' Resurrection transformed everything as far as his followers were concerned, but the novelty of the Gospel did not constitute a rupture with the ministry of Jesus, and *the community of disciples*

---

[3] *Jesus of Nazareth: From the Baptism in the Jordan to the Transfiguration* (New York: Doubleday, 2007), written by Joseph Ratzinger/Pope Benedict XVI. The Holy Father began the book before his election, and he makes it clear that it presents his own personal opinions and is not to be seen as an expression of papal teaching. The Jewish author is Jacob Neusner, author of *A Rabbi Talks with Jesus*, originally published in 1994.

was the guarantor of that continuity. At the beginning of the Acts of the Apostles, Saint Luke describes how Peter and the community chose Matthias to take the place of Judas among the Twelve. Peter's criteria for candidacy are very interesting. He says to the community: "So one of the men who have accompanied us during all the time that the Lord Jesus went in and out among us, beginning from the baptism of John until the day when he was taken up from us—one of these men must become with us a witness to his resurrection" (Acts 1:21–22). The new apostle is to be a witness to the Resurrection of Jesus, but he is to be chosen from among the disciples who had accompanied Jesus throughout his public ministry. Saint Paul was a notable exception, of course; most of the earliest preachers of the Gospel, however, were men and women who had known Jesus in his lifetime, and could testify not only to his Resurrection, but also to his teaching and miracles. The Twelve held a privileged place among these witnesses. Curiously, we know little about most of them apart from their names. Legends surround them, and tradition associates them with the evangelization of various places, many quite distant from Palestine. What we do know is that late in the second century Saint Irenaeus could affirm that the same Creed was professed in Spain, Gaul, Egypt, Libya, and the East, and that these communities had received the Gospel from the apostles and their disciples (*CCC*, nos. 173–74).

Mention of Irenaeus brings us to the third stage of continuity: between the first disciples and later generations of believers. Irenaeus himself serves as a good example. He was born sometime in the first half of the second century and grew up in Smyrna, in Asia Minor. There he heard the preaching of the bishop Polycarp, who suffered martyrdom around the year 155. Polycarp was in his eighties when he died, and he claimed to have learned the Gospel from "John the elder" and other apostolic witnesses. Scholars disagree as to whether this John was the author of the fourth Gospel, but whoever he is, Polycarp describes him as an eyewitness to the life of Jesus. Irenaeus died at the beginning of the third century, that is to say, 170 years after Christ. This is a long time, and yet Irenaeus learned about Jesus from a man who had heard about him from an eyewitness! He and Polycarp illustrate the link between later generations of Christians and the first disciples. In fact, Irenaeus appealed to this continuity in his debates with the Gnostics: he pointed out that the subsequent leaders in the communities founded by the apostles were known, and none of them had taught the doctrines that Gnostics claimed were "apostolic". Christians living almost two centuries after Jesus still preserved the apostolic witness, and, as with Irenaeus, some had learned the living Gospel from those who had received it from eyewitnesses.

Some biblical scholars today speak of a Jesus "movement" in the first two centuries, by which they mean a wide variety of diverse (and sometimes conflicting) communities inspired in some way by Jesus. He may have influenced many disparate groups, but as Catholics we do not agree that this movement predated the Church. We hold that Jesus and his followers belonged to the Jewish people; that his disciples remained together after his death and Resurrection; and that as they carried the Gospel throughout the world, they preserved a sense that they belonged to one community, the Church. This community accommodated various views about Jesus' life and death, and those differences naturally created tensions, but the importance of maintaining the unity of the one Body of Christ was recognized. There may well have been other groups as far back as the first century who identified themselves with Jesus and defined themselves differently. But this understanding of the continuity of the one Body of Christ—the apostles and other disciples of Jesus forming the nucleus of the ongoing community of the Church— is, I believe, the predominant perspective found in the New Testament, and it has been the self-understanding of the Christian community in Rome from the first century to the present day.

Although Irenaeus tells us that Christian communities throughout the world traced their origin back to the apostles, he does not offer a clear picture of how they were related to one another. The New Testament speaks of "churches", or of "the church of God at such-and-such a place", but it also refers to "the Church" as a universal body, and the term "the Catholic Church" appears at the end of the New Testament era in the writings of Saint Ignatius of Antioch (*CCC*, no. 830). Irenaeus grew up in Asia Minor and died as the Bishop of Lyons in southern France, which indicates that communication existed between Christian communities that were geographically quite distant from one another. The Christian writers of the second century under stood "the Church" to be more than a loose aggregation of local communities; it was the one Body of Christ, and for this reason it was important to maintain effective communion between congregations.

The See of Peter and the Unity of the Church

Of the churches founded by the apostles, one had a distinctive role in fostering this communion, the community in that city where Peter and Paul had laid down their lives. At the beginning of the second century, Ignatius of Antioch wrote that the church of Rome "presides in charity" among the Christian communities.[4] The Christian churches of the second century were very conscious of their origins, and Irenaeus noted that many of them could trace the line of their leaders back to the apostles themselves. However, he recognized that the community sanctified by the martyrdom of the two most glorious apostles, Peter and Paul, held a certain preeminence in this regard, and for this reason, he taught that "the whole Church, that is, the faithful everywhere, must necessarily be in accord" with the Roman church.[5] The leaders of that community inherited Paul's solicitude for all the churches and Peter's charge from the risen Lord to feed his sheep. Sometimes the exercise of this responsibility was welcomed: the church at Corinth read the Letter of Clement (ca. 95) in its liturgical assemblies (as did some other communities) even up to the fourth century. At other times, as in a second-century dispute regarding the date for Easter in Asia Minor, Roman intervention was resisted.[6] The nature and extent of Rome's authority was debated, but its authority came, not from the fact that Rome was the capital of the empire (an empire that was persecuting the Church), but from its association with the apostles Peter and Paul. The mosaic of the four rivers flowing out to the whole world from the Cross was placed in the apse of Rome's cathedral to symbolize that the one Church of Christ is called to preach

[4] St. Ignatius of Antioch, *Epistula ad Romanos*, 1, 1: *Apostolic Fathers*, II/2, 192, quoted in *CCC*, no. 834; cf. *LG*, no. 13.

[5] St. Irenaeus, *Adversus haereses*, 3, 3, 2: *PG* 7/I, 849, quoted in *CCC*, no. 834; cf. Vatican Council I: DS 3057.

[6] Irenaeus' high regard for the church of Rome did not prevent him from remonstrating with its bishop on this question. In most places (including Lyons, where Irenaeus was bishop), Easter was celebrated on Sunday; in Asia Minor (where he grew up), it was celebrated at Passover, on whatever day of the week it fell. This had been a source of some tension throughout the second half of the second century, but the matter came to a head when Pope Victor I (189–198) excommunicated those who refused to observe Easter on Sunday. Irenaeus wrote to Victor and pointed out that none of his predecessors had taken such a drastic step, and that Pope Anicetus and Polycarp of Smyrna had disagreed on the matter, yet remained in communion. Irenaeus did not say that the Bishop of Rome could not excommunicate the churches of Asia Minor, but that he should not.

the Gospel to the whole world, and that the successor of Saint Peter must be solicitous for the whole flock of Christ.

Is this image of the Catholic Church as a living Gospel, whose waters flow untainted down through the centuries, overly idealistic? Let us recall the words of the Second Vatican Council cited above: "For as the centuries succeed one another, the Church constantly moves forward toward the fullness of divine truth until the words of God reach their complete fulfillment in her" (*DV*, no. 8). Many would consider this assertion naïve. Their principal objections are two: first, such an optimistic statement ignores the reality of sin in the Catholic Church; second, it implies that the Catholic Church *always* moves forward in doctrinal matters. To the first objection, any Catholic with even a nodding acquaintance of our history would plead "guilty"— sinfulness as well as holiness marks the members of the Church. To the images of the Church as Virgin, Mother, and Bride, the Fathers sometimes added a fourth: "Chaste Prostitute"—sinful by her selfishness, the Church is sanctified by her Spouse.

Some would find the description of the council fathers easier to accept if every occupant of the bishop's chair beneath that Roman mosaic had been a paragon of sanctity and learning. There have been popes who were great saints; there have been popes who were accomplished theologians; a few have been both. Most popes have been diligent, a number have been mediocre, and some have been corrupt, venal, or immoral. In short, they have reflected in microcosm the field of the Church, where weeds and wheat grow together. Even the apostle chosen by Jesus himself to feed his flock was marked by weakness and failings. The Catholic Church is not a gathering of the elect; the community that has preached the Gospel for two thousand years is no stranger to the humiliation of failing to live up to the message she proclaims. But it is this actual community, with its lights and shadows, that has handed on the Gospel. Somewhere Chesterton suggests that it is inconsistent to claim an association with Saint Francis of Assisi if one is not willing to also admit a connection with Pope Alexander the Sixth.[7] The Catholic Church is very much an earthen vessel.

---

[7] Pope Alexander VI (Rodrigo Borgia) was pope from 1492 to 1503. His family name is synonymous with Renaissance intrigue—poisonings, sexual license, and nepotism—so that this pope has come to symbolize for many the worst excesses of corruption. And he might not take the prize as the worst pope.

The second objection—that it is simplistic to claim that the Catholic Church moves forward unfailingly toward the fullness of divine truth—calls for a nuanced response. Throughout this book, we have seen how the Church's understanding of the Gospel has deepened over time. Often this insight was the fruit of controversy. Even something as simple as the canon of Scripture became clear only gradually; theological issues like the Incarnation and the Trinity had even more complex histories. We Catholics believe that the Holy Spirit guides the Church into all truth and prevents her from falling into error in her fundamental dogmatic faith, but this guarantee does not keep her from exaggerated emphases or the neglect of other important doctrines. Controversy tends to focus attention on one aspect of the truth to the detriment of other aspects. Exponents of contradictory views all believed that they were being faithful to the apostolic tradition, and it is not always readily apparent where the truth lies. This wrangling is distasteful to those who prefer to picture the Church lifting up jewel after jewel of doctrine over the centuries and admiring them serenely. The actual process of "constantly moving forward toward the fullness of divine truth" can be messy and rancorous, and it is rarely serene. The Holy Spirit keeps the Church from going off the rails; he does not guarantee that it will be a smooth ride.

In describing how the Catholic understanding of the apostolic faith has grown, I have tried to show that the Church has exercised restraint when making dogmatic definitions of that faith. At times, such definitions were required in answer to teachings that challenged the deposit of faith, for example, the great Christological definitions of the first several ecumenical councils and the decrees of the Council of Trent regarding the sacraments. At other times, as with the Immaculate Conception and the Assumption, the pope proclaimed a doctrine to be held as divinely revealed at the insistent request of the People of God, and only after the Church's understanding of the doctrine had matured over many centuries. The Catholic conviction that the pope and the college of bishops carry on the teaching office of the apostles creates ecumenical difficulties; when other Christians reject Catholic teaching, it is because they consider it to be an addition to, or worse, a corruption of, the apostolic faith. But we believe that Christ must have intended his Church to have a living teaching authority; otherwise, the one Body of Christ would disintegrate into hundreds of sects professing contradictory beliefs about Jesus. There would be a Jesus "movement", but no Church.

It will not be easy to overcome this ecumenical impasse. From the Catholic perspective, the "claims of Rome" are based on the *fact* of Rome: since the end of the New Testament era, that church and its leaders have maintained that the See of Peter exercises a unique role in safeguarding the unity of the worldwide Church, and no other community or individual has ever made a like claim. In the fourth century, Church unity came to be identified with the Byzantine Empire, but this excluded churches beyond the empire. The communities that emerged from the Reformation found their unity in their role as national churches, or by shared theological convictions that differentiated their adherents not only from the Catholic Church, but also from other Protestant denominations. Only in our own day are we experiencing the end of what is sometimes called "the Constantinian Church", by which is meant an ecclesial body wedded to a political system. Formerly Christian countries are now avowedly secular. This change creates an opportunity to foster a unity among Christians that is not dependent on (or enforced by) the state.

Structures of Church unity based on king, country, or ethnic identity are fading fast in the lands traditionally associated with Christianity; at the same time, the living Gospel is enjoying remarkable vitality in the southern hemisphere. How can the Church take root in new cultures while at the same time assuring her unity in faith? Freed from the temptation to find this unity in a "state church", the way is open to recover a more profoundly *sacramental* basis for Christian unity. As we saw in chapter six, the understanding of the one Church as a communion of churches is founded on the mystery of the Trinity. This unity and diversity were expressed in the bonds uniting Peter and the other apostles, a dynamic that has continued in their successors by means of the complementary structures of primacy and collegiality. In his encyclical on ecumenism, *Ut unum sint*, Pope John Paul II expressed the hope that the improved climate of dialogue among Christians may now provide an opportunity to reach a shared understanding of the Petrine ministry. He made this appeal to other Christians:

> Could not the real but imperfect communion existing between us persuade Church leaders and their theologians to engage with me in a

patient and fraternal dialogue on this subject, a dialogue in which, leaving useless controversies behind, we could listen to one another, keeping before us only the will of Christ for his Church and allowing ourselves to be deeply moved by his plea "that they may all be one ... so that the world may believe that you have sent me" (Jn 17:21)? (no. 96)[8]

Along with this invitation, the Holy Father acknowledged that although the papal office should be a form of service, it has sometimes manifested itself in a different light. Thus his invitation to dialogue demands on the Catholic side a willingness to study our history and distinguish between the proper and the improper exercise of primacy in the past. Pope John Paul articulated very forcefully the Catholic commitment to ecumenism; he clearly believed that this dialogue represents an occasion for the Church to "move forward toward the fullness of God's truth".

The Riches of the Gospel Reveal Themselves over Time

The living tradition of the Church is not simply a matter of handing on formulas; rather, the Church comes to a deeper understanding of the fullness of God's truth by contemplating the perennial truth of the Gospel in new situations. The vertical arm of the Cross—the continuity of the Church's witness through time—is complemented by the horizontal arm: a wider and deeper comprehension of the meaning of the Gospel. We see this dynamic at work already in the New Testament, notably in connection with the question of the acceptance of Gentiles into the Church. From a Jewish perspective, to exempt such converts from the observance of the Law was tantamount to a rejection of Israel's faith; and some refused to accept the decision of the apostles in this matter. Yet the apostles saw the matter differently: God's blessings to the chosen people were now, in Christ, being extended to the Gentiles as well. To assert that Jesus was both "the glory of Israel" and "a light for revelation to the Gentiles" (Lk 2:32) meant that God had fulfilled his promise to the chosen people *and* that this salvation exceeded Israel's expectations. New circumstances revealed new facets of the Good News.

[8] English translation from Vatican website.

The mosaic in Saint John Lateran provides an interesting illustration of this "rereading" of tradition. The Cross of Christ is flanked by several important figures: Mary, John the Baptist, and the apostles Peter, Paul, Andrew, and John. Art historians disagree about how faithfully the thirteenth-century artists copied the ancient mosaics. Had those saints been part of the original composition, or were they added later? And if so, when? Where the artists clearly broke new ground was in placing two contemporary saints, Francis of Assisi and Anthony of Padua, next to our Lady and John the Baptist. They are much smaller than the great biblical figures, but their presence proclaims that the streams of water flowing from the Cross of Christ continue to irrigate the soil of the world and produce the fruit of holiness. As mendicants, Francis and Anthony represented a novel form of religious life in the thirteenth century, yet their placement in the apse of Rome's cathedral showed that this new way of life was genuinely apostolic, and "traditional" in the most authentic meaning of that word.

Throughout this book, I have described how the Church's understanding of the apostolic faith grew over the centuries and how these dogmas are related to one another. The First Vatican Council spoke of the *nexus mysteriorum* (connections between mysteries), and the Second Vatican Council spoke of a "'hierarchy' of truths".[9] At the heart of the Church's faith stands the mystery of the Trinity, and the doorway to that mystery is the Incarnation of the Son of God. Everything else the Catholic Church professes flows from these two mysteries. The salvific meaning of Jesus' death is inextricably linked to his two-fold identity as the eternal Son of God and the Word-made-flesh. We profess that the Church must be a visible community on earth because the logic of the Incarnation calls for this; this community is both one Church and a communion of local churches because she is a created reflection of the mystery of three Persons in one God. Our sacramental system derives from the mystery of the Incarnation, as does our veneration of images and relics: the material world is a vehicle of divine grace. What we believe about Mary emerges from contemplation of the awe-inspiring event of the Incarnation, and of her relationship to the Trinity and to the rest of the Church.

---

[9] See *CCC*, no. 90, which cites for the former, Vatican Council I: DS 3016; and for the latter, *LG*, no. 25, and *UR*, no. 11.

What is true of the Church's dogmatic pronouncements is true of her whole life: the Trinity and the Incarnation are the foundation of what we believe and what we do. Catholic liturgical rites and devotional practices, poetry and architecture, charitable works and educational enterprises—all find their meaning and purpose in the conviction that the Church is the Body of Christ and his Bride, and that through the outpouring of the Spirit our relationship to the Father and to the rest of creation is radically changed. This is true of our moral life, too, although this is something most Catholics may not advert to sufficiently. The Catholic Church can defend traditional morality on the basis of natural law, and often does so in engaging the wider society. For example, we oppose abortion because of the innate dignity of human life, which is certainly not a uniquely Catholic conviction. But when we consider the human person in light of the mysteries of the Trinity and the Incarnation, how much richer the Church's moral teaching appears! Many religions teach us to love God and neighbor, but the Incarnation gives this twofold exhortation a special meaning, because God incarnate assures us: "Truly, I say to you, as you did it to one of the least of these my brethren, you did it to me" (Mt 25:40). And, if marriage is a created reflection of the mutual love between the Persons of the Trinity, then the complementarity of man and woman in the conjugal union is no mere sociological construct—it pertains to the essence of what it means for the two to become one flesh. If spousal love reflects divine love, then it is fitting that the unitive and procreative aspects of the marriage act are inseparable.

In presenting the dogmatic teachings of the Church in this book, I have proposed "implications"—suggestions as to how the truth of Christ sets us free. But each of us must apply the Good News to our own lives. The fathers of the Second Vatican Council did not limit tradition to the teaching of the pope and bishops. Growth in understanding "happens through the contemplation and study made by believers, who treasure these things in their hearts" and "through a penetrating understanding of the spiritual realities which they experience" (*DV*, no. 8). The mosaic of the Tree of Life is composed of countless individual stones. In the same way, each individual believer reflects some unique aspect of the liberating truth of Christ. Every member of the Body of Christ shares in the mission of the Church as a whole: to hand on the living Gospel "which was once for all delivered to the saints" (Jude 3).

The Truth of Life Is Seen through the Eyes of Faith

Saint Paul told the Corinthians that "the word of the cross is folly to those who are perishing, but to us who are being saved it is the power of God" (1 Cor 1:18). Faith is needed to see in Christ the Truth who sets us free. Without faith, we perceive only the dead wood of the Cross: Jesus is at best a good but tragic figure, the Church merely one institution among many in the pageant of human history. Faith opens our eyes to see the green buds of new life emerging from the wood of Christ's Cross. Faith opens our ears to hear the invitation of Jesus, dying of thirst, who yet can say, "If any one thirst, let him come to me and drink" (Jn 7:37). Faith allows us to proclaim the truth that makes us free: "See how the Cross of the Lord stands revealed as the Tree of Life!"

Appendix A

The Joy of Dogma

"THE TRUTH SHALL MAKE YOU FREE." These words are inscribed in bold letters over the entrance to City College of San Francisco. Knowledge liberates: technology frees us from drudgery; art and literature free us from cultural insularity; scientific advances free us from disease. No doubt the students passing beneath that motto seek the truth for different reasons, but they would find the maxim appropriate for their college. I wonder how many of them could identify the author of the quotation? It was not a great philosopher or scientist, a Plato, a Descartes, or an Einstein, who said, "The truth shall make you free"—it was Jesus Christ (Jn 8:32). The truth he came to teach concerns our relationship with God and with one another; the freedom he promised was deliverance from sin, despair, and death itself.

Jesus not only taught that the truth will make us free—he claimed to *be* that truth: "I am the way, and the truth, and the life" (Jn 14: 6). No other religious figure in history has made such an audacious assertion. Every philosopher assumes that the human mind can learn some truth about the most fundamental questions: Where have I come from? Why am I here? Where am I going? Every religious sage assumes that some kind of spiritual being or agency is an essential part of the answer to those questions. Only Christians believe that the Creator himself came into the world as man to teach us the truth.

The truth that Jesus is, and teaches, is *saving* truth: that is, it not only answers our deepest questions; it restores us to communion with God and with all that God has made. This truth truly does set us free—it frees us from our petty self-reliance; it frees us from our sins; it frees us from death itself. In the Catholic tradition, we call this saving truth "dogma".

257

Objections

The word has negative connotations for some. Many people today describe themselves as spiritual, but not religious; and *dogma* is a churchy word indeed. But dogma is Good News: if Jesus has conquered death by his Resurrection, this is good news; if God is not some impersonal force, but an eternal communion of love, this is good news; if we are destined for glory far beyond anything we can now imagine, this is good news. This is why I have entitled this Appendix "The Joy of Dogma"—it is another way of saying, "The truth shall make you free."

Admittedly, the word may not immediately convey a sense of freedom to people today. On the contrary, dogmas strike many as oppressive, obscurantist, and divisive. The first objection is that dogma violates the supremacy of the individual conscience. Critics point out that popes call upon governments to allow believers freedom to practice their faith, and yet deny some scholars the freedom to teach as Catholic theologians. Smoldering in the background of this objection are the embers of the Inquisition, which demanded at least external compliance if not internal agreement in doctrinal matters.

The Inquisition is an egregious example of the tendency to use religious identity as an instrument of social unity. This kind of coercion is still found in some parts of the world; the countries where this is *not* found are primarily those that are historically Christian. Nations that were formerly Catholic, Orthodox, or Protestant today allow the free practice of any religion or none. Precisely because such freedom of conscience exists, it is necessary for religious bodies to determine criteria for membership. I exercise freedom of conscience by choosing to belong to a particular faith community or not; if I cannot in conscience embrace the fundamental beliefs of that community, I am free to leave it. As Pope Benedict XVI frequently points out, the Catholic Church does not impose, she proposes.

Another hurdle is that dogmas are considered "unscientific". The contemporary secular outlook assumes that there is an inherent conflict between science and religion. But if there is a war, it is unilateral; many of the greatest scientists throughout history have been believers, and many are believers today. While there is no opposition between scientific and religious truth, there is an important difference: dogmas do not contradict scientific knowledge, but they do represent truth of a different order. As I will explain in a moment, in the Catholic understanding, dogma is truth that cannot be discovered by unaided human reason, but only by a revelation from God. This does not mean that such beliefs are irrational, or that no reasons can be given to justify them; it simply means that they are inaccessible to reason alone. For example, I can look at the marvels of the world around me and come to believe in a Creator, but that there is in the one God a Trinity of Persons can be known only by revelation. Each kind of knowledge, scientific or religious, has its own proper principles and procedures. And even revealed truths are received with human minds and are the subject of much debate and discussion before their meaning clearly emerges. I hope that this book affords a glimpse into the laboratory of Christian tradition, where we can see how a theological "experimental method" applied to certain fundamental truths over the centuries has yielded deeper knowledge of those truths. This is one way that the Holy Spirit guides the Church into all truth.

Finally, some object that dogmas create divisions between Christians. A familiar slogan has it, "Doctrine divides, service unites." This sentiment is particularly persuasive in a culture that prizes pragmatism. Would it not be better to forget the dusty debates of the past, which quite frankly mean little or nothing to most believers today, and simply rejoice in our common Christian identity? Since the beginning of the ecumenical movement in the late nineteenth century, some have suggested that doctrinal differences simply be ignored. This is in fact an ecumenical cul-de-sac: if the only virtue is "inclusiveness", the Gospel is emptied of its meaning and the followers of Christ abandon their mission, which is to bear witness to the truth. Authentic ecumenism entails the hard work of wrestling with the doctrines that divide us, so that our unity is founded on a shared faith in Christ, and not simply on some vague allegiance to "the Christian ideal". I would amend the slogan to this: "Doctrine unites, service witnesses." Contemporary ecumenical efforts follow the path of dialogue, which entails a respectful listening to the other's point of view. Fruitful ecumenism demands that we deal with dogmas, not ignore them.

The Meaning of Dogma

What, then, is the Catholic understanding of *dogma*? The term has come to have a specific definition in recent centuries, but its fundamental meaning is rooted in the New Testament. Dogma is the Gospel, the Good News revealed by God that we accept in faith. Saint Paul wrote to the Romans: "If you confess with your lips that Jesus is Lord and believe in your heart that God raised him from the dead, you will be saved" (Rom 10:9).

But what is this Gospel? Who is Jesus Christ? What does it mean to call him Lord? It is not surprising that a message with life-and-death consequences quickly generated competing expressions. Within thirty years of the death and Resurrection of Jesus, Saint Paul had to warn the Galatians: "If any one is preaching to you a gospel contrary to that which you received, let him be accursed" (Gal 1:9).[1] The Second Letter of Saint John conveys a similar caution: "For many deceivers have gone out into the world, men who will not acknowledge the coming of Jesus Christ in the flesh; such a one is the deceiver and the antichrist" (2 Jn 7). The first Christians realized that what united them was a shared understanding of the ministry, death, and Resurrection of Jesus Christ. This common understanding was not univocal, because no one interpretation could do justice to the mystery; this is evident from the fact that there are four Gospels in the New Testament, each of which relates to the life of Jesus in a different way. But from the very beginning, the community found it necessary to set boundaries and to reject some interpretations of Jesus as not merely partial, but wrong.

The arbiters in such matters were the apostles, who had been commissioned by Christ himself to preach the Gospel. He had given to the Twelve, and to Peter among them, the authority to lead the community of disciples and to determine their doctrine and life. The glimpses we get of the apostles in the New Testament suggest that there were disagreements even within this select and preeminent group. They relied

---

[1] The Greek word translated as "accursed" is *anathema*, and it means to be ostracized from the community. The term subsequently came to be applied to those who held views contrary to the faith of the Church. The exclusion was intended to be medicinal, that is, a temporary state of affairs to be lifted when the individual came to agree with the understanding of the Gospel professed by the community.

on the assistance of the Holy Spirit in their deliberations, but the deliberations themselves were very human, and could be rather heated. Any idea that God's revelation was conveyed in some kind of mystical trance is belied by the evidence of Scripture: from the outset, understanding of the truth God revealed in Christ has demanded intellectual effort, spirited debate, and a great deal of patience.

After the apostles died, their communities handed on the Gospel they had received from them, and their leaders bore witness to that belief. In the second century, Saint Irenaeus and others spoke of "the rule of faith", the core beliefs professed by Christian communities throughout the world. This nucleus of doctrine was expressed in various local creeds, of which the Apostles' Creed is a good example. As in the New Testament, so in succeeding centuries, we find diverse theological views about Christ, but also the awareness that some ideas must be rejected if a meaningful common profession of faith is to be preserved. This unity-in-diversity has been fostered in many ways: an agreed-upon collection of sacred books; formal and informal communication between the leaders of local communities; shared liturgical customs and creedal statements; devotional practices, hymns, artistic works, and so on. A mother teaching her child to make the sign of the cross is as integral to the process as the bishops gathered in solemn council. But at the heart of all this tradition stands "the rule of faith", the constitutive beliefs of the Christian religion, that we call dogma.

Over the past several centuries, the word has taken on a precise meaning in Catholic theology: a dogma is a divinely revealed truth, recognized as such by the teaching authority of the Church, and binding on all the faithful. Let us consider each of the three characteristics in turn.

Divinely Revealed Truth

Jesus Christ himself is the final and complete revelation of God; he is "the way, and the truth, and the life" (Jn 14:6). The doctrinal truths we profess are secondary expressions of the primary truth of the Father's love for us, the forgiveness of sins that he offers through Christ's death on the Cross, and the divine life we receive from the Holy Spirit. Put simply, what is revealed to us by Christ is the mystery of Trinity, and the remarkable invitation to enter into the communion of love that is the Father, the Son, and the Holy Spirit. This is *saving* truth because it opens our eyes to the reality of God's infinite, unconditional love for each and every person and the eternal life he offers us in Christ. We could never discover this truth for ourselves, and the only way to receive it is by faith: we believe this is true because God has revealed it to us. Dogmatic truths are expressions of that fundamental truth, and we believe *them* because we believe *him*. As the fathers taught at the First Vatican Council: "What moves us to believe is not the fact that revealed truths appear as true and intelligible in the light of our natural reason: we believe 'because of the authority of God himself who reveals them, who can neither deceive nor be deceived.' " [2]

Recognized by the Church

Secondly, these truths are recognized by the Church as divinely revealed. Sometimes this recognition is made in a solemn manner, especially when settling a theological dispute that threatens to divide the faith community. An example is the Nicene Creed that is recited by millions of Christians every Sunday. That Creed was written in the fourth century to safeguard belief in the complete divinity of Christ, and its clauses hammer home this truth: "God from God, Light from Light, true God from true God, begotten, not made, consubstantial with the Father". When a dogma is solemnly taught, we speak of it being "defined". But not all dogmas have been defined in this way. One of the most fundamental truths of the Christian faith is that Jesus Christ rose from the dead. This is an article of faith, but it has never been the object of an explicit, solemn definition because it has never been called into question by believers.

Binding on All the Faithful

Finally, in the Catholic understanding, dogmas are considered binding on all the faithful. This seems to be a tautology. Are not "the faithful" those who profess the faith of the Church? From an ecumenical perspective, however, this statement raises difficulties: How can Orthodox or Protestant Christians be "bound" by Catholic dogmas? The basic point to be made here is that there is an ecclesial component to determining what truths are revealed by God, and this is recognized by

---

[2] *CCC*, no. 156, citing *Dei Filius*, no. 3: DS 3008.

Orthodox and Protestant Christians, too. Also, while the Catholic tradition affords a significant role to the teaching authority of the Church, our ultimate reason for believing a dogma is not the authority of the Church that proclaims it, but the authority of God who reveals it. Thus, there may be more common ground here than seems apparent at first.

An example may help to make my point. All Christians believe that the four Gospels contained in the New Testament, and only those Gospels, are canonical. God inspired the sacred authors, and only God can make known which writings are inspired; there is no Geiger counter to determine inspiration. All of us, Orthodox, Protestants, and Catholics, believe that God has made known which Gospels are his inspired word; human investigation or scholarly research could not ascertain this. At the same time, this truth came to light through the experience of the Church: of the many Gospels circulating throughout the second century, these four alone came to be recognized as the word of God. When we affirm that these Gospels are Sacred Scripture, we are making an act of faith in a truth revealed by God, and we are recognizing that such an affirmation involves the judgment of the Church.

Doctrinal disagreements between various Christian confessions must be faced resolutely. But when dealing with dogmas, there is an important principle to keep in mind, supported by no less a Catholic authority than Saint Thomas Aquinas: our assent to a dogma is given ultimately to the truth itself, not to its formulation. Formulations are necessary, of course, but words are historically conditioned and their meanings change. For example, I have given a Catholic definition of *dogma* as a saving truth revealed by God and accepted as such by the Church. But the word was used in the Gospel of Luke to describe the census decree of Caesar Augustus; it was used by the Second Council of Constantinople to condemn the "impious dogmas" of those who denied that Jesus Christ had a human will; and it was used by Melchior Cano at the Council of Trent in reference to "Lutheran dogmas". So, as late as the sixteenth century the term *dogma* did not have the precise meaning in the Catholic lexicon that it has come to possess since. It would be misleading to find the word used in the sixth century, or the sixteenth century, and presume it meant then what it does now. One service theologians perform is to examine the doctrinal statements of the past and ask: What did these words mean *then*? What truth was this council or that pope seeking to articulate? We want to get beyond the rind of the formulation to the fruit of the truth. Words are essential: they ensure that we hold the same fundamental beliefs, and they are necessary if we are going to share those beliefs with others. But ever since the Tower of Babel, language has both united and divided the human family. Pentecost represents the undoing of Babel. As the disciples proclaimed the Resurrection of Christ, devout pilgrims from every nation under Heaven said, "We hear them telling in our own tongues the mighty works of God" (Acts 2:11). Dogmatic truths are the mighty works of God, their formulation is the expression "in our own tongue" for believers in each particular time and place.

To embrace Catholic dogma is to enter into solidarity with a community of believers, past and present. It is an instance of fidelity to tradition, which G. K. Chesterton described as "the democracy of the dead". When properly understood, Catholic dogmas do not constrict, they liberate. They are the "Good News" of Jesus Christ as that message has been reflected on and shared for two thousand years. The Bible itself is the primary norm of the Church's faith because it is the inspired record of the encounter the first disciples had with Christ. Scripture is the mirror into which the Church gazes throughout the ages; dogmas must be rooted in the word of God. But the wildly divergent interpretations of Jesus circulating today as in the past show how misleading it is to read the New Testament without the rule of faith.[3] For two millennia, the same Holy Spirit who inspired the sacred authors to write has assisted the community of believers to understand the meaning of what they wrote. This is what Jesus himself promised on the night before he died: "The Counselor, the Holy Spirit, whom the Father will send in my name, he will teach you all things, and bring to your remembrance all that I have said to you" (Jn 14:26). Acceptance of the dogma handed down to us manifests our conviction that Christ has been true to his promise: the Holy Spirit has continued to teach the followers of Christ the truth that makes us free.

---

[3] The integral connection between Scripture and the rule of faith was recognized as far back as the second century. Irenaeus likened those who attempted to interpret the Scriptures without the Creed to a man taking apart a beautiful mosaic of a king, rearranging the pieces into the picture of a dog, and then proclaiming it to be the image of the king (*Adversus haereses*, 1, 8, 1). All the pieces may be there, but their proper relationship has been destroyed.

Appendix B

The Catechism of the Catholic Church

In 1985, twenty years after the close of the Second Vatican Council, Pope John Paul II convened a synod of bishops to explore the spiritual riches of the council and examine its teachings in greater depth. The years since "the sixties" had been tumultuous in both Church and society, and many bishops at the synod expressed a desire for some kind of catechism or compendium of Church teaching. In 1992, thirty years after the opening of the council, the first edition of *The Catechism of the Catholic Church* was published. The second, and final, edition was promulgated on August 15, 1997.

This latest *Catechism* follows a traditional four-part structure: (1) what we believe, with a presentation of the twelve articles of the Apostles' Creed; (2) how we worship, with a survey of the seven sacraments; (3) how we live, with a review of the Ten Commandments; and (4) how we pray, with a reflection on the seven petitions of the Lord's Prayer. Yet *The Catechism of the Catholic Church* is very much a product of the Second Vatican Council: its extensive biblical references, citations of liturgical texts and spiritual writers from the East as well as the West, and frequent quotation of the conciliar texts themselves all reflect the vision of Vatican II.

As rich a resource as it is, *The Catechism of the Catholic Church* is only a tool, and like any tool, its effectiveness depends on the skill of the person using it. Certainly the *Catechism* could be consulted as a kind of almanac, for a quick answer to the question, "What does the Catholic Church teach about ... ?" But this approach only scratches the surface of this resource.

The four parts of the *Catechism* are mutually related, and it is when we make the connections between them that we begin to appreciate how useful this volume is. What we believe shapes our worship; the grace of the sacraments strengthens us to live the mystery we celebrate and nurtures our spiritual life. In this book, I have presented the dogmatic beliefs of the Catholic Church, the truth that makes us free. The *Catechism* makes this observation about them: "There is an organic connection between our spiritual life and the dogmas. Dogmas are lights along the path of faith; they illuminate it and make it secure. Conversely, if our life is upright, our intellect and heart will be open to welcome the light shed by the dogmas of faith" (no. 89; cf. Jn 8:31–32). Applying the teaching of the Church to our lives is a crucial enterprise: it is the difference between learning facts and living truth.

One very simple way to make these connections is by referring to the other paragraphs listed in the margins of the *Catechism*. For example, the Catholic Church professes that Jesus Christ laid down his life for every human person without exception (*CCC*, no. 605). In the margin of that paragraph, the reader is directed to paragraph number 2793, where we are told that when we pray to "our" Father, we should bring before God all those for whom he gave his beloved Son over to death: "God's love has no bounds, neither should our prayer." God's love and care for all men and the whole of creation finds its fullest expression in Christ's perfect self-offering; the *Catechism* reminds us that this dogmatic truth should move us to make our prayer truly universal in scope.

The sentence just quoted from paragraph number 2793 has a footnote: "Cf. *NA* 5", which refers to the "Declaration of the Relation of the Church to Non-Christian Religions" (*Nostra Aetate*) of the Second Vatican Council. This citation illustrates another treasure in the *Catechism*: the wealth of quotations from Scripture, the Fathers of the Church and other spiritual writers, the liturgical texts and magisterial teachings of the Church. In order to mine the riches of the *Catechism*, it should be read in conjunction with the Bible and other resources, at least the documents of the Second Vatican Council. There are many fine modern translations of the Bible, with insightful notes and commentary, and these can be used with the *Catechism* to explore the scriptural foundations for our Catholic faith. Similarly, a study of the documents of Vatican II provides a context for the teachings presented in the *Catechism*. A very useful resource is the *Companion to the Catechism of the Catholic Church*, published by Ignatius Press (1994), which provides the texts referred to, but not quoted, in the *Catechism* itself.

The authors of *The Catechism of the Catholic Church* envisaged their work in this way: "This catechism is conceived as *an organic presentation* of the Catholic faith in its entirety. It should be seen therefore as a unified whole" (*CCC*, no. 18, italics in original). This goal will be achieved if we take advantage of the many elements the *Catechism* offers: the Glossary and Analytical Index, cross-references to other parts of the *Catechism*, and the sources referred to in the footnotes.

Mention also should be made of the *Compendium of the Catechism of the Catholic Church*, which was issued in 2005. This useful resource summarizes the *Catechism* in a lucid and succinct manner, with references to appropriate paragraphs of the *Catechism* for each point. The interested inquirer will find in the *Compendium* a good starting point for an exploration of the teachings to be found in the *Catechism* itself.

In this Appendix, I will indicate the principal references in the *Catechism* to the basic dogmas of the faith we have examined in this book. I invite the reader to follow their lead into the riches of our Catholic faith to be found in *The Catechism of the Catholic Church*.

Chapter One: The Resurrection of Jesus

The Resurrection of Jesus is the crowning truth of our faith in Christ (no. 638). Christ truly died and experienced the separation of soul and body (no. 624). The Resurrection is historical, and it transcends history (no. 643). Evidence: the empty tomb (no. 640) and appearances to disciples (nos. 639–44). Christ's human nature was glorified by his Resurrection (nos. 645–46, 999). We are destined to share in his Resurrection (nos. 654–55).

With regard to relationships to Christ, the Church is the Mystical Body of the risen Christ (nos. 792–95) and his Bride (no. 796); he is the New Adam (no. 359), whose obedience undoes the effects of Adam's disobedience, original sin (nos. 402–4). There is a mutual indwelling between the risen Christ and Christians (no. 521).

We are born into the new creation through faith and the sacraments (nos. 790, 1002–3). The paschal mystery of Christ's death and Resurrection is present to us in the liturgy (no. 1085), and especially in the Eucharist, which is the sacramental Body of Christ (no. 1375). The Church gathers to celebrate the Eucharist on the Lord's Day because this is the day of his Resurrection (nos. 1166–67).

Chapter Two: Christ's Redemptive Death

Christ freely embraced his death in obedience to the Father's will (nos. 606–9). He gave his life for the whole human race (no. 605), including those who had already died (nos. 634–35). By his obedience, Christ undid the effects of Adam's disobedience (no. 615). He is both Priest and Victim (nos. 608, 662, 1544), and by his one perfect sacrifice we are redeemed (nos. 613–14) and justified (no. 1992). The Cross is the perfect expression of God's love for us, and mankind's love for God (no. 613). All sinners, not the Jewish people, are the authors of Christ's death (no. 598). While the existence of suffering poses a great problem (no. 312), it can become life-giving when united to the redemptive suffering of Christ (no. 618).

Chapter Three: The Incarnation of the Son of God

The Incarnation is the distinctive sign of Christian faith (no. 463). Christ's relation to the Father is central to his identity (nos. 606–7): he is "Son of God" in a unique way (nos. 441–45). In the face of various heresies (nos. 464–69), the Church affirms that the Son of God is eternally begotten of the Father and shares the divine nature completely. In the mystery of the Incarnation, the Son of God became truly man (no. 470), with a human body (nos. 476–78), soul (no. 471), intellect (nos. 472–74), and will (no. 475). He is thus one Person, the Son of God, with two natures, divine and human (nos. 479–83). The Word became flesh to reconcile us with God (nos. 459, 614), manifest God's love to us (no. 458), serve as a model of holiness for us (nos. 459, 520), and allow us to become partakers in his divine nature (nos. 460, 521, 1997). The incarnate Christ is present to us when we invoke his name (nos. 432–35, 2667–68); he is reverenced in icons and images (nos. 477, 2132); the Sacred Heart fittingly manifests his human and divine love for us (nos. 478); and he is present sacramentally in the Eucharist (no. 1374), which for this reason properly receives our adoration (no. 1378).

Chapter Four: The Most Holy Trinity

We believe in one God (nos. 200–202), who is almighty (no. 268) and is truth and love (nos. 214–21). Through the events of salvation history, the mystery that this one God is a communion of three Persons was gradually revealed (no. 684). In retrospect, we perceive a trinitarian pattern in the work of creation (nos. 290–92), although the work of creation and salvation are common to all three Persons (no. 258). It is through the sending of the Son and the Holy Spirit that the mystery has been revealed to us: the Spirit is revealed by the Son (nos. 243–44), and the Spirit reveals the Son (nos. 683, 687, 690). While the Holy Trinity is one in nature (no. 253), the three Persons are truly distinct from one another (no. 254) and relative to one another (no. 255).

The Trinity is central to Christian faith (no. 234), and historically, the Church gradually developed a language to express her faith in this mystery (nos. 245, 251–52). The Western theology states that the Holy Spirit proceeds from the Father and the Son, while the East professes that the Holy Spirit proceeds from the Father (nos. 246–48). The goal of God's saving plan is to bring all of creation into the communion of the Trinity (no. 260).

Chapter Five: The Church

In the Creed, we do not profess that we believe "in" the Church in the same way we believe in the Father, Son, and Holy Spirit (no. 750). Nonetheless, the saving missions of the Son and the Holy Spirit are continued in the Church (no. 257), and the trinitarian work of redemption brought the Church into existence (no. 759). The Church is the universal sacrament of salvation (no. 774), a community both visible and spiritual (no. 771). The mystery of election runs through salvation history (nos. 762, 781), and the Church's origins are rooted in the Old Testament (nos. 761–62). The Church is related to Christ as his Body (nos. 787–95) and his Bride (no. 796), and his mission as Priest, Prophet, and King continues in her (nos. 787–95). She is the Temple of the Holy Spirit (nos. 797–98), and so is each individual member (no. 1265).

In the Creed, we profess four "marks" of the Church: she is one (nos. 817–22), holy (nos. 823–29), catholic (nos. 830–31), and apostolic (nos. 857, 861). The Church of Christ "subsists" in the Catholic Church (no. 816), but there are ecclesial elements to be found in other Christian communities (no. 819), and degrees of incorporation among all the baptized (nos. 836–38).

The one Church is made up of a communion of churches; each particular church is the Catholic Church manifested in a particular location (nos. 832–34). The Catholic Church is dedicated to the work of deepening unity among all Christians (nos. 820–22). Because Christ is the only Savior, and the Church is his Body, she has been established by God as the sure means of salvation, but God is able to give eternal life to those beyond the visible community of disciples (nos. 847, 1257, 1260).

Chapter Six: The Pope and the Bishops

Jesus called the twelve apostles, associated them with his saving mission, and prepared them to lead the community of the Church (nos. 551, 858–60). Their role as witnesses to the Resurrection and founders of churches is unique to the apostles, but the bishops succeed them as pastors and teachers (nos. 861–62). Peter possessed a unique charism as leader of the Twelve, and this role has been handed on to his successors, the bishops of Rome (nos. 551–52, 881–82). Each bishop is responsible for his own particular church and the welfare of the universal Church (no. 886); the college of bishops as a whole, united to the successor of Peter, share responsibility for guiding the Church (nos. 880, 883–84). There is thus a twofold pattern of Church leadership willed by Christ: the collegiality of the bishops and the primacy of the pope. In this way, both the variety and unity of the Body of Christ is fostered structurally (no. 885), in keeping with God's saving plan to bring all creation into the communion of the Holy Trinity (no. 810).

The bishops succeed the apostles not only as pastors, but also as teachers (no. 77); this teaching office is known as the Magisterium (nos. 85, 890). The Holy Spirit guides the whole Church in understanding the saving truth of revelation, and in these matters, the belief of the Church is protected from error (nos. 84, 92, 889). Each bishop exercises his teaching office within his own particular church, and the college of bishops together with the pope does so for the universal Church (no. 883). The ordinary teaching of the pope and bishops is authoritative and should be embraced by the faithful (nos. 87, 2034), but when exercising the supreme teaching office to define dogma by the solemn teaching of an ecumenical council (no. 88) or an *ex cathedra* teaching of the pope (no. 891), such teaching is divinely protected from error and is held to be infallible (no. 891).

Chapter Seven: Sacred Scripture

The canonical books of the Bible (no. 120) are held to be inspired, so that, while they are truly the product of human authors (no. 106), we also believe that God is their author (no. 105). For this reason, they teach without error the saving truth God wishes to reveal (no. 107).

They are properly interpreted under the guidance of the same Holy Spirit who inspired them (no. 111), which means that particular passages are understood in light of the whole of Scripture (no. 112), read within the living tradition of the whole Church (no. 113), with attention to the "analogy of faith"—the relation of truths to one another and the whole plan of revelation (no. 114). Jesus Christ is the key to the whole Bible, both the Old Testament and the New (nos. 65, 101–2).

By a "literal" interpretation, we understand what the human author intended to convey (no. 110), and all other meanings are based on this (no. 116). As the successors of the apostles, the pope and college of bishops are called upon to teach the meaning of the word of God authoritatively (no. 85), but the Magisterium must always be the servant of that word (no. 86).

The Church venerates the word of God as she does the Eucharist (no. 103) and sees in her liturgical celebrations an important context for understanding the meaning of God's word (no. 1100).

Chapter Eight: The Life of Grace

Everything God has created is good (nos. 299, 337–44), and he sustains everything in existence (no. 301). Man is unique among earthly creatures because he has the capacity to know and love his Creator (no. 356).

As a result of the Fall, mankind lost certain preternatural gifts, and human nature was wounded, but not totally corrupted (no. 405). By his death and Resurrection, Christ has restored our communion with God (no. 1992): by the grace of conversion, we are justified, so that our sins are forgiven (nos. 1989–90) and our human nature is sanctified (no. 1995).

Grace is divine life that restores our communion with God (no. 1997), bestows on us filial adoption as sons and daughters of God (no. 1265), raises us to a supernatural relationship with God (no. 1999), and heals us from sin (no. 1266). Grace is at work at every moment, from initial conversion (no. 2001) to final perseverance (no. 2016). Grace does not negate our human freedom: rather, grace and freedom work in harmony (no. 1993), and our ability to do good improves with practice (no. 1773), so that cooperation with grace increases our freedom (no. 1742).

Justification is a pure gift that no one can merit (no. 2010); however, God has chosen to associate us in the work of salvation (no. 2008), so that once justified we can deepen our holiness, share our spiritual gifts with others, and help ourselves and others attain the gift of eternal life (no. 2010).

Baptism removes all sin, even original sin (no. 1263), transforms our human nature (no. 1265), and bestows on us the theological virtues of faith, hope, and charity (nos. 1991–92). In addition to the graces needed for our personal sanctification, the Holy Spirit bestows charisms for the good of the Church (nos. 799–801).

Chapter Nine: The Sacraments

Jesus Christ instituted the seven sacraments (nos. 1114–16, 1210) for our sanctification, as a means of building up his Body, the Church, and as the highest form of worship we could offer to God (no. 1123). The "sacramental economy" prolongs the saving mission of the Father, Son, and Holy Spirit (no. 1076). All life comes from the Father, and our worship is directed to him (nos. 1077–83) through the Son (nos. 1084–90), in the communion of the Holy Spirit (nos. 1091–109). This pattern of receiving life from the Trinity and offering worship in the Trinity is a hallmark of Christian prayer (nos. 1083, 2627).

The unity and diversity of the Trinity finds liturgical expression in the unity of faith and diversity of rites in the Church (nos. 1200–203), the complementary relationship of priests and people (no. 1120), the variety of ministries in the liturgical celebration (no. 1144), and the dialogical patterns in the liturgy (no. 1153). The sacraments are properly understood within their communal liturgical context (no. 1108) in which the sign value of the sacramental rites is expressed (nos. 1145–52).

Because Christ himself is the minister of the sacraments (nos. 1088, 1115, 1128), they are actions that effect what they signify and impart the divine life of grace (no. 1127). Their efficacy is not affected by the worthiness of the human minister (nos. 1128, 1584), but their fruit-fulness presumes the faith of the Church and their recipient (no. 1124), whose dispositions can limit or augment the effect of the grace given (no. 1128).

The seven sacraments are organically connected, and at their center stands the Holy Eucharist (no. 1211). Three sacraments (baptism, con-firmation, holy orders) make a permanent change in their recipient, and for this reason cannot be repeated (no. 1121). The whole way of life of the Christian community hands on the apostolic faith (nos. 81, 83); in addition to the sacraments instituted by Christ, we have sac-ramentals instituted by the Church that prepare us to receive the grace of the sacraments and dispose us to cooperate with the grace we receive (nos. 1667–73).

Chapter Ten: The Holy Eucharist

The glorified human body of Jesus is at the right hand of the Father (no. 663), but the Church is his Mystical Body, and in the Holy Eucha-rist, the Body and Blood of Christ are present sacramentally. So pro-found is the union between the ecclesial and sacramental Body of Christ that it can be said that the Eucharist makes the Church (no. 1396).

Christ is present in many ways in our liturgical assemblies (no. 1088)—in the community, in the priest who acts in his name, and in the word of God in which Christ himself speaks to us—but his presence in the Eucharist is unique, because there he is present truly, really, and substantially (nos. 1374, 1376). For this reason, it is appro-priate that we worship Christ present in the Eucharist (no. 1378).

The Eucharistic celebration is also the one perfect sacrifice offered by Christ on the Cross, re-presented and memorialized in our midst (nos. 1357–67). Christ is for all time Priest and Victim (no. 1367), even in Heaven (nos. 662, 1137). The Church shares in offering this sacrifice, not because anything must be "added" to Christ's sacrifice, which is sufficient of itself (nos. 614, 617), but because Christ desires to unite all the members of his Body, the Church, to his perfect sac-rifice (nos. 618, 1368–70). The offering of this sacrifice not only sanc-tifies the members of the Church on earth; it also benefits those who have died who are undergoing their final purification as they enter the presence of God (no. 1371).

Chapter Eleven: The Communion of Saints

Communio sanctorum refers to both a sharing in holy gifts and a communion of holy people (no. 948), which finds its most complete expression in the Eucharistic celebration (nos. 1090, 1409). The saints in Heaven, the souls in Purgatory (nos. 1030–32), and the members of the Church on earth are all united in the one Body of Christ (nos. 954, 1475). Christ unites us to his prayer of intercession: the saints in Heaven strengthen us by their prayers, and we assist the souls of the faithful departed who are experiencing their final purification (nos. 956, 958, 1032, 2683). Because we are truly one in Christ, we can make satisfaction for the sins of others and share our merits with them (nos. 1459–60, 2010). The Church grants indulgences, which lessen the penance needed to be performed in order to make amends for our wrongdoing (nos. 1471–79). We venerate the saints and honor their images (nos. 956–57, 1161), but God alone is deserving of worship (no. 2628).

Angels are associated with the communion of saints: they are purely spiritual beings possessing intellect and will (no. 330). The angels play a part in the events of salvation history (no. 331), offer spiritual protection to us (no. 336), and unite with us in worshipping God (no. 334). Devils are fallen angels, beings who were created good (no. 391), but who have radically and irrevocably rejected God (no. 392). Although they are superior to us by nature, their power is limited, and Christ has broken their reign on earth (no. 395).

Chapter Twelve: Mary, Virgin and Mother

The Incarnation of the Son of God was brought about by God's initiative (no. 503), but was made possible by Mary's cooperation (no. 494). She is the "New Eve", whose obedience prepared the way for Christ, just as Eve's disobedience had prepared the way for Adam's sin (nos. 411, 494, 726). She said her Yes on behalf of the human race (no. 511) and miraculously conceived the Word of God by faith (no. 506).

Mary conceived as a virgin, gave birth as a virgin, and remained a virgin after the birth of Jesus (nos. 496–99, 510). Her virginal maternity is reflected in the Church, which is Virgin Mother (no. 507). While Jesus defended the sanctity of marriage, he also called some followers to live a life of virginity for the sake of the Kingdom (no. 915), and from apostolic times, virgins and widows who do not marry again for the sake of the Kingdom have been an integral part of the Church (no. 922); marriage and virginity are complementary (no. 1620).

Because she gave human birth to the eternal Son of God, Mary is rightly called "Mother of God" (nos. 466, 495). She is also the spiritual mother of all the redeemed (nos. 501, 968–69, 2674), because, like Abraham, her faith has helped to bring about a family of believers (nos. 145–49). It was above all at the foot of the Cross that Mary manifested this maternal faith (no. 964).

Chapter Thirteen: Mary's Origin and Destiny

Mary's cooperation with God's will was so complete that she is free from sin (no. 411). She was so completely sanctified by Christ (no. 492) and the Holy Spirit (nos. 493, 722) that she was preserved from original sin (nos. 490–93). In her holiness, Mary is an image of the Church as the holy Bride of Christ (no. 972). At the end of her life, Mary was taken body and soul into the glory of Heaven (no. 966). She is a sign that we are to share in the Resurrection (no. 972), and an eschatological icon of the Church in glory (nos. 829, 972). Given to the beloved disciple as Mother by the dying Christ, Mary continues to exercise her maternal care for us from Heaven (no. 969), but this influence is always subordinate to Christ, the one Mediator, and totally dependent on him (no. 970).

Chapter Fourteen: Life Everlasting

We believe that Christ will return at the end of time as Judge of the living and the dead (nos. 628–29, 1038–40). The universe itself will be transformed (nos. 1040–42), and every man will receive a glorified body (nos. 989–90, 999–1000). This judgment implies that it is possible to forfeit the joy of Heaven: Hell is a state of definitive self-exclusion from communion with God (nos. 1033–35). Heaven is communion with the Holy Trinity and the saints (no. 1024), in which we will see God face-to-face (nos. 1023, 1028). Salvation comes from union with Christ in the Holy Spirit, but we believe that God somehow offers the possibility of partaking in divine life to every human person (no. 1260).

Abbreviations

CCC Catechism of the Catholic Church

DS Denzinger-Schönmetzer, *Enchiridion Symbolorum*

DV *Dei Verbum* (Dogmatic Constitution on Divine Revelation)*

GS *Gaudium et Spes* (Pastoral Constitution on the Church in the Modern World)*

LG *Lumen Gentium* (Dogmatic Constitution on the Church)*

PG *Patrologia Graeca*, ed. J. P. Migne

PL *Patrologia Latina*, ed. J. P. Migne

SC *Sacrosanctum Concilium* (Constitution on the Sacred Liturgy)*

UR *Unitatis Redintegratio* (Decree on Ecumenism)*

*Citations of Vatican Council II documents are taken from the English translation provided by the Holy See on the Vatican website (www.vatican.va).

Index of Biblical Passages

Subject Index